ROMAN HISTORY

TWO STUDIES
ON THE
ROMAN LOWER CLASSES

M. E. Park and M. Maxey

ARNO PRESS

A New York Times Company

New York — 1975

Editorial Supervision: MARIE STARECK

◆

Reprint Edition 1975 by Arno Press Inc.

Copyright © 1975 by Arno Press Inc.

Reprinted from copies in
  The Swarthmore College Library

ROMAN HISTORY
ISBN for complete set: 0-405-07177-9
See last pages of this volume for titles.

Manufactured in the United States of America

◆

Library of Congress Cataloging in Publication Data

Main entry under title:

Two studies on the Roman lower classes.

    (Roman history)
    Reprint of M. E. Park's The plebs in Cicero's
day, printed by Cosmos Press, Cambridge, Mass.,
1921, which was the author's thesis, Bryn Mawr,
1918; and of M. Maxey's Occupations of the lower
classes in Roman society, published by the University of Chicago Press, 1938, which was issued
also as the author's thesis, University of Chicago,
1936.
    Bibliography: p.
    1. Plebs (Rome) 2. Labor and laboring classes--
Rome. 3. Rome--Occupations. I. Park, Marion
Edwards, 1875-1960. The plebs in Cicero's day.
1975. II. Maxey, Mima, 1885-   Occupations of
the lower classes in Roman society. 1975.
III. Series.
DG83.3.T9 1975   301.44'42'0937   75-7347
ISBN 0-405-07069-1

CONTENTS

THE
PLEBS IN CICERO'S DAY

A STUDY OF THEIR PROVENANCE AND
OF THEIR EMPLOYMENT

A Dissertation

PRESENTED TO THE FACULTY OF BRYN MAWR COLLEGE

By MARION EDWARDS PARK

IN PARTIAL FULFILLMENT OF THE REQUIREMENTS
FOR THE DEGREE OF DOCTOR OF PHILOSOPHY
MAY 1918

THE COSMOS PRESS
CAMBRIDGE, MASSACHUSETTS

CONTENTS

THE PLEBS IN CICERO'S DAY

CHAPTER I

A STUDY OF THEIR PROVENANCE

During the last two hundred years of the Roman Republic far-reaching changes took place in the racial composition of the plebs. The foreign element so greatly increased that in 64 B.C. Rome could be called by a contemporary a state made up of an assembly of the nations,[1] and Appian and Suetonius in describing events of 44 could note, one a universal mixture of foreign blood in the plebs,[2] and the other the presence in the city of different nationalities preserving their individual customs.[3] Simultaneously with the increase in foreign stock occurred a corresponding decrease among the native Italians. But neither increase among the foreigners nor decrease among the Italians is stated in numerical terms by any classical writer. Sometimes the one fact or the other is referred to but more often it is only implied in accounts of new legislation, shifting social standards, or readjustments in face of economic conditions. The magnitude of the change is clear but its processes are often obscure. It is worth while to put together all the fragments of evidence from literary or inscriptional sources bearing on so important a subject. If a fairly definite idea can be obtained of the extent to which foreign stock in Italy replaced native-born a surer basis will be given to discussions of the changes in government, in religion, and in national temper in the late Republic and the Empire.

---

[1] *Roma est, civitas ex nationum conventu constituta . . . . Video esse magni consili atque artis . . . esse unum hominem accommodatum ad tantam morum ac sermonum ac voluntatum varietatem.* Q. Cicero, Pet. Cons. 54.

[2] παμμιγές τε γάρ ἐστιν ἤδη τὸ πλῆθος ὑπὸ ξενίας καὶ ὁ ἐξελεύθερος αὐτοῖς ἰσοπολίτης ἐστί. Appian, B. C. II, 120.

[3] *Exterarum gentium multitudo circulatim suo quaeque more lamentata est praecipueque Iudaei* (after Caesar's assassination). Suet. Jul. 84, 5.

The inward and outward movements in the shift of population from 200 to 31 B.C. are closely connected. In spite of inevitable repetition clearness is gained if we examine separately the decrease in native population and the increase in immigration. This arrangement has, therefore, been adopted.

A. The Decrease of Native Stock
FROM 200 TO 31 B.C.

I. THE DIRECT INFORMATION OFFERED BY THE CENSUS FIGURES.

The information on Italian population yielded by literary and inscriptional sources is in general in the form of vague and disconnected statements. But in the case of a single section of Italians, the Roman citizen body, a series of statements direct and fairly consecutive exists, the figures of the Roman census.[1] It is necessary, therefore, before attacking the more general question to try to define the value of the information contained in the census figures and to present it in a clear tabular form.

In two respects the Roman census figures are inadequate. In the first place, the range of information given is restricted. They include citizens only, that is, until the census of 86–5 only a minority of the inhabitants of Italy; of the citizens they include only one class, a class whose limits are disputed and whose ratio to the whole body remains therefore undetermined;[2] further, within this class they do not indicate the way in which the citizenship was secured, whether by birth,

[1] For compilations of the census figures see Beloch, *Bevölkerung*, Chap. VIII, *Der röm. Census;* lists pp. 340, 343–4, 346–8, 370–1; Nissen, *Ital. Landeskunde* II, pp. 99 ff; lists pp. 110–4, 116.

[2] Beloch (*op. cit.*, p. 319) concludes that all adult Roman citizens of the male sex came under the Republican census without reference to class or age. Greenidge (Hist. of Rome, pp. 60–1) includes *iuniores* and *seniores*, but takes no account "of those citizens whose property did not entitle them to be placed among the *classes.*" So Kubitschek (*Census*, R. E. VI p. 1917). Mommsen (St. R. II, p. 411) includes only the *iuniores*, i. e., those of the proper class and age who were competent for field service; so Nissen (*op. cit.*, p. 112).

manumission, or act of government. In the second place, the traditional figures are not altogether a safe basis on which to build conclusions. They are available only at second hand in the historians and means are rarely offered by the narrative for more than general verification or correction.

On the other hand their information is unique. They record the numbers of a given group of Italians at fairly regular intervals during a long period, and the very length of the series furnishes some margin for correction of the separate figures.

CENSUS FIGURES FOR THE YEARS 234-28 B.C.

Year.	Figure recorded.	Figure corrected.
234-3	270,713 [1]	
(225	291,300)[2]	
209-8	137,108	237,108 (Beloch)[3]
204-3	214,000	
194-3	143,704	243,704 (Beloch, Nissen)
187-6	258,318	
179-8	258,794 [4]	
174-3	269,015	
169-8	312,805	
164-3	337,452	
159-8	328,316	
154-3	324,000	
147-6	322,000	
142-1	327,442	
136-5	317,933	
131-0	318,823	

[1] Census figures for the generation previous to 200 are added to indicate the losses caused by the Second Punic War.

[2] There is no stated census figure for 225. The number is derived from Polyb. II, 24. See Momm. R. F. II, 400–1.

[3] Beloch (*op. cit.*, pp. 349–50) corrects the traditional figure (Liv. XXVII, 36, 7; Epit. XXVII) on the ground that the normal increase of the years 234-18 plus the generous use of the power of manumission during the Second Punic War accounts for the relatively small loss in men of military age in the period 234-08. The recorded figure is, however, accepted by Nissen (*op. cit.*, p. 112) and it may well be correct.

[4] The standstill of population in this decade is perhaps to be accounted for by the pestilence of 187–79. Beloch (*op. cit.*, pp. 350–1) on insecure grounds raises the figure to 280–290,000.

Year.	Figure recorded.
125–4	394,736 [1]
115–4	394,336
86–5	463,000 [2]
70–69	910,000
28	4,106,300 [3]

An examination of these census figures shows that in spite of the limitations in the information which they convey, they make a contribution to the solution of the general problem of change in the Italian population. They constitute for the years 200–131 a record of the changes of number in a special group of Italians; they show that this group steadily increased from the close of the Second Punic War at the rate of about 1.3% a year for forty years, and that from 165 to 131 it steadily decreased at the rate of about .25% a year.[4] There is no

[1] Mommsen (R. G. II⁴ p. 100) and Greenidge (op. cit., p. 150) accept the recorded figure for 125–4 and attribute the increase (76,000) to the numbers of new settlers on the land, previously capite censi and not appearing in the lists. They would not, therefore, infer an absolute gain in population. Beloch (op. cit., p. 351) corrects the figure for either 125 or 115 to 294,336.

[2] Beloch (op. cit., 352) corrects this figure to 963,000 to represent the additions to the list of Roman citizens at the close of the Social War. This would allow for a loss of 53,000 in the next fifteen years which include the period of the Civil War of Sulla and Marius. Nissen (op. cit., p. 116) regards the figure as too uncertain for discussion.

[3] This census with its great numerical increase is of a different character from those held under the republic. Beloch (pp. 376–7) includes here the entire free population, men, women and children; that is, in terms of the previous census, the figure represents 1,500,000 male citizens of military age. Within the period between 70 and 28 the area of country whose inhabitants were Roman citizens greatly increased: 200,000 to 250,000 Transpadanes, and 350,000 to 400,000 residents of colonies in the provinces had received citizenship. On the other hand the losses of the Civil Wars fell most heavily on the area included in the census. Beloch estimates that 900,000 of the 1,500,000 were descendants of the 910,000 appearing in the census of 70–69, while 600,000 had received the citizenship at a later date. Nissen (pp. 117–8) includes in the 1,500,000 the names of all independent persons; that is, he supposes that the object of the censors was no longer to make a list of those liable to military service but rather to record the property of the person registered. The names of most women and children would therefore still be omitted, but a few who were independent property-holders would now be included.

[4] The average yearly increase from 204 to 164 was 3,000 (see, however, p. 14, n. 1); the average yearly decrease between 164 and 131 was 565. In the records of the census in 125, 115 and 85, the figures are disputed;

reason for not regarding this group as typical of the whole body.

Where the census figures fail there is no substitute. During the last years of the Republic, for Roman citizens as well as for the main body of Italians, we must use fragmentary and indirect evidence.

II. THE INDIRECT INFORMATION OFFERED BY A STUDY OF FACTORS IN THE DECREASE OF NATIVE STOCK.

During the second and first centuries both Roman citizens and Italians in general were subject to various conditions which either directly reduced their numbers or tended to prevent a normal increase.

1. The long absences from Italy of men of military age on military service caused a direct decline in the birth rate and lowered it indirectly by bringing about bad economic conditions in Italy.

2. Men of military age were killed in the wars.

3. Lack of opportunity at home and more favorable conditions abroad caused a steady emigration of Italians to the provinces and the outlying districts subject to Roman influence. Such emigrants became permanent residents of their new homes.

4. Disinclination toward marriage and a tendency toward small families among those who married was manifested among the poorer classes as a natural result of unsettled or actively bad economic conditions; yet childlessness became general also among the upper classes whose situation was

---

the figure for 70 covers a large and undetermined addition to the number of citizens and cannot be brought into direct connection with the previous figures, and the same is true of the figure for 28.

The population of modern Italy has increased from 26,801,000 in 1872 to 36,740,000 in 1918. The percentage of yearly increase between 1872 and 1911 ranged from .61 to .73; between 1911 and 1916 from 1.04 to 1.18; in 1917 it was .46; in 1918, .06. See Statesman's Yearbook 1920, p. 984.

unaffected or even bettered by the changes in the centuries following the Second Punic War.

These factors, it need hardly be said, were not mutually exclusive. They acted together in many cases and one often intensified the effect of another. For the losses in war, the absences in military service, and the emigration rough data can be collected and an attempt to do this has been made in the following pages, in the hope that the figures, although of necessity inaccurate, will serve to suggest the processes which were going on.

1. **Military Service.** The drain on population caused by frequent military service on the part of the younger and more vigorous men readily suggests itself as a factor in the weakening of the stock. The details of the military duty required by the republic during this period are known with some fullness and there exist in the historians occasional enumerations of the soldiers on service in a given campaign, or a given year.[1] All Roman citizens and all allies were liable for military service in the second and first centuries but in ordinary times the right of the government to call out soldiers, though theoretically unlimited, was actually limited by various restrictions as to the age, the previous length of service, and the property-rating of the individual.[2] (1) The soldiers must be between the ages of 17 and 46. (2) They must have served less than ten campaigns in the cavalry or, in accordance with the generally accepted views, less than sixteen campaigns in the infantry.[3] (3) In the earlier part of the second century they must have been rated in the previous census as owners of property to the value of 11,000

---

[1] For a summing up of the data, see Marquardt, St. V, II, pp. 319 ff.; Mommsen, St. R. III, pp. 240 ff., 1071 ff., I, 505 ff.; Liebenam, *Exercitus* R. E. 1909; *Dilectus* R. E. 1903; for a general study of changes in the army, O. Seeck, *Ges. d. Untergang d. antik. Welt* (Berlin 1910) I, pp. 234 ff.

[2] For the exemption of certain small classes of citizens see Liebenam, *Dilectus* R. E. pp. 601–2.

[3] The statements of ancient authors here are few and puzzling. The passage in Polybius (VI, 19, 2) is unfortunately corrupt. As it stands it reads: τῶν λοιπῶν τοὺς μὲν ἱππεῖς δέκα, τοὺς δὲ πεζοὺς † ἐξ οὗ δεῖ στρατείας τελεῖν

asses; this minimum was lowered by the middle of the century to 4,000 [1] and all restriction as to property-rating was done away with by Marius in 107 and never restored.[2]

From this body of citizens liable to service a regular number was drawn yearly, made up in a normal year according to the pre-Marian army regulations of two consular armies so-called, that is, four legions in all each consisting of 4,200 infantry and 300 cavalry. With these citizen troops served contin-

---

etc. Lipsius read εἴκοσι here, Casaubon δεκαέξ. The latter reading has been followed by Büttner-Wobst (Leip. 1888) and Hultsch (1892) in their editions of Polybius and by Lange, Marquardt, Mommsen, Liebenam *op. cit.* and Cagnat (Dict. Dar. *Exercitus*). There is no statement for the Marian period. Augustus established first sixteen (Dio LV, 23, 1), later twenty years (Dio LVII, 6, 5). As arguments for the reading sixteen in the Polybian passage, we have (1) its relation to the number of campaigns served by the cavalry, (cf. six infantry to three cavalry campaigns demanded of a magistrate, Lex Jul. Munic. 89 ff. 98 ff.); (2) the statement that in emergencies the soldiers must serve a slightly increased number of campaigns, *i. e.* twenty, (Polyb. VI, 19, 3); (3) the number first established by Augustus (16). It is curious to note, however, that after much shorter periods the soldiers complained of being detained in service beyond their time. In 180 the soldiers in Spain (Liv. XL, 35, 3–7; 11–12) demanded release saying through their emissaries in the Senate that they had served under A. Fulvius Flaccus (182), and many praetors before him. Gracchus replied (Liv. XL, 36, 10–12) that soldiers whose term of service had expired should be released. Fulvius thereupon was allowed to bring back with him those soldiers who had gone to Spain before 187, and others who had acted with bravery in his own (*i. e.* later) campaigns. In 152 an army of new recruits was sent to Spain to take the place of those who had served six years (Appian, Hisp. 78). In 35 Augustus was forced to discharge soldiers who had served at Mutina (43) and Philippi (42), and whose time had expired. The mutiny in Lucullus's army in 68–7 seems to have been a general one (Appian, Mithr. 90; Plut. Lucull. 33) though Plutarch in Lucull. 34, 35 limits it to the Fimbrian soldiers. The two legions of the latter had served from 86 on; the other three legions only from 74 (Appian, Mithr. 72).

[1] Gellius (XVI, 10, 10) assigns to a time preceding Marius a reduction from 4,000 to 375 *asses*. Greenidge (Hist. of Rome, p. 61, n. 2) suggests that the correct number here is 3,750.

[2] Restrictions on service in the fleet were less severe; *liberti*, that is men of foreign birth, regularly served as well as citizens rated between 1,000 and 1,500 *asses*. It is needless to say also that in emergencies the government promptly overstepped the limits it had itself set. Citizens under and over age were called (Liv. XXV, 5, 8; XLII, 33, 4), *proletarii* and citizens *capite censi* served before 107 (Gell. XVI, 10, 13) and in the Social War *liberti* did at least guard duty on land (Liv. Epit. 74; Appian, B.C. I, 49). See Mommsen St. R. III, 448–9 for a discussion of previous service of *liberti*.

gents of allies in approximately the same numbers,[1] thus increasing the total to about 40,000 men. The census figures show that the quota of citizens serving each year was six out of one hundred;[2] the relation of the allied contingent to its total available number is not known.

After this brief summary of the requirements of military service, we proceed to try to form an idea of the proportion of men who were actually serving at a given time. The figures for ten successive years are given below. They err on the side of understatement. Anyone looking over the sections in Livy devoted to the yearly assigning of troops will notice that the statements are fuller and more accurate for the Roman legions than for the Allies. Clearly Livy often fails to enumerate the official contingents of the latter, although in his narrative of the year's campaigns he may refer to their presence. The total number of troops for any one year, therefore, must often fall short of the truth.

	Census Figures	Roman Citizens	Total Number
(204)	214,000		
200		31,500 [3]	59,500 Liv. XXXI, 8; 10, 5; XXX, 41, 5.
199		31,500	37,500 Liv. XXXII, 1, 1–5.
198		34,800	54,800 Liv. XXXII, 8; 26, 2, 12.
197		30,300	59,800 Liv. XXXII, 28; XXXIII, 4, 6.
196		48,300	86,400 Liv. XXXIII, 25–26.
195		36,000	91,100 Liv. XXXIII, 43; XXXIV, 8, 4; 26, 11.
194	243,704?	36,000	38,200 Liv. XXXIV, 43; 46, 1–2; 52, 2, 11; 56, 13.
193		30,100	59,100 Liv. XXXIV, 56; XXXV, 4, 1; 5, 2.
192		38,350	111,800 Liv. XXXV, 20.
191		59,100	124,600 Liv. XXXVI, 1.

[1] Polyb. VI, 26, 7. Actually the ratio of allied to citizen troops varied considerably. For passages in Livy giving the numbers of both see Weissenborn-Müller on Liv. XL, 36, 6.

[2] Taking 304,138 as the mean of the census figures from 204 to 115.

[3] I have regarded the legion as made up of 4,500 men unless it is otherwise stated.

The rough average of citizens yearly absent on military service during this decade was therefore 37,595 out of 243,704,[1] not 6% but 15.4% of the whole number liable for duty, two and a half times the normal proportion.

Our information does not allow us to calculate the ratio for the Allies. It would probably be still higher for various facts show that they were called on for more troops than they could actually furnish. In 181, a year of pestilence in Italy, when at least 45,000 Allies along with from twelve to fourteen legions of citizens were already in the field, an additional levy of 8,300 men called out by vote of the Senate to suppress rebellion in Sardinia could not be got together.[2] Later in the year reserves up to fifty years of age were called out to form two *legiones tumultuariae*.[3] Again both in 180[4] and in 174[5] there was difficulty in filling out the number of troops voted. During this decade we know that among those who were having difficulties in completing their quotas were the Latin Allies. In 187 on complaint of Latin envoys 12,000 Latin citizens who in 204 or previously had been registered in Latium but who had in the interval gone to Rome and been registered there, were sent back by the Senate to the Latin towns.[6] In 178 envoys again appeared before the Senate. "The sum of their complaints was that many of their citizens had been registered at Rome and had removed thither; that if this were allowed, in a very few *lustra* their deserted towns and country would not be able to furnish a soldier".[7] . . . The Samnites and Paeligni formally complained at the same time that 4,000 of their families had removed to Fregellae, but that their quota of troops remained the same.[8] In 174-3 there were still enough Latins in Rome to cause a

[1] The corrected census figure for 194.
[2] Liv. XL, 19, 6.
[3] Liv. XL, 26, 6-7.
[4] Liv. XL, 36, 14.
[5] Liv. XLI, 21, 5.
[6] Liv. XXXIX, 3, 4-5.
[7] Liv. XLI, 8, 6-7.
[8] Liv. XLI, 8, 8; was this a station so to speak on the underground railroad to Rome?

definite attempt to exclude them from the census lists.[1]
There is no record later of formal complaints, perhaps because
for some time they were asked for less military service or
because they saw some attempt at relief on the part of the
government.[2]

No estimate can be formed of the number of citizen or allied
troops who were serving annually in the years after 167.
There are references, however, which indicate the great numbers called out during special periods.

Large bodies of troops had to be kept in Spain between the
years 154 and 133.[3] In 153, 44,000 were serving there [4] and
though many of these were withdrawn fresh levies were being
constantly sent out.[5] Meanwhile from 149 to 146 an army
of 84,000 men served under Scipio in Africa [6] and a good-
sized army was engaged in Macedonia and Greece.[7] The
Spanish campaigns continued a second decade and called for
the maintenance of large bodies of troops in Spain.[8] In 137
there were 30,000 soldiers in service there,[9] in 134, 60,000
before Numantia alone.[10]

The service required of the men of the next generation in
the last decade of the century was very heavy. A large
army was maintained in Numidia from 111 to 105[11] and in
105 a second and still larger force must have been serving in
the north of Italy, for 40,000 soldiers and 40,000 camp followers

---

[1] Liv. XLIII, 10, 3. Such Italian emigration to Rome helps to explain
the apparent increase in citizen population up to 164; that is, it was partly
at the expense of Italy that the Roman census figures of 194, 189, and 179
were raised.

[2] See p. 45.

[3] Heitland (Rom. Republic II, 176, n.) says that the troops employed
in these wars were probably mainly Allies. Allies are mentioned in the
sources, however, only in the years 145 and 142.

[4] Appian, Hisp. 45–8; 56–7.

[5] Appian, Hisp. 61; Liv. Epit. 52–53; Appian, Hisp. 64, 65; 76.

[6] Appian, Lib. 75.

[7] Liv. Epit. 50.

[8] Orosius (5, 7) says 40,000 men were engaged in the Numantine War.

[9] Liv. Epit. 55.

[10] Appian, Hisp. 97.

[11] Sall. Jug. *passim.*

were killed at Arausio.   On the news of this loss, no man of military age was allowed to leave Italy,[1] and all reserves were drilled in preparation for active service.[2]   Yet in 103 in the midst of the preparations to turn all Italian resources against the Cimbri and Teutons, 17,000 men had to be sent to Sicily, of whom 14,000 were Romans or Italians.[3]   That army had to be continued until 100 although during the same years Marius and Catulus had 54,000 men with them in the north.[4]

Conditions in the first century are too familiar to need comment.   After only ten years of quiet almost every man in Italy must have been drawn into the Social War on one side or the other.   Appian estimates that 100,000 Romans and the same number of Italians besides the garrisons in the towns were put into the field.[5]   The remaining years of the decade saw little disbanding of troops, and in 83–1 Sulla alone had twenty-three legions, 120,000 soldiers, serving under him.[6] The wars, foreign and Italian, filling the middle third of the century and continuous for almost a generation, drained the manhood of the country to a degree which forced recognition of the fact by the state.[7]

In an effort to estimate the permanent loss suffered by Italy from the military service of her native sons, the classes affected must first be borne in mind, and, second, the various ways in which their absence on service affected the figures of population.

Both before and after Marius' changes the armies were drawn almost entirely from men of Italian birth and in the

---

[1] Gran. Lic. p. 21 (Bonn).
[2] Val. Max. II, 3, 2.
[3] Diodor. XXXVI, 8, 1 and 10.
[4] Plut. Mar. 25.
[5] B.C. 79; Velleius (II, 15, 3) estimates the total losses as 100,000, more than Appian's estimate for soldiers serving!   The numbers for the whole period are untrustworthy (Cf. Vell. II, 20, 4 and Liv. Epit. 72–89).
[6] Appian, B. C. I, 100; 104.
[7] Compare the complete readjustments in demands for military service in the early Empire (Marquardt, Mommsen, Liebenam, *op. cit.*).

prime of life. It is true that within these limits the type of soldier varied. In the second century, since the proletarian was barred out and the prosperous artisan of native stock was almost non-existent, the burden of the levy fell on the small farmer. On the other hand, after the reforms of Marius, if normal conditions had prevailed, the weight of military service would have fallen on the poorest classes in the towns. Having nothing to lose by being away from home and everything to gain in the way of pay and plunder, they had responded to the new opportunity by volunteering in such numbers that conscription, though still on the books, promised to be no longer necessary. But as matters turned out, the Social Wars and the long Civil Wars of the last seventy years of the Republic kept not only the city proletariat but for long periods every Italian who could be used in an army away from home on active, often on foreign, service.

During both centuries, because of the type of war which Italy had to wage, the soldiers called to service were obliged to remain away from home continuously for several years; and this necessity not only lowered the birth rate in Italy directly but by contributing to the deterioration of the soldiers' property and the discomfort, often distress, of their families, and by creating in the men themselves a restlessness which made old occupations and old ties less stable, brought about a condition which in all countries and times has lowered the birth rate indirectly. Finally, the long absences on service must have not infrequently resulted in a permanent emigration and residence outside Italy.

2. **Actual Losses in the Wars.** A list follows, arranged by decades, of the losses of the native stock on the battlefield from 201 to 60 B.C.,[1] and where it is possible there is added a rough calculation of the average yearly loss. Such a summary represents only a general estimate. In the first place,

---

[1] From this time on many soldiers from Gaul or elsewhere were included in so-called Roman armies and the figures cease to be valuable for our purpose.

the losses are frequently not reported in numbers. Further, the numbers when reported are often open to suspicion, for, to say nothing of errors of transmission, there were undoubtedly occasional deliberate variations from the truth. The glory of Rome was sometimes best served by an over-estimate or an under-estimate on the part of the historian. Finally, it must be borne in mind that in the sources no reckoning is made of soldiers who died abroad from wounds or from disease, though the addition of these deaths would probably have more than doubled the numbers now recorded.

It is impossible to estimate the percentage of loss. These figures include in almost every case the losses of the citizens and allies indiscriminately, and there are no corresponding exact general figures either for the whole body of citizens and allies subject to conscription or for the number actually serving in any single year between 201 and 60.[1] The Roman losses are not given separately and therefore cannot be compared with the Roman census figures.

Decades B.C.	Yearly Average	Losses[2]
201–190	3,350	7,000 (Liv. XXXI, 2, 9); 2,000 (XXXI, 22, 2); 6,700 (XXXII, 7, 6); 3,000 (XXXIII, 36, 4); 5,000 (XXXIV, 47, 8); half a legion, and *Socii* (XXXV, 1, 2; cf. XXXIII, 43, 7–8); 5,000 (XXXV, 5, 14); 6,000 (XXXVII, 46, 7).
189–180	1,210[3]	*gravis pestilentia* (Liv. XXXVIII, 44, 7); 4,000 XXXIX, 20, 7); 5,600 (XXIX, 30, 6; 31, 15); *gravis pestilentia* (XL, 19, 3–8; 36, 14; 42, 6); 1,000 (XL, 32, 7); 1,500 (XL, 40, 13).
179–170	720[3]	*gravis pestilentia* (Liv. XLI, 21, 5. Obseq. 10); 3,000 (Liv. XLII, 7, 10); 2,200 (XLII, 60, 1); 10,000, but few Italians (XLIII, 9, 6–7; 10, 7; 11, 11).

[1] See p. 12 for the inaccuracy of the total figures for troops serving in any one year.

[2] All losses under 500 are omitted.

[3] Not including those dying of disease, for whom no numerical figure is given. This series of pestilences began the year that Rome's first Eastern army returned from Asia.

169–160		500 (Liv. XLIV, 10, 9); 600 (XLIV, 12, 3).
159–150	3,200[1]	6,000 (Appian, Hisp. 56); 9,000 (Hisp. 56); 6,000 (Hisp. 45); 4,000 (Hisp. 46); 7,000 (Hisp. 58).
149–140	870[1]	Force under praetor (Liv. Epit. 50); 4,000 (Appian, Hisp. 63); many out of 11,300 (Hisp. 64); 1,000 (Hisp. 66); 3,000 (Hisp. 67); 700 (Hisp. 77); 5,000 (Oros. 5, 4, 13).
139–130		Many of Gracchan party (Appian, B. C. I, 16; 200 (Oros. 5, 9); slaughter of troops (Oros. 5, 10).
129–120		Many killed in rioting at Rome (Sall. Jug. 31, 1; 42, 4); 3,000 (Plut. C. Gr. 17); 3,000 in course of trials (Plut. C. Gr. 18; Oros. 5, 12).
119–110		Army of C. Porcius Cato (Liv. Epit. 63, Flor. 1, 38); many of army of Papirius Carbo (Liv. Epit. 63, Appian, Celt. 13).
109–100	8,000[1]	Parts of the armies of M. Junius Silvanus and L. Cassius Longinus (Liv. Epit. 65); part of the army of M. Aurelius Scaurus; 80,000 soldiers and 40,000 camp followers (Epit. 67).
91–80 Social War	17,230	a. Romans: citizens in Asculum (Appian, B. C. I, 38, Liv. Epit. 72); 7,700 (Appian, B. C. I, 41); many (1, 43); 8,000 (Oros. 5, 18); many (Appian, B. C. I, 44); most of 35,000 (I, 45); many (I, 52). b. Italians: 6,000 (Appian, B. C. I, 42); 6,000 (I, 46); 8,000 (I, 48); 10,000 (I, 50); 23,000 (I, 50); many (I, 51, 52); 15,000 (I, 52). Total losses: over 100,000, (Diodor. XXXVII, 29, 5, and sum of Appian's figures); 300,000 (Vell. II, 15, 3).
Civil Wars		10,000 (Plut. Sert. 4; 13,000, Licin. 23, 27); many (Appian, B. C. I, 64; 71; Liv. Epit. 80; Dio XXXI, 11); 10,000 (Appian, B. C. I, 91); 50,000 (Appian, B. C. I, 93; Val. Max. IX, 2, 1–2); 6,000 (Plut. Sulla 30); massacre among Samnite men (Strabo V, 4, 11; Appian, B. C. I, 94); 12,000 (Plut. Sulla 32, Cf. Sall. Hist. I, 17; Val. Max. IX, 2, 1); 2,000 (Plut. Sert. 12).
79–70	2,900	5,000 (Appian, B. C. I, 109); 6,000 (I, 110); 3,000 (I, 112); 5,300 (Memnon, F. H. G. 39); many of 10,000 (Plut. Crass. 9); 1,000 (Appian, B. C. I, 120); 3,000 (Dio XXXVII, 40, 1).

[1] Not including those dying of disease, for whom no numerical figure is given. This series of pestilences began the year that Rome's first Eastern army returned from Asia.

The scantiness of our information precludes comment on the figures of this list. Attention can only be called to the heavy losses of the first decades of the second century, the years 160–150, 110–100, and 90–70. What has been suggested in the previous section in regard to the type of soldier serving during these periods[1] should be applied here also.

3. Emigration. There are no direct statements in the sources on the losses of Italy by emigration in the second and first centuries. What facts we have are derived from inscriptions recording the votes of communities of Italians living outside Italy, from references in the historians to similar or less organized groups whose residence outside of Italy is noted in connection with an historical narrative, and from casual references to similar groups or individuals in non-historical writers, especially in Cicero.

It will readily be seen that in such sources the chances are against the mention of emigration in its beginnings. Only communities of some stability record their decrees in permanent form, and only communities of some importance are mentioned in a general historical narrative, while Cicero's references are limited almost entirely to the century in which he wrote. But to the few direct references which we have, we can safely add what is implied as to its beginnings by the known facts of its later development.

For our purpose it is not necessary to differentiate between the Italians who emigrated as Roman citizens and those who left parts of Italy which had not yet received citizenship. Hatzfeld has proved that on the Delian inscriptions of the second and first century Ῥωμαῖος meant simply a man of Italian birth,[2] and it is probable that corresponding inscriptions from other localities would show a variety of origin

---

[1] pp. 15–16.
[2] J. Hatzfeld, B. C. H. 36 (1912) pp. 132–3. Among those given that designation in Delos for instance are a resident of Cumae before 180, an Apulian at the end of the second century, Italians from Greek-speaking Sicily or South Italy (Achilleus in 145, Serdon), and even slaves and *liberti*.

among the "Romans" or even the "Roman citizens" whose residence there is recorded.[1]

As would be expected the Italians resident outside of Italy who are referred to most often by the historians or Cicero are men of some importance from their position or wealth, *publicani*, merchants, owners of *latifundia*, stock raisers,[2] the men who came back to Rome from time to time or who were prominent in their new homes. Poorer emigrants are usually mentioned only in the mass.[3] A few are included among the *familiae* of the *publicani* and the great merchants and landowners. Others carried on for themselves humble branches of the same occupations.

a. Italians Employed by *Publicani*. Employment under the *publicani* drew relatively few Italians away from Italy. The *familiae* were very large,[4] it is true, but the rank and file were slaves[5] and only the few higher positions were filled by free-born Italians.[6]

b. Mercatores and *Negotiatores*. The freemen who left Italy to carry on private business abroad were a much larger class.[7] Their emigration began when the first non-Italian

---

[1] See Athen. V, 213 b. from a speech of Athenio at Athens: τῶν 'Ρωμαίων . . . . οἱ δὲ λοιποὶ μεταμφιεσάμενοι τετράγωνα ἱμάτια τὰς ἐξ ἀρχῆς πατρίδος πάλιν ὀνομάζουσι.

[2] So in Gaul (Cic. Font. 12; 46), in Sicily (Verr. II, 188), in Asia (Cic. Scaur. 35, Manil, 18), in Africa (Auct. Bell Afr. 36) etc.

[3] See for a general reference Cic. Balb. 30: *ductos vidi . . . . nonnullos imperitos homines, nostros civis, Athenis in numero iudicum atque Areo-pagitarum.*

[4] Cic. Manil. 16, *cum publicani familias maximas quas in salinis habent, quas in agris, quas in portibus atque in custodiis . . . .* Pompey requisi-tioned part of the 2,000 armed men whom he secured in Cyprus *ex familiis societatum* (Caes. B. C. III, 103).

[5] Cic. prov. cons. 10, *quo veniret, ibi publicanum aut publicani servum vetuit;* Cic. Verr. III, 188.

[6] In Asia, P. Terentius Hispo, a kinsman of Terentia (Cic. Att. XI, 10, 1, Epist. XIII, 65, etc.); in Sicily, L. Carpinatius, (Cic. Verr. III, 169; P. Vettius Chilo, a knight (Verr. IV, 166); P. Servilius, C. Antistius (Verr. IV, 167); L. Canuleius (Verr. III, 171); L. Vibius, a knight, (Verr. III, 182); in Bithynia, Cn. Pupius (Cic. Epist. XIII, 9, 3); in Africa, P. Cuspius, L. Julius, P. Cornelius (Epist. XIII, 6, 6a).

[7] See J. Hatzfeld, *op. cit.*, and *Les trafiquants Italiens dans l'Orient Hel-lénique*, Paris, 1917; P. Roussel, *Délos, Colonie Athénienne*, Paris, 1916; for general treatment of Italian (and non-Italian) merchants and bankers

regions came under Roman influence or control; indeed if an analogy can be drawn from the situation in Gaul whose process of reduction to a Roman province we know in unusual detail, the legions were everywhere preceded by the *mercator*.[1] Merchants, again, accompanied the armies,[2] sold what they could to the troops and bought the booty.[3] There can be no doubt that such traders were from the lower classes;[4] there was too much risk and too little profit to make frontier trading tempting to the man established comfortably at home. Later on when the balance swung toward safety the more cautious merchant dared make his venture.

For the second century, when one by one large districts were thus being opened to the *negotiator*, a few references are available. By 193, for instance, there were enough Italians at Halaesa in Sicily to make a dedication in honor of the Roman praetor.[5] In 180 there were many Roman citizens and Latin *socii* in Illyricum.[6] The mass of Delian inscriptions mentioning upwards of 350 individuals with Italian *nomina* in business on the island begins with 166.[7] The references for Africa happen to be unusually numerous. There were Italians living in Carthage when the Roman

---

especially in the Empire see V. Pârvan, *Die Nationalität der Kaufleute in röm. Kaiserreiche* (Breslau) 1909; for Italian merchants in Greece, G. Colin, *Rome et la Grèce* (Paris) 1905, pp. 92 ff., 262–7.

[1] See in general Cic. Manil. 2; Verr. VI, 157; for Gaul, Caes. B. G. III, 1, 2; I, 1, 3; II, 15, 4; for Germany, Caes. B. G. I, 39, 1; IV, 2, 1; 3, 3; for Britain, Caes. B. G. IV, 20, 3–4; 21, 5.

[2] For Africa, see Sall. Jug. 44, 5; Auct. Bell. Afr. 75, 3; for Gaul, Caes. B. G. VI, 37, 2; II, 33, 6–7. The merchants in Cenabum (B. G. VII, 3, 1), in Cavillonum (VII, 42, 5) and in Noviodunum (VII, 55, 5), though they may have been longer established, probably came to Gaul with the Roman army. For Cilicia see Cic. Att. V, 20, 5.

[3] The soldiers took to trading in Boeotia in 196 (Liv. XXXIII, 29, 2–4).

[4] The names of two such traders in Gaul are known: L. Publicius, a dealer in Gallic slaves, who came and went from Italy (Cic. Quinct. 24) and P. Umbrenus, a *libertus* (Sall. Cat. 40, 2; Cic. Cat. III, 14). C. Fufius Cita (Caes. B. G. VII, 3, 1) seems to have been a resident merchant who supplied the Roman army.

[5] C. I. L. X, 7459. These men were undoubtedly *negotiatores*.

[6] Liv. XL, 42, 4. These men were undoubtedly *negotiatores*.

[7] Hatzfeld, *op. cit.*, pp. 10 ff.

demands on the city were announced in 150,[1] and Sallust informs us of the large number of Italian and Roman merchants in Cirta, Vaga, and Utica by 112.[2]

But even without contemporary references, the impressive lists of *conventus* and of Roman and Italian *negotiatores* in the first century would establish a large emigration in the previous century.[3] Even though we subtract somewhat from the traditional 80,000[4] to 150,000[5] victims massacred by Mithridates in Asia in 88, the number of the "Italians and Romans, men and children and women, their *liberti* and slaves — all who were of Italian stock"[6] who by that year were resident in Asia was exceedingly large.[7] In 88, 20,000 "most of them Italians," were massacred in Delos and on the coasts near by.[8] By 66 "a great number of citizens" in the province again needed protection;[9] in 59 there were "many Roman citizens" in Pergamon, Smyrna and Tralles.[10] When Cicero made his Verrine speeches (70), he represented not only his Sicilian clients but many Roman citizens; six

[1] Appian, Lib. 92.

[2] Cirta, *multitudo togatorum* (Sall. Jug. 21, 2); *Italici, negotiatores* (26, 1 and 3); Vaga, *forum rerum venalium . . . . ubi et incolere et mercari consueverant Italici generis multi mortales* (47, 1); Utica, *Negotiatores, quorum magna multitudo Uticae erat* (64, 5).

[3] For a list of *conventus* of Roman citizens (and of Italians) cf. Kornemann, R. E., *Conventus*, 1900; Schulten, *de Conventibus Civium Romanorum* (Berlin) 1892. For a list of *negotiatores*, etc., in Sicily see Pârvan, *op. cit.*, p. 8, n. 1; in Greece and the Islands, pp. 8–10; in Macedonia and Thrace, p. 9; in Asia (mostly imperial), pp. 11–16; in Syria (mostly imperial), p. 16; in Africa, pp. 19–20; in Gaul, pp. 22–26; in Germany, p. 27; in Illyricum, p. 31; in Delos, Hatzfeld, *op. cit.*, pp. 10 ff.

[4] Val. Max. 9, 2, 4, Ext. 3.

[5] Plut. Sulla. 24, 4.

[6] Appian, Mith. 23.

[7] Cic. Manil 70, *tota in Asia, tot in civitatibus . . . . (omnis) civis Romanos necandos . . . . curavit;* 11, *tot milibus civium Romanorum . . . . necatis;* Flacc. 60; *illam universorum civium Romanorum per tot urbis . . . . caedem.* These persons were probably not all connected with business houses, but those who lived in the cities — and most of them did (cf. special records for Ephesus, Tralles, etc. Appian. Mithr. 23) — were likely to be so connected.

[8] Appian, Mithr. 28; cf. Hatzfeld, *op. cit.*, pp. 119–20.

[9] Cic. Manil. 18.

[10] Cic. Flacc. 70.

hundred in addition to various individuals specified testified
that they had been victims of Verres's graft.[1]   More than a
hundred were members of the *conventus* at Syracuse,[2] and
there were Roman knights everywhere in the other towns.[3]
In fact to a modern reader the conduct of the Roman praetor
in Sicily is no more surprising than the number of Roman
citizens who were his victims.   In 69 Gallia Narbonensis was
filled with Roman merchants and *publicani* and farmers.[4]
In 57–6 Roman citizens carrying on business in Achaia,
Thessaly, Athens, Dyrrachium, Apollonia, Ambracia, Par-
thus, Bulis, Epirus, Locris, Phocis, Boeotia, Acarnania,
Amphilochia, Perrhaebia, Athamania, Macedonia, Aetolia,
and Dolopia suffered from the Roman governor of Macedonia.[5] The presence of many Italian merchants in Africa
at the end of the second century has been noted and in 46
again the African *conventus* are spoken of as *firmi atque magni*.[6]

   We know from several passages in Cicero that many
merchants did not themselves remain abroad;[7] undoubtedly
the owners of the large business houses came and went, while
their clerks and agents and the owners of the smaller businesses avoided the long and expensive journey by settling
down in the places of their occupations.   From the Delian
inscriptions we can form some idea of the composition of
the isolated Roman commercial communities in which they
established themselves.

---

[1] Cic. Verr. III, 119.
[2] Cic. Verr. VI, 155.
[3] Cic. Verr. VI, 27.
[4] Cic. Font. 11; 12; *maximus numerus c. R.* 13; 15; 46.
[5] Cic. Pis. 96.
[6] Cic. Lig. 24.
[7] See for Asia, Cic. Manil. 18: *ex ceteris ordinibus homines gnavi atque
industrii partim ipsi in Asia negotiantur, ... partim eorum in ea pro-
vincia pecunias magnas conlocatas habent;* for Sicily, Cic. Verr. II. I, 6:
*quod multis locupletioribus civibus utimur, quod habent — provinciam,
quo facile excurrant, ubi libenter negotium gerant; quos illa partim mercibus
suppeditandis cum quaestu compendioque dimittit, partim retinet, ut arare,
ut pascere, ut negotiari libeat, ut denique sedes atque domicilium conlocare;
quod commodum non mediocre rei publicae est, tantum civium numerum tam
prope a domo — detineri;* in general, Cicero's letters of introduction
(Epist. XIII), largely for subordinates in charge of business offices abroad.

One hundred and fifty-three *nomina* appear in Hatzfeld's list;[1] that is, at least 153 different Italian families were represented in Delos. Among the 389 individuals of these families there are 116 who so far as can be told were of free stock, 103 *liberti*, and 54 slaves. The status of the remaining number (116) is doubtful, but they are probably rather *ingenui* or *liberti*[2] than slaves. The preponderance of *ingenui* and *liberti* is probably due not solely to a less frequent recording of slave names but also to the fact that the type of work demanded in the commercial houses could be done only by Italians or by an intelligent class of slaves, and such a class tended in time to secure its own manumission.[3]

Many of the men engaged in trade in Delos were *ingenui*. The size of the business houses is roughly indicated by the number of individuals using the family *nomina* in their signatures, and the larger the establishment, the greater proportion of libertine and slave names we should expect to find. Yet in the lists of the families whose *nomina* are represented by seven or more individuals[4] twenty per cent are freemen.[5] In several cases freemen from more than one generation of the family are mentioned in the inscription.[6] The great majority of *nomina*, however, are represented by very few individuals. Almost half of the free men (50) are either

---

[1] Hatzfeld, *op. cit.*, pp. 10 ff.

[2] An equivocal form of the name, for example, Λεύκιος 'Αιμίλιος Ποπλίου is very common. Some of the users of the form are certainly *ingenui*, some *liberti*, (Hatzfeld, *op. cit.*, p. 137) but where no second definite signature exists by which the first can be interpreted, the status of the man remains doubtful.

[3] Cato the Elder was thus represented in trade by his *libertus*, (Plut. Cat. Maj. 21).

[4] Aemilii, Audii, Aufidii, Caecilii, Castricii, Egnatii, Gerillani, Granii, Maecii, Paconii, Pedii, Sehei, Stertinii, Tutorii.

[5] Twenty-six out of 132. The presence in Delos of still other freemen is implied by the fact that slaves manumitted by members of the family who do not themselves appear on the Delian lists occur in every group. Among the Granii, for instance, no *ingenuus* is actually recorded in Delos but *liberti* of six different *patroni* appear. It is altogether likely that among such *patroni* some were *ingenui* and resided in Delos, though the fact is not recorded. Others may never have left Italy.

[6] Cf. the Audii, Cotii, Gerillani, Plotii.

sole representatives of the *nomen* or they share it with only one other person; that is, about one-half of the whole number of Italians in Delos were either owners of small businesses which they managed with the aid of a partner or a *libertus* or a few slaves, or they were at work in the offices of the larger firms. There was evidently room in the foreign field for the man of small capital. This indicates the motive which drew many Italians of the poorer classes out of Italy.

The Italian homes of the Delian merchants are rarely indicated.[1] Six *nomina* are noted by Hatzfeld as Latin, four from the neighborhood of Puteoli and nine more from South Italy and Sicily.[2] It is certain that they were employed in banking, and the exportation of Italian oil [3] and it seems likely that Delos was a clearing house for many other Italian and eastern exports and imports.[4]

c. *Aratores* and *Pecuarii*. The owners of the *latifundia* outside of Italy apparently worked them with slave labor. On a stock farm in Epirus owned by Atticus,[5] he raised 800 sheep besides cattle and horses, employing a flock master, and a shepherd for every hundred sheep.[6] A certain Alexio was apparently in charge [7] and through him or other stewards money and clothing were furnished to Cicero.[8] Atticus does

---

[1] One citizen names himself Lanuvinus (Hatzfeld, *op. cit.*, p. 20) and a freeman (or *libertus*) φρεγελλανος (p. 78).

[2] pp. 131–2.

[3] See Hatzfeld's summary, pp. 140–146.

[4] We know for instance that Roman companies were managing the slave trade at the end of the second century (Diodor. XXXVI, 3, 1) and that from 146 on, Delos was the great slave market (Strabo XIV, 5, 2). Pârvan's statement (*op. cit.*, p. 36) that the Italians confined themselves to the banking business and the importation of grain is naturally to be restricted to the larger houses. The petty *mercatores* carried about what their customers wanted. (Wine, Diodor. V, 26; and other things, *ea quae ad effeminandos animos pertinent*, Caes. B. G. I, 1, 3; II, 15, 4; 14, 2, 6).

[5] Varro, Rust. II, 2 ff. It was apparently considered a typical stock farm (II, 1, 6).

[6] Varro, Rust. 2, 20; 10, 10.

[7] Cic. Att. XIII, 25, 3; VII, 2, 31. His name indicates libertine or slave status.

[8] Att. XI, 2, 4.

not hint that his *familia* differed from the usual Epirote *familiae* made up of slaves under *praefecti*.[1] We know also a few details of a large farm [2] near Narbo which as early as 81 had already been owned by three Quinctii in succession, a father [3] and two sons. One son who actually lived on the farm formed a partnership with a connection by marriage, an ex-*praeco*, and together they raised for sale [4] "the ordinary Gallic products." [5] They employed slaves owned jointly and slaves owned by Quinctius alone,[6] and apparently themselves acted as overseers. Here again there is no trace of the employment of Italian freemen of the poorer class; in the course of the narrative of a lawsuit in which tenants or free employees would have been valuable witnesses for the owner none are mentioned.

There is no question, however, that at least during the last century of the republic a certain number of poorer Italians did go out from Italy and take up land. That the oversea colony was not so popular as homestead distribution in Italy is witnessed by the succession of agrarian laws from the Sempronian to the Julian, and it was not thoroughly successful until Julius Caesar made it so.[7] Earlier than this, however, Italians had taken up land outside Italy. In 122, 6,000 Roman citizens were settled on the site of Carthage; [8] colonists were sent to Narbo in 118,[9] and in Corsica, to Colonia Mariana and to Aleria under Marius and Sulla respectively. Though there were no early colonies in Spain, Metellus

---

[1] Varro, Rust. I, 17, 5.

[2] *Pecuaria res ampla et rustica sane bene culta et fructuosa* (Cic. Quinct. 12).

[3] Cic. Quinct, 98.

[4] Cic. Quinct. 11.

[5] Cic. Quinct. 12, *societatem earum rerum quae in Gallia comparabantur.*

[6] Cic. Quinct, 28; 90.

[7] For list of Caesar's colonies see Kornemann, *Coloniae* R. E., (1900) pp. 526–533.

[8] See Kornemann, p. 532.

[9] See Cic. Font. 12, *ex tot negotiatorum, colonorum, publicanorum, aratorum, pecuariorum numero*, etc. *Coloni* are omitted from a similar list (Font. 46) being summed up as *Narbonensis colonia.*

Balearicus removed 3,000 Romans who had settled there by 121 to the newly conquered Balearic Islands.[1] Under Pompey especially veterans were encouraged to settle with their families in permanent homes outside Italy. Large numbers were left by him in the East, as, for instance, at Nicopolis in 65.[2] In 49 he called out a legion of veterans from Cilicia,[3] a legion from Crete and Macedonia, and two from Asia.[4] In 48 a legion was made up in Pontus from reserve soldiers.[5]

If we fill in a picture from these isolated facts, we realize that during the second century and the first half of the first century numbers of individuals and families were leaving Italy not for temporary but for permanent residence in some other part of the world.[6] The emigration from the lower classes was not only greater than from the upper, but such settlers left Italy without the idea of an ultimate return. The drain on this stratum of population in Italy was correspondingly greater. Toward the end of the republican period it was apparently increasingly easy to persuade them to go,[7] but the habit was by that time more than a century old.

4. Decline in the Birth rate. According to Plutarch, in the years after the law which restricted holdings of public land [8] fell into neglect and before 151, the Italian peasants evicted from their holdings "neglected the rearing of children" so that all Italy soon perceived the decrease in the free population.[9] A similar statement dealing with the succeeding generation who by 133 formed part of the city proletariat

[1] Strabo III, 5, 1. Cf. also the foundation of Carteia to provide for 4,000 children of Roman soldiers by Spanish mothers (Liv. XLIII, 3).
[2] Dio XXXVI, 50, 3; XXXVII, 20, 2; Appian, Mithr. 115.
[3] Cicero had held a levy of Roman citizens in Cilicia in 51 (Att. V, 18, 2).
[4] Caes. B. C. III, 4, 1–2.
[5] Bell. Alex. 34, 5. For Gabinius's soldiers who had remained in Alexandria, see Caes. B. C. III, 110.
[6] Cf. Cic. Balb. 28.. *Multi etiam superiore memoria civis Romani sua voluntate, indemnati et incolumes, his rebus relictis alias se in civitates contulerunt.*
[7] Cf. Cic. leg. agr. II, 42, of the Egyptian proposal of Rullus, *dicitur — demigraturos in illa loca nostros homines propter agrorum bonitatem et omnium rerum copiam.*
[8] See p. 44, n. 2 for its probable date.
[9] Plut. T. Gr. 8.

is made by Appian in the account of Ti. Gracchus's speech
on his agrarian law.   The poor supported Gracchus's asser-
tions by declaring that they were being reduced from comfort
to extreme poverty and from that to childlessness because they
could not bring up children.[1]   But the form in which Gracchus
cast his legislation shows his belief that deliberate childlessness was only a secondary cause for the decrease in Italian
population and that if the primary causes were dealt with
successfully the secondary would right itself.   He may have
been right; his attitude is not controverted by the fact that
legislation on the subject was introduced two years later by
the censor, Metellus Macedonicus,[2] for the latter's action
seems to have been aimed not at the poor but at the better
educated and wealthier classes.   In their representative,
Lucilius[3] and in Afranius[4] we catch an echo of the talk
stirred up by Metellus's proposition, and the speech in which
he proposed compulsory marriage *liberorum creandorum causa*
and publicly rebuked its avoidance became famous enough
to be used at second-hand by Augustus a century later.[5]

Though we have Cicero's word that by the middle of the
first century the problem had again to be taken up,[6] we are
ignorant whether celibacy and deliberate childlessness had
by that time become customary among the lower classes as
well as the upper.   Caesar's remedy, however, which consisted of prizes to fathers of large families,[7] implies that he

---

[1] Appian, B. C. I, 10.

[2] Liv. Epit. 59.

[3] Lucil. 676–687 M; see Cichorius, *Untersuch z. Lucil.* pp. 133 ff.

[4] Afranius, Prol. to Vopiscus, 360–2 C. R. F.[2] p. 211; Marx on *Afranius*,
R. E. pp. 708–10.

[5] Gell. I, 6, 2; Suet. Aug. 89.   His line of argument seems to have been
the duty of the individual citizen to rear children for the good of the state.

[6] Cic. Marc. 23. *propaganda suboles . . . . omnia, quae dilapsa iam
diffluxerunt, severis legibus vincienda sunt.*

[7] Dio XLIII, 25, 2.   Though the provision of Caesar's agrarian law of
59 that the recipient of land must have at least three children (Dio
XXXVIII, 7, 3; Suet. Jul. 20, 3; Appian, B. C. II, 10) is puzzling if the
recipient is also to be a veteran, it seems certain that some preferential
treatment was to be given to fathers of families, whether veterans or civil-
ians.   This supports the idea that child-bearing had to be artificially
encouraged among the poorer people.

was attacking a situation which was common among the poor. It seems probable that what in the second century had been at least among the lower classes merely a result of other conditions had in the first century become a primary cause of the decline of native stock in Italy among lower and upper classes alike.

B. THE INCREASE OF FOREIGN STOCK IN ITALY
FROM 200 TO 31 B.C.

Such losses among the native stock as those recorded in the first section of this chapter were numerically more than made good. Large numbers of non-Italians were constantly arriving in Italy and they became permanent residents. This was true of all parts of Italy. Because our literary sources deal with the history of Rome, and with general Italian history only in its connection with Roman, we happen to know more details of the newcomers' relation to Roman than to general Italian conditions, but the presence of foreigners throughout Italy and their economic importance everywhere is implied where it is not stated.

I. INCREASE BY FREE IMMIGRATION

There were among such foreigners both free immigrants and slaves.[1] The records of the non-Italian free immigration are, however, so scanty as to be of little use,[2] although the names of a few individuals in the second and first centuries, largely professional men and artists, who took up an Italian residence and in some cases received the citizenship are known.[3] It is likely that the number of free immigrants

---

[1] Compare Augustus's limitation of manumission, *magni praeterea existimans sincerum atque ab omni colluvione peregrini ac servilis sanguinis incorruptum servare populum* (Suet. Aug. 40, 3).

[2] Compare for instance the vague fact of the expulsion of Greek teachers from Rome in 161 (Suet. Rhet. 1, p. 120 R; Gell. 15, 11).

[3] See the list of Greeks in Rome in Hillscher, *Hominum Litteratorum Graecorum in Urbe Roma Commoratorum.* NJklA. Supp. 18 (1892) pp. 356 ff.

was actually at all periods a small one.[1] Few opportunities
in industry were open to free labor at Rome or in Italy generally and for the free poor outside Italy, therefore, a possible
betterment of their economic condition did not figure as a
stimulus toward emigration.   The difficulty and insecurity
of travelling, moreover, hindered the less resolute.

II.   INCREASE BY SLAVE IMMIGRATION

There was always, on the other hand, a market for slave
labor, and persons other than the emigrants themselves over-
came the difficulties of transportation.   About 200 the demand
for slaves became very urgent;[2] as was natural at the close
of a long war, there existed both an unusual shortage of labor
and an unusual need for it.   Great numbers of Italians had
been killed, disabled or enslaved, and the fact that when the
government tried to relieve the survivors from further service,
many re-enlisted for the new armies shows that the long cam-
paigning had begun to breed disinclination for a life of routine.[3]   Further, it happened that successive wars in Macedonia, Spain, and elsewhere kept the next generation also
pretty steadily under conscription.   At the same time there

---

[1] For the slave origin of the ordinary trader of oriental stock in Italy,
see Pârvan, *op. cit.*, p. 39.

[2] The number of Carthaginian captives sold as slaves during the progress
of the Second Punic war was not large; 2,000 of the garrison in Malta in
218 (Liv. XXI, 51, 2-3), the garrison of Capua in 211 (Appian, Hann.
43), and the beaten army at Baecula, *i. e.* 12,000, less the Spanish auxi-
liaries who were sent home, in 209 (Liv. XXVII, 19, 2 and 8).   On the
other hand, slaves who had served in the Roman army in 216 (Liv. XXII,
57, 11; XXIII, 14, 2) were manumitted, either at once (Appian, Hann.
27) or after serving two years (Liv. XXIV, 14, 3 ff.).   Their number was
8,000 (so Liv., Appian, Macr. Sat. I, 11, 30, 24,000, Val. Max VII, 6, 1),
but their loss was felt heavily, combined as it was with the conscription
of slaves as rowers for the fleets in 210 (Liv. XXVI, 35, 5) and in 206
(XXVIII, 11, 9).   They seem to have remained in service at least till
205 (Liv. XXVIII, 46, 13).

[3] They were assigned land (Liv. XXXI, 4, 1-3), yet re-enlisted (Liv.
XXXII, 8, 2; 9, 1; XXXV, 2, 8).   There was some doubt whether the
2,000 veterans of Liv. XXXI, 14, 2; XXXII, 3, 3-7 were actually volun-
teers.

was desperate need for workers to rebuild and re-cultivate Italy. An increase of the slave labor to which the people were already accustomed would promptly suggest itself as a solution of the difficulty, while successful wars leaving captives and money in the victors' hands made the carrying out of such an idea instantly practical. Once introduced as a necessity of the hour, slave labor increased by its own momentum; originally caused by a lack of available free labor, it lessened the demand for that labor when it again became available. It was thus a factor in preventing the recovery of the native stock from losses by war, military service and emigration which in a country with healthy economic conditions would probably have taken place.

The statements of all the handbooks on the sources of the slave supply need not be repeated in detail. While war captives predominated among the slaves of 200–146 and slaves from the block later, in both periods each source was drawn on and the old fashion of raising slaves in the *familia* continued, a minor but steady contribution to the whole number.

Numerical statistics on the increasing slave importation are even more difficult to collect than similar statistics on the decrease among native Italians. In the following pages may be found some suggestions of the number and nationality of the slaves.

1. **The War Captives.** In spite of the statements that the sale of captives was a regular procedure[1] it would be unsafe to count all Roman war prisoners as slaves.[2] In the following instances, however, actual sale of prisoners is recorded in the sources[3] or it is indirectly proved by the

---

[1] See E. Köser, *de captivis Romanorum*, Giessen (1904); M. Bang, *Herkunft d. röm. Sklaven*, M. R. I. 27 (1912) p. 192. Cato (234–149) habitually selected his slaves from among war captives (Plut. Cat. Maj. 21).

[2] See Köser, *op. cit.*, pp. 68–72 including n. 5, and 98 for war captives, usually those of higher rank, who were never sold but kept in prison or under guard in Italy.

[3] See Köser, *op. cit.*, p. 94, n. 6, for list from which the following references are taken.

appearance of slaves of the nationality in question at Rome soon after the capture of prisoners.

Indication of numbers	Nationality	Date	Source
Slaves in Setia, Norba, Circeii	Carthaginians or Asiatics [1]	198	Liv. XXXII, 26, 5.
500 in Praeneste	————	198	Liv. XXXII, 26, 15–17.
5000 (So Weissenborn-Müller)	Macedonians	197	Liv. XXXIII, 10, 7, 11, 1.
Inhabitants of seven castella	Spaniards	195	Plut. Cat. Maj. 10; Liv. XXXIV, 16, 10; 21, 5.
Inhabitants of Samé	Greeks	189	Liv. XXXVIII, 29, 11.
Inhabitants of Corbio	Spaniards	184	Liv. XXXIX, 42, 1.
5632 inhabitants of Mutila and Faveria	Illyrians	177	Liv. XLI, 11, 8–9.
80,000 killed or captured; numerous in Italy	Sardinians	177	Liv. XLI, 28, 8; Aur. Vict. Vir. III, 57, 2; Fest. 322 M; Cic. Epist. VII, 24, 2; Varro. Sat. Men. 78.
Inhabitants of Mylae	Thessalians	171	Liv. XLII, 54, 6.
Familiae of Thebans	————	171	Liv. XLII, 63, 12.
150,000	Epirotes	167	Liv. XLV, 34, 5.
Many Macedonian slaves at Rome		after 167	Cic. Tusc. III, 53.
————	Dalmatians	155	Zon. 9, 25 end.
9,500	Spaniards	142–17	Appian, Hisp. 68.
Survivors of Carthage	Carthaginians, and their slaves?	146	Oros. IV, 23, 7.
50,000			Appian, Lib. 130.
36,000			Flor. I, 31, 16.
55,000			Oros. 4, 23, 2.
Many Carthaginian slaves in Rome			Cic. Tusc. III, 53.
Survivors of Numantia	Spaniards	133	Appian, Hisp. 98.
60,000 Cimbri 90,000 Teutons [2]	Gauls and Germans [3]	102	Liv. Epit. 68.

[1] "Slaves of Carthaginian hostages" may well have been themselves Asiatic; see Mahaffy, Ha. VII (1890) pp. 167 ff.

[2] 100,000 Teutons, Plut. Mar. 21; 140,000 men (Oros. 5, 16); see, however, Dio, fr. 94.

[3] For summary of discussion on the original stock of the Cimbri, see Rice-Holmes, Caesar's Conquest of Gaul, Oxford (1911), pp. 546 ff.

Indication of numbers	Nationality	Date	Source
Inhabitants of Co-lenda	Spaniards	98	Appian, Hisp. 99.
Slaves of Athenians	Greeks or Asiatics?	86	Appian, Mithr. 38 (see Gran. Lic. p. 33 Bonn).
6,000 inhabitants of Mitylene (or their slaves?)	Greeks (?)	84	Plut. Luc. 4.
Many towns	Asiatics	84	Appian, Mithr. 61.
Great numbers of inhabitants	Pontus	72	Appian, Mithr. 78.
53,000 Aduatuci	Gauls	57	Caes. B. G. II, 33, 7.
All Veneti but senate	Gauls	56	Caes. B. G. III. 16, 4.
Great number of Nervii	Gauls	53	Caes. B. G. VI, 3, 2.
Total number of prisoners 1,000,000[1]			Plut. Caes. 15. Appian, Celt. 2.
Inhabitants of Zeno-dotia	Mesopotamians	54	Plut. Crass. 17.
Inhabitants of Pin-denissus to the value of 120,000 sesterces	Cilicians	51	Cic. Att. V, 20, 5.
6,000 Alexandrians	Egyptians	48	Bell. Alex. 18, 4.
Inhabitants of Tarsus	Cilicians	43	Appian, B. C. IV, 64.

2. Slaves from the Block. There is no doubt that the slave traders early supplied Roman markets with slaves bought from persons who raised them for sale or kidnapped them from districts at peace with Rome. Plautus refers to Egyptian and Syrian slaves who at that date in Rome could only have been products of the slave trade,[2] and Livy ventures

---

[1] For the expectation of additions to the slave markets from Caesar's campaigns see Cic. Att. IV, 17, 6. For Caesar's practice of giving slaves to his troops see Caes. B. G. VI, 3, 2; VII, 89, 5; Suet. Jul. 26, 3; Bell. Alex. 18, 4–19, 1.

[2] *Egyptian*: Plaut. Poen. 1291 is a genuine Roman reference. *Egyptian* or *Syrian* (Merc. 415) and *Ethiopian* (Ter. Eun. 165, 471), may be reflections of Greek originals. Plautus (Trin. 542–546) mentions *Syrian* slaves and goes on to compare them with Campanian. There is no positive evidence that the Campanian reference is not a Roman hit attached to a Greek reference to Syrians, but there may have been Syrian as well as Campanian slaves at Rome at the time.

to apply to the Syrians and Asiatics of 191 the later catch-word, *genera hominum servitate nata*.[1] But Strabo implies that the great period of slave hunting for Italian markets did not begin until the middle of the century.[2] When Cilicia and Syria were defenseless under a weak dynasty, free entrance was given to pirates and slave dealers. Export of slaves became very profitable. The business itself was proverbially easy, and the large market of Delos was near, a centre where 10,000 slaves could be received and forwarded in a single day.[3] Roman wealth acquired after the downfall of Carthage and Corinth sent up the demand for slaves and the regular dealers, the pirates, even the governments of Rhodes and Egypt saw to the supply. Of the number which reached Italy from Syria and Cilicia unfortunately no estimate can be made. There were close to 60,000, largely Syrians and Cilicians in the slave army of 135 in Sicily[4] and that they were also exceedingly numerous in Italy cannot be doubted.[5] By the latter part of the century the importation of slaves for Italy and the provinces had been taken over by efficient Roman companies.[6] They continued to exploit the old fields in the East, and Bithynia was successfully included so that by 104 her king complained that almost all her free popula-

---

[1] Liv. XXXVI, 17, 5; see XXXV, 49, 8 and Cic. prov. cons. 10.

[2] Strabo XIV, 5, 2. Carthage, Greece and probably Sicily had supplied themselves from these districts previously. Mahaffy (Ha. 7 (1890) pp. 169–70) argues that the multitudes of Syrian and Cilician slaves in Sicily by 142 were bought from Carthaginian *latifundia* and had been originally procured directly from the East, Roman slave markets like Delos being avoided.

[3] Phaselis and Side in Pamphylia under Lycian patronage were also well known markets (Strabo XIV, 3, 2).

[4] Diodor. XXXIV, 2, 16. For the nationality of the slaves, see Diodor. XXXIV, 2, 5, 16, 17, 21, 24, 43.

[5] Compare the saying of Cicero's grandfather, "The men of our generation are like Syrian slaves, the better they know Greek the more rascally they are" (Cic. de Orat. 11, 265). Syrians are mentioned three times in Lucilius (*i. e.* between 131 and 102), 128 M (cf. Virg. Copa 1), 497–8, 669–80. The last case is unusually interesting if Marx is correct and "Syrus" is here an equivalent of *faenerator*.

[6] Diodor. XXXVI, 3, 1; Plut. Luc. 20.

tion was working as slaves in the provinces.[1] That slaves were obtained elsewhere, especially in Asia, is certain though no statement to that effect exists.

In the first century these great fields for the slave dealer remained open and new territory was added by Lucullus, Sulla and Pompey. Apparently the importations did not diminish even after the markets were flooded with German and Gallic war captives in the years following 102. The literature of the first century furnishes many references to large groups of slaves or *liberti* as well as to individuals, and not only the main sources of supply but minor sources, nationalities contributing a few individuals, appear. Such references are collected in the following list, the main value of which lies not in striking general statements but in its suggestion of variety as well as of numbers.[2]

Nationality	Any indication of number
Ethiopians	100 *venatores* (Plin. N. H. 8, 131); 3 individuals (Appian, B. C. IV, 134; *Cic. Verr. III, 107 ff; Plut. Cic. 26); 1 literary reference (Auct. ad. Her. IV, 63).
Gaetulians	*bestiarii* (Plin. N. H. 8, 20).
Moors	*iaculatores* (*Sen. Dial. X, 13, 6; Plin. N. H. 8, 52).
Egyptians	1 individual (Athen. I 20 D.); literary reference (Cic. Orat. 232).
Syrians	9 individuals (*Suet. Gramm. 8 and 13; *Plin. N. H. 35, 199; *Cic. Har. Resp. 1; Plut. Luc. 21; Mar. 17; Suidas on Tyrranio Minor; C. I. L. VI, 5639; *10149); literary references (Cic. Pis. 1; Orat. 232; Appian, B. C. II, 74; Macr. Sat. II, 7, 67 et al.).

[1] Diodor. XXXVI, 3, 1; 800 free men were released in a few days in Sicily as a result of his protest.

[2] The list is based on the longer list compiled by Bang (M. R. I. 25 (1910) pp. 225 ff). He uses his references to support the point that so long as Rome was limited in area and involved in foreign conquest captives from outside her territory formed the main body of her slaves; that later when she was making no more conquests her slaves were largely kidnapped or raised for sale in districts controlled by her. I have included here only such references as concern slaves presumably from the block living in Italy in the first century B.C. Some, like the Jews referred to in Cicero's speech for Flaccus, may have been a second or third generation removed from the original slave immigrant. References not found in Bang are marked with an asterisk.

Nationality	Any indication of number
Jews	Numerous in Rome (*Cic. Flacc. 66, 67; *Hor. Serm. I, 4, 142–3; *Suet. Jul. 84). 1 individual (Plut. Cic. 7).[1]
Spaniards	Employed on farms (Varro Rust. II, 10, 4). 1 individual (C. I. L. IV, 1848).
Liburnian	1 individual (C. I. L. IX, 352).
Greeks	1 individual (*Suet. Gramm. 15).
Thracians	Many gladiators (Plut. Crass. 8). 1 individual (Appian, B. C. I, 116).
Bithynians	Literary reference (Catull. 10, 15).
Asiatics	Numerous in Rome (*Cic. Flacc. 17); 5 individuals (*Cic. Verr. V, 30; *IV, 54; *Q. fr. I, 1, 19; *Plin. N. H. 7, 56; I. G. XIV, 666); literary references (Cic. p. red. in sen. 14; S. Rosc. 89; *Hor. Epist. I, 6, 39; Appian, B. C. II, 74).
Pontus	1 individual (*Cic. Att. II, 6, 1 et al., Varro in G. L. 4, p. 529, 10 K).
Gauls or Germans	35,000–36,000 gladiators (Liv. Epit. 97 = Frontin. Strat. 2, 5, 34; Appian, B. C. I, 117); employed on farms, Varro Rust. II, 10, 4). 6 individuals (Sall. Hist. III, 96 D; Frontin. Strat. 2, 4, 7; 5, 34; Plut. Crass. 8; Oros. 5, 24, 1; Liv. Epit. 77; Suet. Gramm. 7; Dio LIV, 21, 3); a Gallic slave dealer (Cic. Quinct. 24).
Indians	Plin. N. H. 2, 170; literary reference (*Hor. Serm. II, 8, 14).
Indefinite	Plin. N. H. 7, 56; 35, 199; *Plut. Comp. Crass. & Nic. 1.

III. SURVIVAL OF SLAVE STOCK IN ITALY

Fragmentary as it is, the direct information at our disposal is enough to establish the fact that the foreign population in Italy was increasing during the years 200–31, but other evidence can also be used in this connection. The history of the servile uprisings confirms both the early date and the great volume of slave immigration. The survival of slave stock in Italy is proved by the records of the Roman *familiae* which show that

---

[1] Cartault thinks the *Apella Iudaeius* of Horace (Serm. I, 5, 100) was a well-known *libertus*. More probably the reference is literary.

the immigrants who remained slaves reproduced or perhaps even increased their original number, and further by the legislation regulating the vote of the *libertini* and the sons of *libertini* which shows that immigrants who emerged from slavery maintained themselves as a formidably large section of the Roman citizen body.

1. **The Servile Uprisings.**[1] *a.* 198–185. The first outbreak of slaves in Italy took place within three years of the end of the second Punic War in the Latin towns.[2] In Setia in 198 *familiae* of Carthaginian hostages conspired with other slaves of their own nationality.[3] The movement threatened Norba and Circeii and five hundred slaves were arrested and punished in Praeneste. Two years later in Etruria a more dangerous uprising occurred.[4] Etruria became for the time being an active menace, and the slaves were dispersed only by the hard exertion of a Roman legion. In Apulia the slaves tried to free themselves by way of brigandage rather than by open outbreaks. Their organization apparently ignored by the government at first became so powerful that when the Roman praetor finally broke up the gangs of bandits in 185 he had condemned upwards of 9,000 individuals.[5]

b. 133. Whether newcomers kicking against the pricks were responsible for the outbreaks of 133 in Italy [6] is not known. For some reason Etruria and Apulia remained quiet, but there was a slight outbreak in Rome itself and at Sinuessa 4,000 slaves were involved.[7] No disturbance in Italy

---

[1] See Rathke, *de Romanorum Bellis Servilibus* (Berlin) 1904. Facts of numbers and nationality are selected here from the historians.

[2] Liv. XXXII, 26, 4 ff.

[3] Probably Asiatic rather than Carthaginian; see p. 32, n.1.

[4] Liv. XXXIII, 36, 1–3. The *latifundia* system was probably spreading fast in Etruria; in 137 it was completely established (Plut. T. Gr. 8). In Apulia it had been introduced still earlier for in 216 two hundred and seventy *pastores* from the region had served in the cavalry (Val. Max. VII, 6, 1); by 36, however, according to Varro (Rust. I, 29, 2) the *latifundia* had begun to give way to small farms.

[5] Liv. XXXIX, 29, 8–10.

[6] See Rathke, *op. cit.*, p. 33 for dates.

[7] Minturnae and Sinuessa, Oros. 5, 9; Rome, Diodor. XXXIV, 2, 19. It

is recorded during 132 while the Sicilian uprising was being
finally put down by Roman armies, nor do we know what
means were taken to avert a disaster so much dreaded.[1]

c. 104. The extent of the outbreaks in Italy during
the years of the second servile uprising in Sicily is difficult
to determine from the material on hand.[2] Diodorus describes
the revolts as πλειοῦς and πολλαί, but the excerpts mention
only two in Campania, and a more serious one in an unnamed
locality,[3] in the course of which the Roman leaders and 3,500
slaves were killed.

d. 73–1. The servile uprising under Spartacus was by
all odds the most dangerous to Rome in its possibilities and
the most serious during its progress. Its course is fairly
clear though contradictions in the historians make questions
of chronology and of the numbers engaged difficult of settle-
ment.[4]

In 73 under the leadership of the Thracian Spartacus and
two Gauls, seventy slave gladiators escaped from a gladia-
torial school at Capua and made their way to Vesuvius.
They attacked and defeated 3,000 soldiers hastily raised in
Campania and, joined by other slaves and by some freemen
from the rural districts as well, they began to ravage Campania. The praetor at first with 4,000, later with more
soldiers, attempted vainly to cut off their forces and restrict
the uprising to a local area, but they eluded him, made their
way to Lucania and spent the winter there. Recruits from

---

is tempting to connect the attempts in this troubled year with the dis-
turbances in Rome, and perhaps with the absence in Rome of many of
the country people (Appian, B. C. I, 10). A chain of servile uprisings took
place in the decade, however, Sicily 135–2, Delos and Attica 133, and the
movement led by Aristonicus of Pergamon 133–129. (For the last date
cf. Appian, B. C. I, 17 with Mithr. 62).

[1] Appian, B. C. I, 9.
[2] Diodor. XXXVI, 2.
[3] This may have been Lucania. See Rathke (*op. cit.*) p. 42. Heitland
(Rom. Rep. II, p. 380) suggests that the force ἐκ δὲ τῆς Λευκανίας (Diodor.
XXXVI, 8, 1) taken by Lucullus to Sicily in 103 may have been raised in
view of expected outbreaks in Lucanian *latifundia*.
[4] See Rathke, *op. cit.*, for discussions of moot points.

Lucanian farms doubled their number. By the spring more vigorous measures were taken by the government and one of Spartacus's lieutenants was defeated, but Spartacus himself going North into Samnium defeated the consuls in turn, and later the consuls and praetor with their combined armies of six legions. Rome itself was now threatened. Spartacus fought two victorious battles, at Mutina and later in Picinum, but he was thwarted by his own soldiers in his plan of leaving Italy by the north, and Crassus, who took command of the Roman troops in July 72, succeeded little by little during the next eighteen months in getting the better of him. He was forced south and finally defeated in Lucania and Apulia.

The number of men serving under him is disputed and cannot be exactly fixed.[1] They were largely Thracians, Gauls, and Germans like their leaders, employed on the great stock farms of southern Italy.[2] The length of time needed to put down the outbreak, the important men associated in command of the government troops, and the panic which the idea of a servile uprising caused during the remaining years of the Republic prove the peril in which Rome felt herself placed.

Accusation of intention to call out the slaves was made thenceforth against every political agitator in turn. Milo and Caelius in their ill-starred attempt in 48 did actually try to put themselves at the head of a slave army.[3] But Catiline in spite of the statements of his enemies and the advice of his friends did not do so.[4] Clodius's famous *servorum dilectus*

---

[1] The tradition followed by Livy and Appian places the numbers very high, 120,000 (Appian, B. C. I, 117; Liv. Epit. 96–7; Oros., Frontin., etc.); Sallust (Hist.) gives no figures. Mommsen accepts 40,000 as a moderate estimate, Heitland 70,000.

[2] Many of them must have been Cimbric or Teuton captives of 102 or the sons of such captives.

[3] Caes. B. C. III, 21–2.

[4] See Sallust's plain statement (Cat. 56, 5): *servitia repudiabat*. Catiline's supporters in the South, however, probably intended to rouse the slaves. See Sall. Cat. 30, 2; 46, 3; Lentulus advised it in the North (Cic. Cat. III, 12). For statements that Catiline actually made use of slaves see Cicero *passim*, Appian, B. C. II, 2; Dio XXXVII, 33, 2.

was in no sense a call to a general servile uprising; it was rather the unusually efficient manipulation of a tool well-known to both his friends and his enemies.[1]   Cicero's charge that Antony freed slaves or added them to his forces [2] may or may not be true; in any case Antony obviously had no intention of starting any general movement among them.   Clearly, the inauguration of such a movement was beyond the consideration of all except the most desperate.   If in times of almost continuous excitement and violence slaves were not enlisted on either side it was because they were so numerous that to every Italian alike, of every political faction, their subordination was of the first moment.

Granted the arrival of many foreigners in Italy, coming as slaves and remaining permanently in their new home, the question arises whether this foreign stock survived or whether it died out after one or two generations, to be replaced by fresh arrivals who in turn failed to perpetuate themselves.

In the scarcity of records [3] a fairly conclusive answer may be reached through the references to the productivity of slaves in the *familiae rusticae* and *urbanae* and through the history of libertine suffrage.

2. The Productivity of Slaves.   Appian makes a strong statement on the conditions among *familiae rusticae* in the period preceding the Gracchi:

> "The possession of slaves brought them (the rich land owners) great gain from the multitude of their progeny who increased because they were exempt from military service. . . . thus the race of slaves multiplied throughout the country." [4]

Curiously enough Cato's contemporary work on agriculture does not confirm this.   An anecdote [5] informs us that the

---

[1] It was an outgrowth of the *familia armata*.
[2] Cic. Epist. XI, 10, 3; 13, 2.
[3] Sepulchral inscriptions of slaves, for instance, date only from the very late republican period.   See Momm. St. R. III, 201, n. 3.
[4] B. C. I, 7.   Translation of H. White, London 1899.
[5] Plut. Cat. Maj. 20.

slaves in his own *familia* had children, but the arrangement
for the labor which he describes on his model estates includes
only one woman, the *villica*,[1] nor does he advise any woman's
work like weaving or spinning on the farms. It is probable
therefore that his *vernae* were children of slaves of the *familia
urbana*, and that he made no plans for breeding slaves among
the agricultural laborers as an investment. Whether Appian's
statement should be read in the light of Cato's practice is,
however, doubtful. A century later Varro refers to women
and children among the *pastores*, and to the increase among
slaves as a definite source of profit: *puerperio familiam faciunt
maiorem et rem pecuariam fructuosiorem*.[2] A general practice
among owners of *familiae rusticae* on moderate sized estates
is indicated.[3]

The conditions prevailing among the slaves in the *familiae
urbanae* are more certain though literary references to the
subject are few.[4] Nepos tells us that Atticus would have
none but *vernae* in his large household,[5] to the individual
members of which he wished to give careful training. And
above all the *columbariae* inscriptions of the great houses of
the late Republic and early Empire give definite evidence
for the frequent *contubernales* and children of slaves recorded
in the *familiae*.[6]

It is certain then that the slave population in Italy was not
increased by fresh arrivals from outside only. Many of those
already in Italy maintained their stock by producing children.

3. The Increase in Voters of Slave Stock.
The ease of
manumission is one of the outstanding facts in the history of

---

[1] Cato Agr. CXLII.
[2] Varro, Rust. II, 1, 26. Columella (50 A.D.) says that a slave woman
on a farm who bore more than three children should be rewarded with
freedom (I, 8, 18).
[3] See also Hor. Ep. II, 65, *vernas ditis examen domus*, and Tib. II, 1, 23.
[4] The letters of Cicero contain only one reference to a *verna* (Epist.
VIII, 15, 2). A woman of Brutus's *familia* was married to Glycon, the
physician of Hirtius (Cic. Br. I, 6, 2).
[5] Nep. Att. 13, 4.
[6] See C. I. L. VI, 3926 ff. for the monuments of Livia, Drusus, Marcella
and the Statilii. See Amer. Hist. Review 1916, pp. 690 ff. for statistics.

slavery at Rome;[1] the ease with which manumitted slaves passed into the citizen class is another. Although they were often included in the suffrage restriction which affected the proletariat as a whole because in a great majority of cases they were rated in it, for a long period they suffered no special political restrictions.[2] It follows that when the *liberti* as a class did suffer special political restrictions, it was because they were increasing enough to make themselves felt and feared.[3]

The first hint of such a situation is shortly before the Second Punic war, probably in 220. In that year the censors restricted all *liberti* and sons of *liberti* to voting in the four city tribes with the non-propertied citizens even though they owned enough property to raise them above that class. That is, even previous to the war, the number of foreigners holding the franchise and owning property was large enough to be felt as a menace by one section of the native-born voters.[4]

We have seen that the number of slaves in Italy steadily

---

[1] Cf. Cicero's remark that a frugal slave could buy his freedom in seven years (Ph. VIII 32). It was applied also by the individual owner, or by the state especially in connection with military service (Macr. Sat. I, 11, 32; Appian, B. C. I, 49; Mommsen on Res. Gest. 72. References to the practice of manumission often imply the existence of large numbers of slaves. Sulla set free 10,000 slaves who as his *liberti* continued to act in his personal interest (Appian, B. C. I, 100); owners of slaves in 59 set them according to Dio (XXXIX, 24) so that the new *liberti* might share in the corn distributions and the owners be thus spared the expense of their living; Augustus actually restricted the number of slaves who might be manumitted (Suet. Aug. 40, 3).

[2] The Lex Sulpicia (Dessau, I. L. 6088, XXVIII) shows that manumission was recognized as free in the Provinces.

[3] For all the facts on libertine suffrage see Mommsen St. R. III, 434–44.

[4] Mommsen (*op. cit.*, p. 437) thinks it was the rising middle class who thus expressed themselves through Flaminius in 220 and Ti. Gracchus in 168. The plebs (Plut. Flamin. 18) which already included many *liberti* opposed such restrictions on its members, and the aristocracy, believing it could control the votes of men still in a measure dependent on the *patronus*, wished such votes to be scattered as widely as possible and disregarded any possibility of danger to the state. This combination succeeded in winning exemption from the restriction for the sons of *liberti* before 189, and the latter class was numerous and powerful enough to prevent its ever being forced back into the city tribes. Sons of *liberti* were generally entered in the tribe of their patron, *i. e.* a rustic tribe.

rose after 200; the number of *liberti* must have risen proportionally. Ti. Gracchus who was himself responsible for a great increase in 177 probably foresaw an increase still greater at the close of the Third Macedonian war. He saw that at once or in the immediate future *liberti* would be able actually to outvote the native stock. He took time by the forelock and nullified their vote.[1] He compelled all freedmen to vote in one of the city tribes which was to be chosen by lot for each *lustrum* and this restriction continued practically unchanged to the end of the republic. The ex-slaves succeeded in raising it only to the extent of voting in all four city tribes, and no one was able to obtain more for them. The passage in 131 of the bill enjoining the use of the secret ballot lost the *liberti* the help of the nobles by ending the control of the client's vote by the patron. Perhaps exasperation at this break of the ex-slaves from their masters' control as well as defiance in the face of their numbers resounded in the bitter taunts of Scipio Aemilianus in that year: "*Et cum omnis contio acclamasset, 'hostium', inquit armatorum totiens clamore non territus, qui possum vestro moveri, quorum noverca est Italia?*"[2] *Orto deinde murmure, 'non efficietis', ait, 'ut solutos verear quos adligatos adduxi.'*[3]

Cicero refers to Gracchus's action in the dialogue *de Oratore* which he imagines to have taken place in 91 and he informs us that the *liberti* were then numerically a preponderant part of the voting body. (Ti. Gracchus) *verbo libertinos in urbanas tribus transtulit, quod nisi fecisset, rem publicam, quam nunc* (91 B.C.) *vix tenemus, iam diu nullam haberemus.*[4] And he would hardly have made such a striking general statement in his dialogue, had it not been equally true in 54, the year in which he wrote.[5]

[1] The hiatus in the text of Liv. XLV, 15, 1 prevents our knowing whether Gracchus's original proposal absolutely deprived the *liberti* as a class of the vote. The best argument for this view is that the "compromise" later forced on Gracchus by his colleague practically shut them out of it.

[2] Vell. II, 4, 4.

[3] Val. Max. VI, 2, 3.

[4] de Orat. I, 38.

[5] For other references by Cicero to the large libertine vote see Att. II, 1, 8;

Further discrimination against *liberti* took place in 88, when they alone remained restricted to suffrage in the four city tribes although the non-propertied citizens with whom they had been voting were transferred to the rural tribes; that is, all *liberti* were now in a political condition less good than that of all *ingenui*. Under the democratic party of 84 they were raised to an equality with the free voter for the brief time in which that party held office, but attempts by the democrats of 67 and 59 toward the same end failed.

C. Facts of Race and Population Derived from the Sources.

It remains in conclusion to quote the few passages from the sources which directly concern conditions of population either in Rome or in rural Italy at any time in the two hundred years. They present a vivid picture of the results following on the outgoing and incoming of population, a study of which has filled this chapter.

The earliest passage is found in parallel versions in Plutarch and Appian,[1] and the period to which it refers has been usually assumed to be earlier than the one with which we deal. Niese [2]

---

written in 60: *Quid faciemus, si aliter non possumus?* (than make broad concessions to the *equites*) *an libertinis atque etiam servis serviamus?* Att. II, 16, 1 written in 59: *quod vectigal superest domesticum praeter vicensimam? quae mihi videtur una contiuncula clamore pedisequorum nostrorum esse peritura.* Sest. 47 *Sin victi essent boni, qui superessent? Nonne ad servos videtis rem venturam fuisse?*

[1] Plut. Ti. Gr. 8; Appian, B. C. I, 7.

[2] Niese, *Das sogenannte Licinisch-Sextische Akergesetz* (H. 23 (1888) pp. 410 ff.). He proceeds to argue that the law referred to by Appian and Plutarch is the so-called Licinian Law described by Livy but that it should be dated not in 367 but within the limits of our period, preferably about 180. Whether we agree with Niese that the law of 180 was an original enactment or whether we regard it as the re-enactment of an earlier Licinian law, his assertion that the description handed down in the Plutarch-Appian tradition belongs in this period cannot be doubted. It may well be that the difficulty in securing soldiers in 181 and 180 forced a reluctant government into action, while the comparatively peaceful years following the return of the Eastern army in 167, by removing the immediate need for soldiers, allowed the provisions of the law to fall into neglect without the govern-

has pointed out once for all that the details of the descriptions
of economic conditions must be assigned to a date between
the conquest of Italy and 167.

Appian after describing the method of assigning land which
came under the control of the government in the course of
the subjection of Italy goes on to say:

"This they did in order to multiply the Italian
race, which they considered the most laborious of
peoples, so that they might have plenty of allies at
home. But the very opposite thing happened: for
the rich . . . . absorbing any adjacent strips and
their poor neighbours' allotments, partly by purchase
under persuasion, and partly by force, came to cul-
tivate vast tracts instead of single estates, using
slaves as labourers and herdsmen, lest free labourers
should be drawn from agriculture into the army.
At the same time the ownership of slaves brought
them great gain from the multitude of their progeny,
who increased because they were exempt from
military service . . . . thus . . . . the race of slaves
multiplied throughout the country, while the Italian
people dwindled in numbers and strength, being
oppressed by penury, taxes and military service
. . . . (8). For these reasons the people became
troubled lest they should no longer have sufficient
allies of the Italian stock and lest the government
itself should be endangered by such a vast number
of slaves. . . . . A law was at last passed with difficulty at the instance of the tribunes, that nobody
should hold more than 500 jugera of this land, or
pasture on it more than 100 cattle or 500 sheep. To
insure the observance of this law it was provided also
that there should be a certain number of freemen
employed on the farms whose business it should be
to watch and report what was going on. Having
thus comprehended all this in a law they took an oath
over and above the law, and fixed penalties for violat-

ment's troubling itself to interfere. In any case both Appian and Plutarch
connect the final passing of the law with the increasing difficulty of finding
allied soldiers. Appian notes that the initiative was taken by the tribunes.

ing it, and it was supposed that the remaining land
would soon be divided among the poor in small
parcels." [1]

Plutarch after giving a briefer version of the above goes on
to describe more fully than Appian the period following the
passage of the law.[2]

> This act for a short time checked avarice and
> was of assistance to the poor who remained where
> land had been leased to them and worked their
> original allotment. But later the rich men of the
> neighborhood got the leases into their own hands
> again by using feigned names, and at last openly
> held almost everything in their own names. The
> poor driven out from their holdings no longer offered
> themselves readily for military service, and neglected
> the rearing of children so that the whole of Italy soon
> felt a decrease in its free population and became
> filled with gangs of half-civilized slaves. By means
> of these the rich proprietors farmed their estates
> after they had driven out the citizen population. C.
> Laelius, Scipio's friend, attempted a reform (150 B.C.),
> but meeting powerful opponents and fearing actual
> disturbances he gave it up, thus earning the name of
> the Wise.[3]

For eighteen years no legislator dared to rush in where
Laelius feared to tread.

The next statement chronologically is that quoted by
Plutarch from C. Gracchus for the district of Etruria in 137.

[1] Appian, B. C. I, 7–8. Trans. of H. White. The standstill in population about 180 is borne out by the facts that the mountainous region of
Samnium was used as a dumping-ground for 47,000 Ligurians and their
families in 181–180 without protests from Roman citizens (Liv. XL, 38,
1–6; XLI, 4); that previous to 172 the rich Capuan lands were not all
rented (Liv. XLII, 19, 1), and that the state was using non-Romans for
citizen colonies (see Liv. XLII, 4, 4), and the inclusion of Ennius among the
colonists of Potentia or Pisaurum in 184 (Liv. XXXIX, 44, 10; Cic. Brut.
79, Enn. Ann. V 169 Vahl.).
[2] Plut. T. Gr. 8.
[3] See Sall. Jug. 41, 7–8 of the period between 201 and 133. *Populus
militia atque inopia urguebatur; — interea parentes aut parvi liberi militum,
uti quisque potentiore confines erat, sedibus pellebantur.*

But his brother Gaius has written that on his way
to Numantia through Etruria Tiberius remarked
that the country was empty and that the men doing
the farming and herding were foreign and un-
civilized slaves, and then he conceived the political
principles which were the beginning of many ills for
them both.[1]

Two facts in regard to this passage are worth emphasizing:
first, that it is actual contemporary evidence; second, that
Ti. Gracchus's own speeches on the presentation of his bill in
133 show that to his mind Etruria was typical of all rural
Italy.

Ti. Gracchus as tribune made a speech [2] about the
Italian race: though they were the finest material
for soldiers and akin (to themselves) they were little
by little declining into poverty and small numbers
(ὀλιγανδρία) and there was no hope of the situation's righting itself. After inveighing against the
slave population, necessarily debarred from military
service and never faithful to its masters, he brought
forward as a warning the recent rebellion in Sicily;
because the slaves had increased as a result of the
agricultural situation, the war waged against them
by the Romans was no light matter and ended only
after a long period and varying successes and defeats.
. . . . The end which Gracchus had in mind was not
the relief of poverty, but the increase of population (εὐανδρία).[3]

Appian again emphasizes the object of the measure [4] in his
account of the government's failure to abide by the provisions
of the agrarian law of C. Gracchus after the latter's death.

This (the renting of the public land) was of some
help to the poor because of the distribution of money,

---

[1] Plut. T. Gr. 8.
[2] Appian, B. C. I, 9. See B. C. I, 10 for a repetition of the same accusa-
tions put into the mouths of the poorer classes.
[3] Appian, B. C. I, 11.
[4] Appian, B. C. I, 27.

but of no help toward increasing the population (ἐs πολυπληθίαν) . . . . The people lost everything (all provisions of the law) completely. As a result there was a further decrease at once of citizens and soldiers.

Such striking statements of the loss in native population do not recur until the period after the Civil War in 46. In that year Caesar took a census of the city of Rome.[1] Appian makes the statement that the population was found to be reduced by one-half,[2] Dio that there was δεινὴ ὀλιγανθρωπία, such that even the ordinary observer saw it.[3]

The country had lost even more in population than Rome, both Sallust [4] and Cicero [5] mention the *vastitas Italiae* which followed the civil wars. The emptiness of Etruria shown by the brigandage prevailing there [6] and the yet more desperate condition of Samnium [7] were due to Sulla. Apparently neither ever regained its lost population.[8] Cicero speaks in 63 of *Italiae solitudo*.[9] Dio says that in 59 (Καῖσαρ) τὰ πλεῖστα τῆς Ἰταλίας ἠρημωμένα συνῴκιζετο.

[1] Suet. Jul. 41, 3.
[2] Appian, B. C. II, 102.
[3] Dio XLIII, 25, 2. The census was followed by a programme of legislation designed apparently to make Rome a comfortable and attractive place for the better class of citizens and their children and a goal for ambitious Italians and Romans who under the former conditions might have sought provincial careers. Building projects on a large scale, the establishment of libraries, the encouragement given to well-educated professional men to settle in Rome, (Suet. Jul. 44, 1-2), the sweeping reduction in the number of recipients of public grain (41, 3), the removal to over-sea colonies of 80,000 of the poorer citizens, in large part *liberti* (see 42, 1; Strabo VIII, 623, Plin. N. H. III, 3, 12 for status of Corinthian, Spanish and African colonists, and for the two latter, Hardy, Three Spanish Charters, Oxford (1912) p. 49, n. 116), were combined to this end with the offering of prizes to parents of large families (Dio XLIII, 25, 2), and the restriction on the absence from Italy of citizens between the ages of twenty and forty (Suet. Jul. 42, 1).
[4] Sall. Jug. 5, 2.
[5] Cic. Epist. X, 33, 1.
[6] Sall. Cat. 28, 4; see also Rosenberg, *Der Staat der alten Italiker* (1913), p. 137.
[7] Strabo V, 11, 20 (250).
[8] For Gabii see Hor. Epist. I, 11, 7; Cic. Planc. 23; for Fidenae Hor. Epist. I, 11, 8; coupled with Collatia and Antemnae Strabo V, 3, 2; for Labi and Bovillae Cic. Planc. 23; for Tibur Hor. Epist. I, 7, 45; for Acerrae Virg. Georg. II, 225.
[9] Att. I, 19, 4.

The currents of population during the last two hundred years of the Republic have been traced. From 200 B.C. on Italians were leaving Italy, many to spend years in military service in the East or West, some to settle permanently in the scene of their campaigns, others to die in the course of their service; still others were emigrating with the immediate purpose of bettering their economic condition in new surroundings. To take their places in agriculture and, further, to meet the ever-growing demand for domestic servants and for workmen, skilled and unskilled, slaves were regularly imported during the whole period: aliens, who, either as slaves or *liberti*, remained with their children as permanent residents of Italy. So completely had this exchange of populations taken place that, from 170 on, citizens of alien stock equalled in number or even outnumbered the citizens of free stock, while beside them stood a still larger body of slaves, constantly passing over into the ranks of the *liberti* and as constantly being recruited from slave immigrants. The wars and proscriptions of the first century by their continuous inroads on the number of free citizens must have further increased the already large proportion of foreign to native stock. We must conclude, therefore, that the plebs who came under the new administrative, social and religious ideas of the Empire were largely step-children of Italy, with no direct inheritance in the principles on which the foundation of the Republic had been laid.

CHAPTER II
A STUDY OF THEIR EMPLOYMENT

Through the facts already presented it is clear that a profound change in the plebs had taken place at the close of the republican period. Evidence corroboratory of the change can be reached through a study of the labor conditions in Italy. Broadly speaking, the laboring classes were included in the plebs, *urbana* and *rustica*. Even slaves who form an apparent exception were always potential voters. Any facts, therefore, dealing with the composition of the world of labor, the origin and the number of individuals who were at work in Italy and Rome, will throw light on the composition of the plebs as a political body, though here again we cannot proceed to an exact estimate of the proportion of foreign to native stock or of the composition of this foreign element.

A. Agricultural Labor.

Two Roman studies of the republican period are extant which deal with agriculture and include certain material on agricultural labor, Cato's *de Agricultura* written in the second century and Varro's *Rerum Rusticarum Libri III* in the first. This material has been carefully collected and analyzed by Gummerus.[1] A brief summary of the conditions which they reflect follows.

I. Agricultural Labor in the Second Century

Cato studied the demands of and the profits from estates worked intensively by their owners for the sake of the return on invested capital. The labor directly and permanently under the control of the owner or his manager was slave

[1] H. Gummerus, *Der röm. Gutsbetrieb*, Klio, VI. (1906) pp. 1–100.

labor, the *familia rustica*.   In proportion to the size of the
vineyard or olive orchard taken by Cato as models, the
number of slaves employed in its upkeep was very small.
Their employment was monotonous and unremitting.   It was
confined to the routine farm work which included the production of their own food, and to the manufacture of the
simplest farm *instrumenta*, such as rough baskets, stakes, etc.
Neither intelligence nor special training was necessary or
desirable; only physical strength and endurance were demanded, and whenever they no longer existed, the laborer
was sold.   The *vilicus* alone must be an intelligent and responsible man, able to arrange and superintend the hiring and
buying which at all important points supplemented the simple
and rough work done by the slaves.   There is, however, no
evidence from Cato that the *vilicus* made use of superior intelligence to secure his freedom; he is invariably spoken of as a
slave.

A surprisingly large part of the farm work was done by
paid labor from outside.   A contractor was engaged to do
all building on a large scale in wood or stone, to make the
furniture, the looms and wooden *instrumenta;*[1] all products of
the flock, as milk, cheese, lambs, and wool, were taken over by
a *conductor*; an *emptor* might buy the fruit on the tree, in
which case he supplied the labor and the transportation; a
contractor might harvest the olives and make the oil.[2]   Such
contractors were themselves certainly freemen; the laborers
they employed were in some instance slaves, in others freemen,
probably the small farmers of the neighborhood.   The owner
or the *vilicus* also engaged laborers by the day [3] and *partiarii*
who cultivated certain crops on shares,[4] probably again from

[1] Raw materials were furnished by the owner and he might also supply
part of the labor to the contractor who paid him for it.

[2] It seems to be only accident that mention of similar arrangements for
the vineyards is omitted.

[3] The *faber ferrarius*, or the *calcarius partiarus* who burned the lime.

[4] A *partiarius* worked the fields between ploughing and harvest time,
and took care of the vineyards.

among the small farmers or the free workmen in the nearby villages. From towns in the neighborhood or from Rome, were bought articles whose manufacture required special outlay in apparatus or labor, including clothing, utensils of pottery, bronze, or iron, ropes and cords.[1]

II. AGRICULTURAL LABOR IN THE FIRST CENTURY

Varro writing more than a century later describes conditions that are singularly unchanged. It is true that he mentions the large estate making use of great numbers of slaves, artisans as well as farm laborers, and the special industry, pottery or cloth factory, established on the farm by the land owner.[2] In general, however, like Cato, he discusses the relatively small and unified estate cultivated to bring the maximum of profit to the owner, a place where the conditions of labor are relatively simple. The basis of the system was still the *familia rustica* with the *vilicus* at its head, a slave over slaves. The slaves of the *familia* again did the routine work of the farm and in the time which could not be spent in out-door work made the simpler tools and apparatus which they used. Contractors with gangs of freemen under them undertook the *opera rustica maiora*, like the vintage and the harvest,[3] and gangs of laborers hired by the day did the necessary work in places where the health of slaves valuable to their owners would be jeopardized. A set of free workmen among whom only *fabri*, *fullones*, and *medici* (!) are specified seem to have made regular rounds on such estates, coming

---

[1] There is no indication of the status of manufacturer or merchant except in the case of two *restiones*, L. Tunnius in Casinum, and C. Mennius L. f. in Venafrum (Cato agr. 135, 3).

[2] In each case Varro refers to a previous treatment of the subject, in the case of the large estate to Cassius's translation of Mago's treatise, in the case of the rural industry to the treatise of the Sasernae.

[3] Compare the legend reported by Suetonius (Vesp. I, 4) as current in regard to the great-grandfather of Vespasian: *e regione Transpadana fuisse mancipem operarum quae ex Umbria in Sabinos ad culturam agrorum quotannis commeare soleant.*

perhaps from villages in the neighborhood, and, each along his special line, attending to the upkeep of the establishment. As in Cato's time, all the important manufactured articles in use were made outside and bought from the makers or from dealers in near-by markets.

In the final analysis then, the work on the country estate described by Cato and Varro in the second and first centuries was divided between a group of slaves living on the estate, slaves not only untrained but relatively few in number and isolated, and a group of freemen living outside who performed not only the seasonal work but all that required special intelligence, special training or special apparatus.[1] There is no indication of the emergence of the *libertus* out of such groups of agricultural slaves; the words *libertus*, manumission, etc. do not occur in Cato or Varro in connection with discussion of the *familia*. Nor are the laborers brought in from outside ever referred to as being *liberti* or of libertine stock. We may conclude that through this channel no significant number of foreigners entered the citizen body.

On the basis of these two studies, how far can we generalize on Italian rural labor as a whole? Two facts must be borne in mind: first, that the type of country estate dealt with by both writers was unique and the conditions of labor represented on it were by no means universal; in the same district with it, for instance, might exist the small farm of the *pauperculus* who employed no slave labor at all [2] and the large estate employing not only great numbers of slaves but also side by side with unskilled farm laborers others with some technical training and, by implication, of higher mental grade; second,

---

[1] The *colonus* or small renter is not mentioned though he may well have existed as early as the second century, and the Sasernae, writing in the period between Cato and Varro, certainly discussed his situation. He may be included in the *mercenarii*, or *partiarii*. *Coloni*, contrasted with slaves and *liberti*, from the estates of Domitius at Cosa manned his seven ships in 49 (Caes. B. C. I, 34 and 56).

[2] *pauperculus cum sua progenie* (Varro Rust. I, 17, 2); cf. also the *fratres ex agro Falisco* who owned one *jugerum* of land (Rust. III, 16, 10); Ofellius (Hor. Serm. II, 2, 115, 128); Virgil's father (Donat. Virg. Vit. 4).

that we have very little information of any kind and no detailed information whatever about these other types. On the whole, however, we may say that the conditions of all slave labor which was employed in the country districts differed radically from the conditions in Rome or in the Italian small town. Slaves bought with an eye to their value as laborers in farming or stock raising would tend to be a rougher and duller lot than the potential artisans or house servants bought for use in town;[1] opportunities for the slave to buy his freedom and for personal relations between master and slave were much rarer; the isolated condition of the farms and cattle ranches encouraged neglect on the part of the owners at best, and at the worst terrible abuse; the stimulus offered by a more varied life, or by the sight of ex-slaves who had effected their manumission was lacking. As a result the status of the laborer was stagnant, the slave did not rise to the condition of *libertus* and the free man was ousted from his place, not by the competition of the individual foreigner who got ahead of him in his job, but by changes in the whole economic system of rural Italy.

B. LABOR EMPLOYED BY A PROFESSIONAL MAN OF MEANS

A certain number of facts which concern the conditions of labor and the political status of the laborer in precisely Varro's period can be sifted out of Cicero's writings.

These facts are fewer and more disconnected than those yielded by a study of Cato and Varro because labor and the laboring classes are only mentioned by Cicero incidentally in the course of what was to him more important and interesting. Further, they differ absolutely in kind. They add nothing to our knowledge of the special field covered by Cato and Varro. Although Cicero owned properties in the country

---

[1] The artisans or house servants employed steadily on great country estates would be relatively too few to affect the general situation.

like the Roman gentlemen for whom the agricultural treatises were written his use of them was different.[1]   His investments represented no serious attempt to increase his income; [2]   he had none of the amateur's interest in intensive farming or the breeding of game and in consequence he did not find it necessary to set up an elaborately organized system of labor.[3] The facts which are offered by a study of Cicero's writings

[1] Cicero inherited from his father *praedia rustica* at Arpinum (Leg. agr. III, 8).   O. E. Schmidt (*Cicero's Villen* N. J. kl. A. III (1899) p. 345) applies to this property Martial's line (11, 48) *jugera facundi qui Ciceronis habet*.   We know that in general the amount of his inheritance was not large (Dio XXXVIII, 20, 4; Ps. Sall. in Tull. 2) but just how much land went with the *Arpinas* we do not know.   The property was rented in small holdings, *praediola* (Att. XIII, 9. 2), but nothing is known of the tenants or of the renting arrangements (Cf. Horace's farm which in his own time or possibly earlier had supported five free tenants, Epist. I, 14, 2).   There is no evidence that Cicero yearned to add field to field. He says of himself in 66, *Quod si adsequor, (libros) supero Crassum divitiis atque omnium vicos et prata contemno* (Att. I, 4, 3).   In 47 he inherited *praedia Fufidiana*, (Att. XI, 13, 3; 15, 4; 14, 3) probably at Arpinum for the Fufidii were connected with the town (Epist. XIII, 11; 12; Att. XI, 13, 3), and in 54 Cicero had described a *Fufidianum fundum* with a villa on it bought for Quintus at Arpinum (Q. fr. III, 1, 3).   Arrangements were made for the sale both of the Fufidiana and the *fundus Brinnianus* inherited in 45.   He had once owned a *fundus* at Frusino and in 48–7 he was anxious to buy it back (Att. XI, 4, 1; 13, 4), but there is no record of his doing so.   The *fructus praediorum* mentioned in his letters (Att. XI, 2, 2) may refer to rents from either country or city property.

Terentia in 59 owned an extensive *saltus* (Att. II, 4, 5) and some untaxed *ager publicus* (Att. II, 15, 3) besides city property (Epist. XIV, 1, 5). Through what forms of renting the income from the country real estate reached Terentia is not indicated.

Quintus owned at one time or another estates in the neighborhood of Arpinum (Att. I, 6, 2); in 67 the Arcanum and the Laterum, both *patrimonia*, which he apparently kept for himself, the Manilianum, a recent possession in 54 (Q. fr. III, 1, 1) and the Fufidianum, which Roby (C. R. I, (1887) 67) and O. E. Schmidt identify with the Bovillanum bought for him in the same year.   This cost 100,000 *sesterces* and the land in connection with it could be drained and would easily give 50 *jugera* of meadow pasturage (Q. fr. III, 1, 3).   Quintus rented his second Roman house in 56 (Q. fr. II, 3, 7), and it seems not unlikely that these two additional Arpinate estates were bought with a view to renting.   We know, however, nothing but the fact of his ownership and improvements.

[2] There were vineyards at Arpinum (Epist. XVI, 26, 2) and flower and vegetable gardens at the Tusculanum and in Rome (Epist. XVI, 18, 2) but no reference to production for sale occurs.   The gardeners who worked on contract or on shares (see p. 73) may have marketed produce.

[3] Many employees at the villas obviously go unmentioned in the letters. *Vilici* and *procuratores* at the Cumanum are spoken of (Att. XIV, 16, 1)

relate to a different field. They throw light on the condition of labor and the political status of the men employed by a professional man, of large interests, with a residence mainly in Rome. Few and disconnected as they are, they are unique of their kind.

Cicero's style of living is too familiar to need detailed description. During the greater part of his official life he owned a large house in Rome, a house in Antium, and five villas in various part of Italy,[1] and during this time his wife, daughter, and son, one or all, shared in the life of these establishments. He himself carried on his own profession, and at various times was occupied with political interests, official and unofficial, and with writing, professional and literary.

He drew on a variety of labor which can be roughly classified as: first, permanent employees, entering his service as slaves and continuing in it often as *liberti*, the *familia urbana*; second, contractors, taking certain kinds of work out of the hands of the household; third, professional men employed temporarily and for special services; and fourth, dealers, from whom finished products were ordered and purchased.[2]

The arrangement of this section follows this grouping. From its nature the material is uneven in value and amount. Wherever possible it has been supplemented from literary and inscriptional sources dealing with Cicero's contemporaries.

---

and a *vilicus*, Nicephorus, on the Laterium of Quintus (Q. fr. III, 1, 5). It may be gathered from Varro's comment on Cato's allotment of labor to estates of a certain size (Rust. I, 18, 3, 5) that the functions of the *vilicus* on such an estate as the Cumanum were different from those on the intensively cultivated estate where only one *vilicus* was advised. Q. Cicero has a *topiarus* who worked both at Rome and Arpinum (Q. fr. III, 1, 5; 6).

[1] At Arpinum, Formiae, Tusculum, Pompeii and Cumae. See O. E. Schmidt, *op. cit.*, pp. 328–467, for dates of purchase and periods of residence.

[2] Of the employees in Cicero's official service in Rome and Cilicia, some were recruited from his own *familia*, others were undoubtedly attached to his service for his terms of office only. For instance, a *libertus* of Lentulus was his *accensus* in Cilicia (Epist. III, 7, 4). The information in regard to the latter is meagre. See the handbooks on the general subject of the assistants to the magistrates.

I. THE FAMILIA URBANA

1. **Its Numbers.** Plutarch defined the style in which Cicero lived as liberal and yet temperate,[1] and the accuracy of the definition is implied not only in the information Cicero lets fall about himself but in his criticisms of others. He could hardly have drawn so contemptuous a picture of Piso's way of life had he not himself had well-groomed, active slaves, a *cocus* and *atriensis* with specialized functions, a *pistor* and a *cella* under his own roof.[2] On the other hand his descriptions of Chrysogonus's household which included not only cooks, bakers and litter bearers, but various skilled workmen and many musicians,[3] of the households of Verres himself, his victim, and his counsel, lead us to conclude that his own menage was notably simpler than theirs.[4]

There is, however, no basis for an inference as to the number of persons whom Cicero permanently employed. In the period of twenty-four years covered by the letters he mentions thirty-one by name but in no single case do we know the length of service; certain employees are referred to, but others equally necessary are never mentioned.[5] He records no purchase or sale of slaves [6] and only one manumission — that of Tiro. The total number undoubtedly varied some-

---

[1] ἐλευθερίως ἅμα καὶ σωφρόνως διῆγε, (Plut. Cic. 8); Cf. 7, 3 and Cicero's own phrase used of Pompey, *non luxuriosi hominis sed tamen abundantis* (Ph. II, 27, 66).

[2] Cic. Pis. 67.

[3] Cic. S. Rosc. 134.

[4] Of Verres, Cic. Verr. V, 54; of C. Malleolus, Verr. II, 92; of Hortensius, Verr. IV, 8. It is true that these references are all from an early period in his career when he had less income himself and was more anxious to strike a popular tone in his attacks. Cf., however, his humorous accounts of his lessons in dining under Hirtius and Pansa in 46 (Epist. IX, 16, 7; 18, 3; 19, 2), a course of study which it is tempting to connect with the passage Fin. II, 23 on the dinners of the refined and elegant *asoti*.

[5] *qui tractant, qui tergunt, qui unguent, qui verrunt, qui spargunt* (Parad. 37).

[6] He moralizes on purchasing slaves in Planc. 62 and quotes moralizing on selling slaves from Hecato's Περὶ Παθήκοντος (Off. III, 91).

what with his fortunes, but there is no reason to think that the fluctuation followed very closely the curve of his income.[1]

2. The Service Rendered by the *Familia Urbana*. The following members of the *familia urbana* are mentioned: [2]

cocus at Rome (Epist. IX, 20, 2); *cocus* sent from Cumanum to Formianum (Epist. XVI, 15, 2).

ianitor at Rome (Planc. 66).

cubicularius (Att. VI, 2, 5).

servus a pedibus Pollex — *s.*

attendants on M. Cicero the younger, Chrysippus *l.*, previously a *librarius;* a slave (A. II, VII, 2, 8).

attendants on Lentulus, *s.* (Att. XII, 28, 3).

medicus, Metrodorus.

lecticarii (Q. fr. II, 8, 2).

nomenclator (Att. IV, 1, 5).

dispensatores Philotimus *l.* at Rome; Ummius (?) *l.* (?) at Formianum.

ratiocinator Hilarus [3] *l.*

librarii [4]

    anagnostae Sositheus *s.;* Dionysius *s.*

    amanuenses Tiro *l.;* Spintharus.

    librarian Dionysius *s.*

    copyists (Att. XIII, 21a, 2; Epist. XVI, 21, 8; 22, 1 *et al); scribae* Laurea [5] *l.;* a slave (Epist. V, 20, 2 Purser's reading); Tiro *l.*, Philotimus *l.* (Att. XIII, 33, 1).

---

[1] Cf. the temperamental Tigellius: *habebat saepe ducentos saepe decem servos* (Hor. Serm. I, 3, 11–12). It is true that in 54, which was perhaps a lean year (Cf. Q. fr. II, 10, 5) Cicero writes to Quintus in Gaul, "I am much obliged to you for your promise of slaves and indeed I am, as you write, shorthanded both in Rome and on the estates" (Q. fr. III, 9, 4), but when he leaves Italy in 58, a bankrupt, he makes no arrangement for the sale of his slaves. Terentia is to do what she thinks just in the case of her own slaves; if the property is confiscated Cicero's slaves are to be manumitted provided they can establish their claim to the position of *liberti;* if the property remains in the hands of the family, all but a few are to keep their slave status (Epist. XIV, 4, 4). In 47 he suggests the possibility of raising money from the sale of plate and furniture, not slaves (Att. XI, 25, 3).

[2] To save space, when the name of the slave or *libertus* is mentioned and Orelli's Onomasticon can be used, reference to the text is here omitted. The status, slave or *libertus*, is added when it appears in the text.

[3] A *libertus* of Cicero but not in his employ when mentioned.

[4] The *librarii* could probably all do the various kinds of secretarial work.

[5] Cognomen in Plin. N. H. 31, 6.

tabellarii [1] Acastus *s.*, Aegypta *l.*, Alexander,[3] Andricus,[2] Anteros,[4] Apenas, Aristarchus, Barnaeus,[5] Demea, Dexippus, Harpalus, Hermia, Mario, Menander,[2] Menocritus,[6] Metrodopus,[5] Phileros,[7] Salvius, Zeuxis[7] and unnamed *tabellarii* or *pueri* of the *familia.*

Special duties uncertain: Eros *l.*,[8] Orpheus *s.*, Phaethon [9] *l.*, Tyrranio *l.*[10]

Apparently Cicero's *familia urbana* was in service both at Rome and in the country. In 49 when Terentia and Tullia were left behind at the Cumanum, *Cicero* suggested that while he was away from Italy, if food was to be dearer, they use the secluded Arpinum estate with the *familia urbana.*[11] In May 45 Cicero wrote from Astura, "But because the household is in a hurry to go home (Rome) I shall go off in order not to appear abandoned"[12] and in July of the same year when he was again in Astura all the upper floor of his house in Rome was empty and he offered the use of it for Atticus's convalescent secretary.[13] When he turned over his Cumanum to Pilia he left "*vilici*, procurators, and house";[14] she apparently brought her own staff of house servants.

A few conclusions can be drawn from this scanty material:

[1] These are *cognomina* of men who actually carried letters between Cicero and his correspondents and in every case the man carried one letter *from* Cicero. It must be remembered, however, that letters were carried by *tabellarii* of friends and of the *publicani* and by travellers of every grade from slaves to senators. There is, therefore, no very sure title to the name of Cicero's *tabellarius.* Names are of course often mentioned merely for identifications of the letters referred to.

[2] Klotz thinks Andricus and Menander (Epist. XIV, 14, 1; 13) identical. On April 4 Cicero awaits letters from Tiro to be brought by "Menander" who has been previously sent to Tiro and on April 5 letters from Tiro are brought by "Andricus." These may be two different men. Various slaves are coming and going, Acastus Apr. 5, Aegypta and Hermia Apr. 6.

[3] Carries an important message (verbal?) for Cicero; can use Greek.

[4] Assigned to M. Cicero the younger.

[5] Carries one letter from Cicero to Atticus.

[6] Carries one letter from Cicero to Lentulus.

[7] Carries one letter from Paetus to Cicero.

[8] Plut. Apophth. Cic. 21.

[9] Carries a letter and a message from M. Cicero to Q. Cicero.

[10] Suidas.

[11] Epist. XIV, 7, 3.

[12] Att. XIII, 26, 2.

[13] Att. XII, 10.

[14] Att. XIV, 16, 1.

First, the *familia* supplied servants who carried on all routine household arrangements, acted as personal attendants and as letter carriers, stewards, and secretaries of various kinds; second, the *familia* did not supply skilled artisans; in a number of instances, certainly, finer pieces of furniture or decoration were bought outright; third, the *familia* did not supply regular artisans, *textores*, *fabri*, etc. On the one occasion where clothing is mentioned Cicero gets it through Atticus's agents;[1] the *faber* or *tector* whose purchase is used as an illustration is probably a handy-man for general employment in the country for he is contrasted with two members of the *familia rustica*, the *vilicus* and the *armentarius;*[2] there is no reference to the making of utensils of wood or metal or of pottery.[3] Indeed, such country estates as Cicero owned would be even less likely to do their own manufacturing than the type represented in the works of Cato or Varro.

3. **The Status of the Members of the *Familia Urbana*.** A glance at the preceding list will serve to show that no hard and fast line was drawn between the employment assigned to the slaves of the *familia* and that assigned to the *liberti*. Yet the two classes differed strikingly in the importance of their position. Of the slaves little but the names are known; of at least five *liberti* of the *familia* some account can be compiled. By putting together these accounts and others

[1] Att. XI, 2, 4. Cato (Agr. 150) advises the sale of all wool from the farm to a *conductor* who apparently sells it again to dealers. Clothing for the slaves on the farm is bought outright: *tunicae, saga, centones* at Rome (Agr. 135.1) *cuculliones* in smaller markets nearby (Cales and Minturnae). *Togae* which are included in the list of clothing to be purchased at Rome must be intended for non-slave members of the *familia*. Varro makes the conventional country housewife spin (Men. 190 Buech.) but says nothing in his general study of agriculture of the making of cloth or even of clothing for the slaves. He does, however, suggest the establishing of work-rooms for cloth-making where there are weavers and weaving-rooms on the farms (Rust. I, 2, 21). Atticus had a great sheep farm in Epirus (Rust. II, 10, 11). His *artifices ceteri quos cultus domesticus desiderat* (Nep. Att. 13.3) may have included *textores* and his agents in Epirus who furnished Cicero with *vestimenta*, may have supplied them directly from such a workshop.
[2] Planc. 62.
[3] If the tile marked *M. Tuli* (C.I.L. XV, 2277) is from the Tusculan estate of Cicero, his workmen may have burned their own roof-tiles.

similar to them an idea can be formed of the kind of slave in the *familia* who obtained his freedom and the kind of use he made of the freedom once obtained.

　　a. The *Liberti* of Cicero's *Familia.*

Seven *liberti,* his own or Terentia's, are mentioned by Cicero, and two by other writers.　Three who were for long periods connected with the household though their patrons were Atticus, Murena and P. Crassus respectively, may be fairly added to the list because of their close connection with Cicero's *familia.*[1]

(1.)　Aegypta, *tabellarius* from 53–45 at least;[2] the only *tabellarius* whose term of service is certainly more than four years.

(2.)　Chrysippus, originally *librarius;* commissioned to buy books for Q. Cicero's library in 54;[3] acted as tutor-attendant of M. Cicero the younger on his journey from Cilicia to Rome in 50.　He abandoned his charge *en route* and in consequence Cicero threatened to take measures to limit his status as *libertus.*[4]

(3.)　Laurea, *scriba;* went with Cicero to Cilicia in 51; kept his official accounts, remaining behind to settle them;[5] in 45 had a certain sum of money in his hands belonging to Cicero;[6] after Cicero's death wrote some verses on the hot springs discovered at the Cumanum.[7]

(4.)　Philotimus, *librarius;* made a declaration for Cicero, in regard to some property valuation.[8]

---

[1] Ummius the *dispensator* at the Formianum, Pescennius, Clodius Philhetairos, and Sallustius, who accompanied Cicero from Rome on his journey into exile may well have been *liberti* of other patrons temporarily in Cicero's employ.　A man named Eros, of unknown status, seems likely to have been a *libertus* of Atticus (see Tyrrell and Purser's Index, Orelli and Eros, R. E.).　Cicero speaks of him as responsible to Atticus, as well as to himself, and he comes and goes between them in the years 46–4.　He receives notes from Cicero in regard to the latter's funds, investigates his debts, and is in general charge of his funds at Rome, his rents, and his payments; Tiro takes his place finally.　Früchtl (*Die Geldgeschäfte bei Cicero*, Erlangen 1912, p. 68) regards him as identical with Eros, the slave of Philotimus (Att. X, 15, 1).　The name is a common one, however, and two different persons are probably referred to in the Cicero passages.

[2] In 53 (Epist. XVI, 15, 1) probably still a slave; *libertus* in 45 (Att. XII, 37, 1).

[3] Q. fr. III, 4, 5; 5, 6.

[4] Att. VII, 2, 8; 5, 3.

[5] Epist. V, 20, 2.

[6] Att. XIII, 22, 4.

[7] Plin. N. H. 31, 6.

[8] See, however, note of Tyrrell and Purser on Att. XIII, 33, 1.

(5.) Tiro; manumitted in 53; services summed up by Cicero, *officia domestica, forensia, urbana, provincialia, in re privata, in publica, in studiis, in litteris nostris*.[1] This statement is borne out in detail. He put the library at Tusculanum in order and made an index;[2] looked after arrangements for the garden and for engaging the garners at Tusculanum,[3] and for entertaining;[4] acted as amanuensis,[5] especially in intimate matters[6] and kept copies of Cicero's letters;[7] supervised Cicero's copyists;[8] in 45–4 attended to Cicero's financial arrangements;[9] represented Cicero in talks with political friends;[10] assisted, perhaps collaborated, in Cicero's literary work;[11] corresponded with Q. Cicero,[12] M. Cicero the younger,[13] Atticus.[14] He bought a praedium in 44.[15]

(6.) Hilarus, *libertus* of Cicero, client of Atticus, *ratiocinator;* with C. Antonius in Macedonia in 61;[16] not mentioned while in Cicero's own employ.

(7.) Philotimus, *libertus* of Terentia, *dispensator;* in charge of upkeep of Roman house in Cicero's absence in 59,[17] and of rebuilding both Cicero's and Quintus's houses in 55–4;[18] acted for Cicero in money payments,[19] and as '*socius*' in purchase of Milo's property by his friends (51);[20] acted for Cicero during the latter's absence in Cilicia, and went to Cicero to report his private transactions in connection

---

[1] Epist. XVI, 4, 3 written in 50; Att. VII, 5, 2; IX, 17, 2; Epist. XVI, 1, 3; 3, 2.
[2] Epist. XVI, 20, 1.
[3] Epist. XVI, 18, 2.
[4] Epist. XVI, 22.
[5] Letters *passim;* used shorthand (Att. XIII, 25 3).
[6] Att. XIII, 9, 1.
[7] With a view to publication, Att. XVI, 5, 5.
[8] Epist. XVI, 22, 1.
[9] Att. XV, 15, 3 and 4; 17, 2; 18, 1; Epist. XIII, 24, 1; XVI, 23, 1.
[10] With Dolabella in 46 (Att. XII, 5, 4) and in 44 (Att. XV, 4, 5; 8, 1); with Plancus in 44 (Att. XVI, 16, 1).
[11] Epist. XVI, 10, 2; acted as critic (Epist. XVI, 17, 1; Gell. VI, 3, 8; XIII, 9, 1). He attempted the composition of tragedy (Epist. XVI, 38, 3). For his later writings and his work as an editor see Schantz, *Röm. Lit.* I, 2, pp. 404–5.
[12] Q. fr. III, 1, 10; Epist. XVI, 26; 27.
[13] Att. XV, 15, 4; Epist. XVI, 21; 25.
[14] Att. XII, 19, 4; 48, 2.
[15] Epist. XVI, 21, 7.
[16] Att. I, 12, 2.
[17] Att. II, 4, 7.
[18] Att. IV, 10, 2; Q. fr. III, 1, 6; III, 9, 7.
[19] Att. V, 4, 3; V, 19, 1; VIII, 7, 3; X, 5, 3.
[20] Att. V, 8, 2 and 3; Epist. VIII, 3, 2.

with Milo's property;[1] in charge of Roman house,[2] and of funds in
49;[3] depended upon as means of information from and communica-
tion with Rome,[4] and with various friends;[5] his slave Eros acted
for him in his absence;[6] went to Ephesus to see Caesar in the
interest of the family of Cicero in 47.[7]

(8.)   Tyrranio, *libertus* of Terentia, originally named Diocles, a Phoenician
war prisoner bought by Dymas, a *libertus* of Caesar, given to Terentia, and manumitted by her; a grammarian.[8]

(9.)   Eros, *libertus* of Cicero. Nothing is known of him but his manumission which is mentioned in Plutarch.[9]

(10.) Dionysius, *libertus* of Atticus,[10] worked in library at Antium as
librarius in 56;[11] with Cicero at Cumanum and Tusculanum in 55;[12]
returned to Atticus;[13] acted as *magister* of M. Cicero from end of 54
to 50;[14] rejoined Atticus on Cicero's return[15] from Cilicia and never
came back to Cicero although in 45 he still regarded himself (by
letter) as *magister* of the two boys.[16] He had in 49 some slaves of his
own, and a little money invested in loans.[17]

(11.) Tyrannio the elder, from Amisus in Asia, war captive from Mith-
radatic war, *libertus* of Murena, in charge of repairing books and
arranging library at Antium in 56;[18] taught Q. Cicero the younger
and the younger Marcus in Cicero's home in Rome in 56;[19] consulted
about purchase of books for Q. Cicero in 54.[20]

[1] Att. VI, 1, 19; 3, 1, etc.
[2] Epist. XIV, 18, 2.
[3] Att. VIII, 7, 3; X, 5, 3; 7, 3.
[4] Att. VIII, 1, 1; 16, 1; IX, 7, 6; 9, 3.
[5] Atticus (Att. VII, 22, 2); Ser. Sulpicius (Epist. IV, 2, 1).
[6] Att. X, 15, 1.
[7] Att. XI, 23, 2; 24, 4; Epist. XIV, 24.
[8] Suidas on Tyrranio, the younger. Tyrranio was a member of Terentia's *familia* in 29, fourteen years after Cicero's death. He was a pupil of
the elder Tyrranio and edited some of his teacher's writings. See Susemihl,
Gr. Lit. alex. Zeit II 183, [186].
[9] Plut. Apophth. Cic. 21.
[10] M. Pomponius Dionysius. The *praenomen* chosen in compliment to
Cicero (Att. IV, 15, 1).
[11] Att. IV, 8, 2.
[12] Att. IV, 11, 2; 13, 1.
[13] Att. IV, 14, 2.
[14] Att. IV, 19, 2; V, 3, 3; VI, 1, 12.
[15] Att. VII, 7, 1.
[16] Att. XIII, 2, 3.
[17] Att. VIII, 10.
[18] Att. IV, 4a, 1; 8, 2; in consultation as early as 59 (Att. II, 6, 1), and as
late as 46 (Att. XII, 6, 1); G. L. IV p. 529 K. Cf. Usener, *Münch. Sitz. ber.*
1892, 582.
[19] Q. fr. II, 4, 2.
[20] Q. fr. III, 4, 5; 5, 6.

(12.) Apollonius, *libertus* of P. Crassus, as a young man much in Cicero's house studying with the Stoic Diodotus; after Crassus's death with Cicero in Cilicia in some capacity requiring *fides* and *prudentia;* later joined Caesar in Alexandria; in 45 wished to write on account of Caesar's exploits.[1]

By the accident of their employment in Cicero's household the foregoing fragments of personal histories of a few slaves have been transmitted to us, and if all information stopped here, we should still guess that by the road of personal relations and intelligent service in the *familia* many slaves in many *familiae* reached the same goal. As a matter of fact we have Cicero's testimony that this phenomenon was a common one for surprisingly often the names of *liberti* of his friends, known to him personally or by reputation, occur in his letters.

b. The *Liberti* of Cicero's Acquaintances.

The *liberti* so mentioned can be roughly divided into two groups, the first in the service of the politicians, the second in the service of men of business. In many cases the reference is of the briefest and unsupported by any further information. With the analogy of Cicero's own *liberti* before us, however, we may say with assurance that the first and some of the second group emerged from the slaves of the *familia urbana.*

(1.) *Liberti* in the Service of Politicians. The tone of Cicero's references shows that often the *liberti* of his political friends had won an intimacy and influence with their patrons suggestive of his own relations with Tiro;[2] they had undoubtedly travelled to freedom by the same path.[3] M. Fadius Gallus is to beware of telling a political confidence "even to his *libertus* Apella;"[4] Philargyrus, the freedman of A. Torqua-

---

[1] Epist. XIII, 16.

[2] The relations of Statius and Alexis to Quintus and Atticus are directly likened to those of Tiro and Cicero (Epist. XVI, 16, 2; Att. XII, 10).

[3] The career of Timarchides, the *libertus* of Verres, is an equally good illustration of the point made above. (Cic. Verr. *passim.*)

[4] Epist. VII, 25, 2.

tus,[1] Dardanus of C. Furnius,[2] Rupa of C. Curio,[3] Theudas of
Trebianus,[4] apparently acted as their patrons' representatives
in Rome when the latter were away, attending to their interests
and taking part in conferences with their friends.[5] Statius
acted as secretary for Quintus Cicero in Asia previous to his
manumission; [6] later his influence with Quintus in provincial
politics became dangerously great and on his arrival in Rome
he was almost a political figure.[7] Later still he adapted
himself to Quintus's lessened political importance and made
himself useful in the oversight of his private affairs.[8] Phania
and Cilix, two freedmen of Ap. Claudius Pulcher, are warmly
commended, the first for his admirable grasp of the political
situation of the moment,[9] the second for his agreeableness.[10]
Apella was sent by Lepidus to Plancus in 43 as a hostage of
his good faith.[11] Philo, a freedman of Sex. Pompey who is
merely referred to Cicero,[12] is described elsewhere as a violent
upholder of his patron's party.[13] Demetrius of Gadara, who
appears only casually in Cicero[14] had a well-known political
career of his own.[15] To these references from Cicero we may

[1] Epist. VI, 1, 6.
[2] Epist. X, 25, 3.
[3] Epist. II, 3, 1.
[4] Epist. VI, 10, 1.
[5] A "Decius, *librarius*," though not spoken of as P. Sestius's *libertus*,
represents his interests with Cicero (Epist. V, 6, 1). He receives the
typical freedman's adjective *frugi*, and is probably a freedman and in
Sestius's employ.
[6] Q. fr. I, 2, 8; cf. I, 1, 17.
[7] Q. fr. I, 2, 1–3.
[8] Att. V, 1, 3; Att. XV, 15, 1. One is tempted to attribute in part
to the influence of this *dedecus* of the house (Att. XII, 5, 1) the unscru-
pulous character of the younger Quintus. Cf. Att. VI, 2, 1–2 and XV,
19, 2 for their intimacy.
[9] Epist. III, 1, 1; cf. also Epist. II, 13, 2.
[10] Epist. III, 1, 2.
[11] Epist. X, 17, 3.
[12] Att. XVI, 4, 1.
[13] Bell. Hisp. 35, 2.
[14] Cic. Phil. XIII, 12; Epist. XVI, 17, 2; Epist. VIII, 15, 2; cf. O. E.
Schmidt, *Briefwechsel Cic.* p. 368.
[15] Plut. Pomp. 2, 4; 40, 1–5; Cat. Min. 13, 2–3; cf. Sen. de Tranq.
Anim. 8, 6; Plin. N. H. 35, 200; Josephus. Bell. Jud. 14, 175; Dio
XXXIX, 38, 6.

add from Plutarch the names of Cato's political secretary, Butas,[1] Antony's *libertus*, Hipparchus, whose partisanship was transferred from Antony to Octavian,[2] and the two freedmen of Octavian, Thyrsus and Epaphroditus, whom he used in confidential missions.[3]

(2.) *Liberti* in the Service of Business Men. Cicero's political preoccupations put at our disposal more information on the *liberti* whose patrons were first and foremost politicians than on the second group who were employed in business. Yet the very fact that the business agents of an individual or a firm figure so often in such a source goes to prove not only their numbers but their importance.[4]

---

[1] Plut. Cat. Min. 70.

[2] Son of Antony's *dispensator* (Plut. Ant. 67, 7; 73).

[3] Plut. Ant. 73; 79. Inasmuch as many of these *liberti* are referred to in connection with the political activities of their patrons, it would be interesting to know whether they themselves had influence among voters of their own status and used it to the patron's advantage. There is no positive evidence here unless Q. Cicero's advice to gain the thorough good will of your *liberti* and slaves be thus construed, *"nam fere omnis sermo ad forensem famam a domesticis emanat auctoribus"* (Pet. Cons. 17). Philotimus arranged for the entertainment in Rome of Cicero's *tribuli*, who were, however, not his own (Q. fr. III, 1, 1). In a few cases the political bias of the *libertus* is clear. Tiro seems to have shared Cicero's views (Epist. XVI, 21, 2). Philotimus (Att. X, 9, 1) and Philo (Bell. Hisp. 35, 2) were aristocratic in their politics. Apollonius seems to have been a Caesarian; *"propter memoriam Crassi de tuis"* (to Caesar) *unus esset"* (Epist. XIII, 16, 3). It is probable that their interests were those of their old masters and their interference in politics was from the upper side. (Caesar) *ex reliquo quoque ordinum genere vel invitatos vel sponte ad se commeantis uberrimo congiario prosequebatur, libertos insuper servulosque cuiusque prout domino patronove gratus qui esset* (Suet. Jul. 27, 1). The great mass of *liberti*, however, apparently voted on the popular side. Cf. Cic. Sest. 97, *sunt etiam libertini optimates*, and a special commendation of their attitude in 63 (Cat. 4, 16). If the republic had not gone to pieces over their heads and a new regime less hospitable to them begun, there might have emerged a group of freedman statesmen and diplomatists with as thorough an education in high politics as a Caelius or a Brutus. The influence of the *liberti Caesaris* was already strong in 45–3 and evidently growing (Cic. Att. XIV, 5, 1; Appian, B. C. 3, 11; Cic. Ph. II, 94). The striking part, political and military, played by the *liberti* of Sextus Pompey is well-known (Appian, B. C. V, 71 ff).

[4] The general subject of the employment of foreigners by Roman commercial houses and the close connection of such employment with the development of provincial branch houses need not be entered on in a presentation of facts regarding slaves or freedmen who were actually so employed.

Liberti mentioned in Cicero's writings who acted as business agents away from Rome:

Agents of Atticus:
>in Epirus   Alexio, undoubtedly *libertus* though not so designated, and others (Att. XI, 2, 4) probably in charge of the sheep ranches, etc. Through them Cicero could get money and clothing.
>
>in Corcyra   Araus, Andromenes, Eutychides, probably in close connection with Epirus as Alexio appears in both places.
>
>in Asia   Philogenes, Democritus, Seius, and others (Att. V, 13, 2)
>
>in Athens   Philadelphus (?).

Agents of other patrons:
>in Sicyon   C. Avianius Hammonius, *l.* of M. Aemilius Avianius.
>
>in Achaia   L. Cossinius Anchialus, *l.* of L. Cossinius.
>
>in Sicily   Hilarus, Antigones, Demonstratus, *l.* of Cn. Otacilius Naso.
>   L. Livineius Trypho, *l.* of L. Livineius Regulus.
>
>in Asia   C. Curtius Mithres, *l.* of C. Curtius Postumus.
>   T. Ampius Menander, *l.* of T. Ampius Balbus.
>
>in Africa   Eros, *l.* of Q. Turius.
>
>in Puteoli   *liberti* of P. Granius, in charge of ship and merchandise (Verr. VI, 154).

Less certain cases where the information on the status or business position is not given:
>in Asia   Cn. Pompeius Vindullus, *l.* of Pompey, in business (?).
>   L. Nostius Zoilus, *l.* in business (?).
>   Procurators of Cluvius of Puteoli,[1] *liberti* (?).
>
>in Africa   L. Julius, *l.* (?), procurator of C. Cuspius.
>   P. Cornelius, *l.*, procurator of C. Cuspius.

It is of course impossible to determine whether the *liberti* of this list had been originally members of the *familia* of the patron. Eutychides, the agent of Atticus at Corcyra, was without much question a member of the Roman *familia* at one time;[2] in other cases information which would decide the question is lacking. But by going back to the records of Cicero's own *liberti* we find a starting point. Three who

---

[1] Epist. XIII, 56, 3.
[2] Att. IV, 15, 1; V, 9, 1.

never formally engaged in business but remained connected with the household interested themselves in investing their own funds: Tiro bought an estate in the country,[1] Dionysius had money out at interest and perhaps trained slaves for hire,[2] and Philotimus, Terentia's *dispensator*, even had something of a financial career.[3] He appears from the beginning in charge of the family property and from time to time of Cicero's personal property, he was a '*socius*' in a friendly arrangement to save the remains of Milo's property,[4] and he certainly went into some commercial bypaths of his own necessitating a visit to the Chersonese [5] and involving him in a law-suit in Ephesus.[6] He owned a slave who was trained along his own line.[7] Whether he acted independently in supervising the work on Quintus's houses in Rome and Arpinum [8] cannot be told. He seems to have remained with Terentia after the separation but he kept up some connection with Cicero as late as 45.[9] In a similar way *liberti* in other *familiae* attended to the financial affairs of their patrons. Nicias, the *libertus* of M. Fadius Gallus, seems to have been concerned with the renting of his house,[10] Philo, the *libertus* of M. Caelius Rufus, was sent to Asia to collect payment on a bond,[11] Antiochus, *libertus* of the elder Flaccus, acted for the son in money matters.[12] A *libertus* was sent to Gaul to collect sums owed to his patron,[13] and another to Asia;[14] a

[1] Epist. XVI, 21, 7.
[2] Att. VIII, 10.
[3] Cicero never speaks of a *dispensator* of his own. He borrowed Eros from Atticus after he ceased to use Philotimus (46–44) and in the last references to business matters (44), Tiro seems to have been acting for him (Epist. XVI, 23; 24, 1; Att. XV, 15; 18.
[4] Att. V, 8, 2 and 3; Epist. VIII, 3, 2.
[5] Att. VI, 1, 19.
[6] Att. XI, 24, 4.
[7] Att. X, 15, 1.
[8] Q. fr. III, 1, 6; III, 9, 7.
[9] Att. XII, 48.
[10] Epist. VII, 23, 4; cf. also the renting of a house for Piso by his *libertus* (Pis. 61).
[11] Epist. VIII, 8, 10; II, 12, 2.
[12] Flacc. 89.
[13] Epist. XIII, 14, 2.
[14] Flacc. 47.

libertus was in charge of buying supplies for Faustus Sulla's troop of gladiators.[1]

With these instances of the independence and responsibility of the ex-slave in mind, we may conclude that often in the small beginnings of big business a clerk or manager or agent was found in some member of the *familia* who had been trained to buy in Roman markets and to deal with Roman banking systems and who could also contribute a knowledge actual or instinctive of the regions open to commerce beyond Italy.[2] It goes without saying that when Roman business houses multiplied and even in the later development of a single business house such a source of supply would become inadequate. The majority of upper clerks and managers would be promoted from the ranks of the slaves directly employed in the business.[3] But the transfer of intelligent slaves from the domestic *familiae* into the business houses must always have continued at the same time.

Several points can be noted on the status of the members of the *familia urbana*. First, the *liberti* mentioned in the foregoing lists emerged from groups of slaves employed in occupations demanding alertness, intelligence and versatility,

---

[1] Sulla 55. *Procuratores*, perhaps of libertine status, were sent from Rome by individual patrons to collect debts in Illyricum (Epist. XIII, 42, 1) and in Asia (Epist. XIII, 72; Q. fr. I, 2, 11).

[2] The first step may have been a post as assistant to the *dispensator;* cf. Eros the slave of Terentia's *dispensator* Philotimus. Cf. also the career of Trimalchio (Petron. 75–77).

[3] That the *libertus* business agent occasionally became a partner in or even the head of the firm is clear though the references are few. Attius Dionysius seems to have been at the head of a firm doing business in Africa, with a procurator, M. Pinarius. P. Umbrenus, a *libertus* (Cic. Cat. III, 14), was in business in Gaul and had a wide acquaintance among native chiefs (Sall. Cat. 40, 2). In Puteoli as early as the decade 80–70 *liberti* were *mercatores, homines locupletes atque honesti,* employing other *liberti* (Verr. VI, 154). How often this final step was taken is much less clear. Cicero's letters of introduction which are largely concerned with business firms in the provinces offer no instances of it. One slave is mentioned as the holder of a post as agent. The business of a Roman knight at Philomelium and elsewhere, is regularly managed by an *ingenuus* (Epist. XIII, 43, 1). It cannot be determined whether the slave Anchialus is in charge of a branch house or in temporary charge of the whole business (Epist. XIII, 45).

usually from the *librarii* and *dispensatores*. Second, among such slaves manumission was common. Third, it occurred early in the relation between employer and employed. Thus the manumission of Tiro and Statius is almost the first thing we know about them. Dionysius is first mentioned in 56 and manumitted before 54. Eutychides is mentioned in 58 as a slave and is manumitted by 54. It seems fairly evident that as soon as a slave became important to his master he ceased to be a slave. He was either given his freedom or was allowed to buy it himself. Fourth, even those *liberti* who did not actually sever their connection with the *familia*, tended to more or less independence of it. The step to complete independence was a short one.

II. THE CONTRACTOR.

It will be remembered that in the second century on a carefully managed country estate such as Cato describes the contractor not only attended to such specialized work as building but took care of the by-products from the estate and gave whatever expert attention was necessary to the main products, and that in the first century on Varro's farms the labor was organized with the same dependence on the contractor. In the city large contractors, men like Crassus and to a lesser degree Atticus, were prepared to carry on building, the handicrafts, and even the work of secretaries and caterers on the scale of public work.[1] It is not surprising, therefore, to find casual references in Cicero informing us that in his establishments both in town and country work was turned over to regular employees who carried it out not on the wage but on the contract system.

The status of these half-independent employees is not certain; in a majority of cases the fact that they have Greek

---

[1] Plut. Crass. 2.

cognomina indicates that they were *liberti*.[1] There follows a list of the instances in which labor was done by contract in some one of Cicero's establishments or in a similar establishment of his brother Quintus.

1. **Contract Labor used for Building, Irrigation, Gardening.**

   a. Contractor, a Member of *Familia*.

   (1.) A *vilicus* of Q. Cicero at Laterium, Nicephorus, intended to take the contract for the building of a certain *aedificatuncula* on the place, but on the raising of the requirements without corresponding rise in payment he gave it up. He was to have received 16,000 *sesterces* for the job.[2] This instance is interesting as revealing the system. The owner does not trust his *vilicus* to conduct an expensive piece of work unless the *vilicus* will take the contract and assume the responsibility. This apparently means that most extra jobs on an estate would be done by contract.

   b. Contractor Independent of *Familia*.

   (1.) Longilius contracted for the construction of Q. Cicero's house on the Palatine and in March 56 was paid one-half of the amount promised him although the house did not promise completion before winter. *Multi structores* were being used in April.[3] Others were working in M. Cicero's house at the same time.[4]

   (2.) A slave, Cillo, was engaged to come from Venafrum to do some digging on the Arpinum estates. He employed at least four other slaves.[5]

---

[1] It may be that the few intelligent slave laborers or artisans on the large estates (p. 54) obtained their manumission and continued to work on contract. Domitius had slaves, *liberti* and *coloni* on his estates at Cosa (Caes. B. C. I, 34; 56).

[2] Q. fr. III, 1, 5. Whether this particular building was turned over to some one else and thus included in the notice of the completion of the *res rustica* . . . . *Lateri* a month later (Q. fr. III, 3, 1) is uncertain.

[3] Q. fr. II, 5, 3. In March Cicero wrote Quintus that the work could be pushed forward if Quintus would authorize it. *Si te haberem, paullisper fabris locum darem* (Q. fr. II, 4, 3).

[4] Att. IV, 7, 3. On the Alban estate of Clodius a thousand men were engaged in building at one time (Cic. Mil. 53).

[5] Q. fr. III, 1, 3.

c. Relation of Contractor to *Familia* Uncertain.

(1.) Diphilus was engaged in rebuilding Q. Cicero's Manilianum in 54.[1] Being found wanting, he was not trusted with
proposed additions to the Arcanum.[2]

(2.) Mescidius and Philoxinus introduced an irrigation
system at the Arcanum in 54, and Mescidius was willing to
take a contract for the Bovillanum (Fufidianum?) at three
sesterces a foot.[3] Philoxinus was probably a freedman; the
status of Mescidius is uncertain. The men may have been
permanent employees of the Arpinum estates or they may
have been called in from outside.

(3.) Workmen engaged in building at the Tusculanum in
44 arranged for their own living and were not, therefore, of
Cicero's own *familia*.[4] The work was probably being done
by contract.

(4.) Four gardeners are referred to,[5] three with Greek names
and probably therefore freedmen.[6] There are no means of
deciding whether or not they were regular members of the
familia. They seem to have worked for Cicero as *partiarii*,
supplying him with fruit and vegetables over and above a
cash rent for the garden.[7] At Rome in 44, Motho was in
charge of the garden which furnished Cicero with flowers.
At the Tusculanum in 44, Helico, *holitor*, had previously
rented the garden without improvements and without a house
(*casa*) for himself for 1000 *sesterces*. Helico's successor paid
less rent for the garden with improvements and furnished no

---

[1] Q. fr. III, 1, 2. Caesius seems to have had some supervision of the
work.
[2] Q. fr. III, 9, 7.
[3] Q. fr. III, 1, 1 and 3.
[4] Att. XIV, 3, 1. *Ecce autem structores nostri ad frumentum profecti,
cum inanes redissent, rumorem adferunt magnum Romae domum ad Antonium
frumentum omne portari.* If they had gone to Rome to receive corn doles
they must have been at least of freedman status.
[5] Epist. XVI, 18, 2.
[6] A *coronarius* at Molae was a freedman (C. I. L. I, 1193); two *holitores*
at Rome, father and son, were freemen (C. I. L. I, 1057).
[7] Flower and vegetable gardens near Rome were early recognized as a
profitable investment. See Cato Agr. 8, 2; Varro Rust. I, 16, 3.

fruit and vegetables for the house. If he continued to be unsatisfactory Cicero proposed to replace him by Parhedrus who was understood to be willing to rent the garden.

2. **Contract Labor used in Publishing.** Cicero's own copyists prepared the manuscripts of his speeches and philosophic and rhetorical works[1] but the actual business of publication was taken over entirely by Atticus.[2] His list of employees must have been long for in addition to the work of his publishing house he purchased and sold libraries[3] and single books[4] and he had branch houses or agents in Athens and other Greek cities.[5] Nepos refers to the careful professional training of his slaves while they were still members of the domestic *familia*. (Atticus) *usus est familia, si utilitate iudicandum est, optima, — namque in ea erant pueri litteratissimi, anagnostae optimi et plurimi librarii, ut ne pedisequus quidem quisquam esset, qui non utrumque horum pulchre facere posset.*[6] The correspondence of Cicero makes it possible to add the names and the special tasks of a few of these employees: *anagnostes*, Salvius; *librarii* in general,[7] Salvius, Antaeus, Pharnaces; *glutinatores*, Menophilus, Dionysius; *librarii* especially employed in reference work, Antiochus, Syrus, Satyrus, Thallumetus.[8] The *cognomina* indicate that the men were slaves or *liberti*. Though there is no further indication of status except in the case of Dionysius who was manumitted in 54, it is unlikely that his promotion was

---

[1] Att. XIII, 21a, 4; Epist. XVI, 22, 1.

[2] See Usener, G. G. N. 1892, pp. 197–206. There were other contemporary publishing houses (Att. XIII, 22, 3), and a little later Horace mentions the firm of the brothers Sosii (Hor. Epist. I, 20, 1). Atticus published not only ordinary but special gift editions, *macrocolla*, and illustrated editions (Plin. N. H. 35, 11).

[3] Att. I, 10, 4; 4, 3.

[4] Att. II, 4, 1.

[5] Att. II, 1, 2.

[6] Nep. Att. 13, 3. Crassus also trained in his own house the slaves whom he offered for hire (Plut. Crass. 2, 6).

[7] Cf. Att. XII, 6, 3 *et al.*

[8] Usener (*op. cit.*) suggests that Tyrranio was in charge of the Greek publications and Nepos of the Latin (cf. Fronto. Ep. I, 7, 20 Nab.), and that Varro was called in for special consultation.

unique among men who were necessarily responsible and intelligent.

III.   THE PROFESSIONAL MAN

The variety in social position and political status among the particular physicians, architects, teachers and librarians on whose services Cicero drew is probably typical of the general situation at that time.

1. Architects employed by Cicero.   Cicero interested himself in building and the references to building projects both on his own property and his brother's often include the names of the architects.[1]

a. Cyrus, whose name indicates that he was a *libertus*, built the Amaltheum (?) at Arpinum in 61,[2] rebuilt Quintus's Roman house in 56[3] and Cicero's from 57 to 54.[4]   He died in 52 leaving a legacy to Cicero and a second to Clodius[5] who had perhaps employed him in his extensive building plans.

b. A *libertus* of Cyrus, Vettius Chrysippus, was consulted about repairs in Cicero's Roman house in 59,[6] reported to Cicero on a possible purchase in 45,[7] and was in charge of rebuilding the *insulae* at Puteoli in 44.[8]   He had been in Gaul with Caesar in 53[9] (perhaps drawing plans for building

---

[1] Under whose direction his other building was done is not known. While the Roman house was being built, the Fornianum and Tusculanum were being rebuilt (Att. IV, 2, 7), the Cumanum was being built (Q. fr. II, 8, 3), and repairs were being made in other houses (Q. fr. II, 4, 3).   Cicero himself suggested changes in the buildings on Quintus's estate (Q. fr. III, 1, 1) and perhaps in other cases for the simpler kinds of building he acted as his own architect though he recognized the danger thus run by both building and owner, "*sicut mali aedificii domino glorianti se architectum non habuisse*" (N. D. I, 72).

[2] Att. II, 3, 2.
[3] Q. fr. II, 2, 2.
[4] Att. IV, 10, 2.
[5] Mil. 48.
[6] Att. II, 4, 7.
[7] Att. XIII, 29, 2.
[8] Att. XIV, 9, 1.
[9] Epist. VII, 14, 1-2.

the Basilica Julia?), and was in Epirus in some capacity in 48.[1]

c. The slave or *libertus* of Balbus, Corumbus, was apparently to carry on some work at the Tusculanum in 44, which had already been begun.[2]

d. Cluatius drew the plan for a shrine to Tullia in 45.[3]

e. Numisius drew a plan for some building in 56.[4]

2. *Physicians* **Employed by Cicero.**

a. A *libertus*,[5] Alexio, mentioned only at his death in 44, when he may have left Cicero his heir.[6] There is no indication that he was a freedman of Cicero himself.

b. Metrodorus, of status unknown, perhaps a slave in Cicero's *familia.* Tiro was under his care at Tusculanum in the winter of 44.[7]

c. A *medicus* at Cumae in 53; apparently not of the *familia* as a fee was paid.[8]

3. *Librarians* **and Teachers Employed by Cicero.**

a. A slave, Dionysius, had charge of Cicero's books in 46.[9]

b. A *libertus* of Murena, Tyrranio, see p. 64.

c. A *libertus* of Atticus, Dionysius, see p. 64.

For purposes of comparison a list of other professional men of the period arranged according to their status is added. References are not given where Orelli's Onomasticon can be used.[10]

A majority of these men seem to have been of slave stock

---

[1] Att. XI, 2, 3.
[2] Att. XIV, 3, 1.
[3] Att. XII, 18, 1.
[4] Q. fr. II, 2, 1.
[5] He made a will (Att. XV, 2, 4).
[6] Att. XV, 2, 4.
[7] Epist. XVI, 20, 1.
[8] Epist. XVI, 14, 1. Asclapo, a Greek physician in Patrae, attended Tiro in 50 (Epist. XVI, 4 and 9) and was recommended to the notice of Servius in 46 (Epist. XIII, 20).
[9] Epist. XIII, 77, 3. Dionysius absconded with a large number of books (*loc. cit.*, and Epist. V, 9, 2; 10, 1; 11, 3).
[10] a. Slaves
    architects: Hospes at Caiatia (C.I.L. I, 1216).
    physicians: Glyco (Cic., Suet. Aug. 11); slave of Caesar (Suet. Jul. 4, 1); Sarpedon (Cat. Min. 1, 3); Strato (Cic.). See also Hor. Serm. II, 3, 147.

but the *liberti* at least were practising their professions independently. Those who had been originally slave members
of a *familia* or slave apprentices[1] undoubtedly emerged
quickly for their training demanded shrewdness and intelligence and they were brought into direct relations with a rich
and powerful class whose gratitude they could promptly earn.
The Greek tradition was a good one and *peregrini* practised
in Rome. ´Cicero spoke of the professions with approval:
(*artes*) *ut medicina, ut architectura, ut doctrina rerum hones-
tarum; hae sunt iis, quorum ordini conveniunt, honestae.*[2]
But, on the other hand, the approval was lukewarm. The
professions continued to lack dignity and attraction for the
better class of *ingenui* because their ranks were full of *liberti*
and constantly recruited from slaves.[3]

---

b. *Liberti*

physicans: Cleanthes (Plut. Cat. Min. 70); Menecrates (C.I.L. I,
1256); Nicia (Diehl, *Altlateinische Inschriften*, 360);
Pamphilus (C.I.L. I, 1059); *l.* of Domitius (Suet. Nero
11, 2).
So probably Antistius (Suet. Jul. 82, 3), Cleophantus
(Cic.) Craterus (Cic., Hor. Serm. II, 3, 161); S.
Fadius (Cic.); A. Rupilius (Cic.); *medicus* of M.
Antony (Cic. Phil. II, 101).

teachers, grammarians, etc. Daphnis (Suet. Gramm. 3), Epicadus
(Suet. Gramm. 12), Epirota (Suet. Gramm. 16),
Eros (Suet. Gramm. 13); Gnipho (Suet. Gramm. 7);
Lenaeus (Suet. Gramm. 13); Praetextatus (Suet.
Gramm. 10); Sphaerus (Dio XLVIII, 33); so proba-
bly Andronicus (Suet. Gramm. 8).
Slightly later in date, Aphrodisius (Suet. Gramm. 19);
Crassicius (Suet. Gramm. 18); Flaccus (Suet. Gramm.
17); Hyginus (Suet. Gramm. 20).

c. *Ingenui* or *Peregrini*

architects: T. Vettius Q. *f.* Ser. (C.I.L. X, 8093); an Athenian
architect employed by Caesar (Att. XIII, 35, 1).

physician: Cornelius Artemidorus of Perga, a tool of Verres (Verr.
IV, 69).

teachers, grammarians, etc., cf. Hillscher, *Hominum Litteratorum
Graecorum in Urbe Roma Commoratorum*, N. J. Kl A.
Supp. 18 (1892) pp. 356 ff.

[1] Like Vettius Chrysippus, the *libertus* of Cyrus the architect, Strato, the
slave of A. Rupilius the physician, and Sex. Fadius, the pupil (*libertus?*)
of Nico the physician.

[2] Off. I, 151.

[3] Caesar tried to make the professions of medicine and teaching at Rome
more honorable by giving citizenship to *peregrini* practising them (Suet.
Jul. 42, 1).

IV. THE DEALER.

Though it is obvious that manufactured articles of every kind must have been bought from their makers or from merchants by Cicero and his household,[1] he refers to such purchases and to the dealers supplying them very rarely. The references obtainable are concerned almost entirely with the acquisition of objects of art from Greece.[2] Atticus on one occasion supplied Cicero with clothing for himself and his slaves,[3] and on another with book-shelves and parchment for book labels.[4] Cicero contemplated buying the marble columns for Tullia's shrine from Apella the Chian in Rome.[5] Statues and a table were bought from the sculptor Avianius direct.[6]

In default of a catalogue of the dealers from whom Cicero himself bought a list follows of the names of tradesmen mentioned by him in any connection with additions from the inscriptions.   Status is added where it is possible.

unguentarii	Plotius *l.* or *ing.* in Puteoli (Cic.); *l.* in Rome (C.I.L. I, 1065); 2 *l.* in Capua (I, 1210); *l.* in Venusia (I, 1268).
pigmentarius	Attius *l.* or *ing.* Cic.
thuriarii	*l.* at Rome (C.I.L. VI. 5638–9; *l.* at Rome (I, 1092); 3 *ing.* but evidently of libertine stock at Rome (I, 1091).
pharmacopola	(*circumforanus*) L. Clodius *l.* or *ing.*, at Ancona (Cic.) Cicero speaks of the Seplasia in Capua, the quarter of the *unguentarii* etc. as having a lively interest in politics (Pis. 24).

---

[1] See pp. 60–61.

[2] *Signa Megarica* and Herms (Att. I, 8, 2), reliefs (*typi*) and fountain bases (*putealia*, Att. I, 10, 3) bought in 67 by Atticus in Greece were brought by freight ships to Formiae and later moved to the Tusculanum.   Pliny (N. H. 13, 92) records that Cicero paid 500,000 *sesterces* for a citrus-wood table.

[3] Att. XI, 2, 4.

[4] Att. IV, 4a, 1; 8, 2.

[5] Att. XII, 19, 1.   A studio of Sopolis the painter, in which among the apprentices employed, was a *libertus* of A. Gabinius (Att. IV, 18, 4), is mentioned in Rome in 54, and an *ergasterium* of workers in marble in 44 is mentioned by Appian (B. C. III, 9).

[6] Epist. VII, 23, 1–3.

copo	A Bivius *l.* or *ing., de Via Latina,* Rome (Cic.)
popa	Licinius *l.* or *ing. de Circo Maximo,* Rome (Cic.)
lanii	*l., ab luco Lubent.* (C.I.L. VI, 33870); *l. de Colle Vimi-nale* (I, 1011); *l.* and *s.* (?), *magistri* of *collegium* at Rome (VI, 168); 4 *l., magistri* of *collegium* at Praeneste (XIV, 2877); 2 *l., magistri* of *Lanii Piscenenses,* at Rome (VI, 167).
holitores	2 *ing.* at Rome (C.I.L. I, 1057).
coronarius	*l.* at Molae (C.I.L. I, 1193).
macellarius	Mindius, *l.* or *ing.* Cic.
mercatores	*bovarius, ing. de Campo* at Rome (Diehl *Altlateinische Inschriften,* 581); *pecuarii,* 1 *ing.,* 1 *l., magistri* of *collegium* at Praeneste (C.I.L. XIV, 2878); *margaritarius, l., de sacra via,* at Rome (I, 1027).
pistores	*redemptor, l.* at Rome (C.I.L. VI, 1958); *similaginarius, l.* at Rome (VI, 9812).

The abbreviated forms of the name in the literary source often make it impossible to distinguish between free and libertine status.   The fuller forms of the name in the inscriptions show out of a total of twenty-eight, twenty *liberti*, one slave and seven *ingenui* of whom three are almost certainly of libertine stock.   With more information at our disposal we should probably be ready to identify the great majority of retail dealers at Rome as *liberti* or of libertine stock.

C. LABOR EMPLOYED IN THE ARRETINE POTTERIES.

On the small estates discussed by Cato and Varro and in the city and country houses of the type of Cicero's all but the simplest manufactured articles were bought outright. Even the large estates managed on the plantation system, except where they were remote from markets, were also on the list of consumers,[1] and the poor in both city and country must always have bought, not made, their clothing, utensils and tools.   To meet the demands of a large consumption at a time when production relied mainly on hand labor we

[1] Varro, Rust. 1, 16, 4.

must postulate an army of workmen, and in view of the cheapness and abundance of slave labor we should expect to find that army largely composed of slaves. Such slaves clearly would live under conditions different from those of the agricultural laborer, and no conclusions drawn from a study of the latter type can be applied offhand to the former. Unfortunately for the investigator in most cases all trace of the workmen disappeared with the cloth and tools they made. It is only in a few industries where the products were of a durable material and where the name of the maker could be attached that there is any basis for investigation of numbers, origins and conditions of the workmen.

Such an industry was the manufacture of Arretine vases. The earlier ware was formerly dated in the first half of the first century B.C.,[1] but two facts point to a later general dating: first, the discovery of numbers of vases with Arretine stamps in the Rhine Valley and, second, the establishment of a new *terminus ante quem*, 12 B.C. instead of 52-1, for the Arretine fragments found on Mt. Beuvray. These indications have been confirmed by Oxé's application of his study of forms of slave nomenclature to the chronology of Arretine vases;[2] he has arrived at the dates 40-20 B.C. for the earlier Arretine potters and has roughly grouped the succeeding potters from that date into the reign of Tiberius. His chronology is accepted here.[3]

Data are furnished by stamps on the ware which contain the name of the owner of the pottery or of the workman or

---

[1] Dressel C.I.L. XV, p. 702; Dragendorff B. J. 96 (1895) pp. 40, 49-50; B. J. 113 (1905) p. 252.

[2] Oxé, R. M. 59 (1904) pp. 108 ff.

[3] Not earlier than 40-20 B.C.: Basilius, Calidius, Domitius, Hertorius, Mesienus, Paconius, Publius, Rasinius, Saufaeus, Maecius and Naevius (Oxé, *op. cit.*, p. 130).

Not earlier than 30-20 B.C.: M. Perennius, L. Tettius, C. Annius, A. Sentius, A. Vettius (p. 132).

Later than 30-20 B.C., the signatures of the last six probably to be dated under Tiberius: L. Iegidius, L. Nonius, C. Sestius, C. Tellius, L. Titius, C. Titius, P. Cornelius, T. Rufrenus, C. Cispius, C. Memmius, L. Umbricius (pp. 132, 139).

both. Long forms of the name were undoubtedly eliminated
by the convention artistic or otherwise that the inscription
should occupy little space, and the official status whether of
the owner of the pottery or of the workmen is, therefore,
rarely revealed.[1] Further, while many forms of the Roman
slave name are distinctive [2] and the majority of the slaves
can, therefore, be recognized as such, the corresponding
nomenclature of the *liberti* and *ingenui* is ambiguous and the
two can be distinguished only where some other factor is
introduced as for instance the use of *cognomina* with distinct
free or libertine implication.[3] As a result statistics on the

---

[1] Slaves are so designated in C.I.L. XV. 5676, 5694; XI, 6700[727,737];
liberti, in C.I.L. XI, 6700 [386]; XIII, 10009 [294]; XV, 5414 *et al.*

[2] As *Cerdo Anni, Cerdo C. Anni, Acastus A. Vibi Scrofae, Eros Calidi
Strigonis.*

[3] Names of the form *Cn Atei Hilarus* can be variously interpreted: (1) as
belonging to slaves, i. e., *Cn Atei (s) Hilarus*, or (*ex figlinis*) *Cn Atei,
Hilarus (fecit)*; (2) to *liberti*, i. e., *Cn. Atei (l) Hilarus;* or (3) as the equivocal form *Cn Atei (us) Hilarus*, assigned according to context to a *libertus*
or a freeman.   The form is extremely puzzling.   (1) It occurs side by side
with the same name in distinctly slave form, as *Rufio T. Rufren ( )* and *T.
Rufren ( ) Rufio*, with no clue as to whether the two are equivalent signatures or whether the second form indicates that a change from slave to
libertine status has been made.   (2) In certain potteries it occurs so often
in the case of a single individual that we must regard him as the principal
employee, perhaps the owner, and certainly not a slave.   (3) On the other
hand it occurs in certain potteries in the case of a large number of individuals — so large that it is hard to regard them as all *liberti.*

Dressel (*op. cit.*, p. 703) somewhat hesitatingly assigns the form to
liberti. Oxé (*op. cit.*, pp. 136–140) holds that in particular instances in
inscriptions on earlier vases the form is certainly to be read *Cn Ateius
Hilarus*, and he does not hesitate to allow the use of the form even to
freemen (p. 138) as well as to *liberti;* on later vases, however, he would
not attempt finally to decide whether the employee designated as *Cn.
Atei Hilarus* was a slave or a *libertus*, though he tends to the *libertus*
explanation. Chase (Catalogue of Arretine Pottery, Museum of Fine
Arts, Boston 1916 p. 17) regards the form as in all probability indicative
of the slave status because if all those who use it are counted as *liberti*,
the proportion of the latter to workmen remaining slaves is unduly raised.

In order to get an idea of the relative importance in the potteries of the
workmen who are proved *liberti* and the workmen who use the doubtful
signature, I have counted in C.I.L. XI, XII and XV the signatures of
all of both classes whose names appear in the lists on pp. 82, 85, 86, exclud-
ing the names of pottery owners.   The 21 *liberti* sign 195 times, an average
of 9 signatures each.   The 42 possible *liberti* sign 171 times, an average
of 4 each.   That is, the workmen using the doubtful signature seem to
have signed vases much less frequently than the proved *liberti* and their
average approaches that of the slaves who average 2–3 signatures each.

status of the workmen are incomplete and inexact. Nevertheless the scarcity of information on industries in general justifies the collection of all possible information in this field which will help to estimate the rate at which slaves and *liberti* were replacing free labor, and the rate at which slaves were being manumitted and thus merging in the plebs.

I. The group of earlier Arretine potteries manufacturing from 40 to 20 B.C. includes a variety of establishments, from those employing at least two to those employing at least thirty-nine workmen.[1]

Owner	Slaves, 123	Workmen, 132 Liberti, 8	Possible *Libertus*, 1
Basilius	4	....	....
P? Calidius	20	2 Eros, Synhistor	1 Protus
P. Domitius	3	....	....
P. Hertorius	2	....	....
P. Mesienus	1	4 Amphio, Menophilus, Sindanos, Helenus	....
A. Paconius	1	1 Aphroditus	....
Publius	24	....	....
Rasinius	39	....	....
L. Saufeius			
Gaius or Gausa	15	1 Celer	....
Maecius	2	....	....
N. Naevius			
Hilarus	12	....	....

Paconius, the one freeman among the potters who sign these earlier vases,[2] is probably identical with the owner of the pottery, Q. Paconius. The number who sign as *liberti* is strikingly small, only 1 in 19; in fact if we exclude the pottery of Mesienus, where conditions seem to have been

[1] It is assumed that the number of extant signatures from any one pottery bears a general relation to the actual number of workmen employed and to their output.

[2] *Paconius f.* (C.I.L. XIII, 10009[185]). L. Saufeius may also have been a working potter.

unusual, only four slaves out of a possible one hundred and twenty-six were certainly manumitted, that is, 1 in 32; from three of the large potteries there are no signatures of *liberti*. The position of the few *liberti* varies. Aphroditus, Celer and Eros sign rarely; the frequent signatures of Calidius's slave, later *libertus*, Synhistor, and the fact that he owned slaves himself make it probable that he held a place of authority in the pottery; Protus who never signs as a *libertus* but who owned three slaves and is conspicuous by the number of his signatures may also have been the manager of a branch pottery or of some division of the main pottery to which he supplied laborers. The small pottery of P. Mesienus deserves special mention for its working force was made up of three, possibly four, *liberti* and one slave.[1] In most cases the owners seem to have been freemen.[2] But while Hilarus is indicated as the owner of his pottery by the use of the signature, *N. Naevi Hilar*, which is unique in the pottery [3] and by the initials *N. N. H.* signed on two vases his *cognomen* plainly implies that he was a *libertus*, and the same probability exists in the case of *L. Saufei Caius* (*Gaius* or *Gausa*).[4] Neither man's cognomen appears in definite slave form. The explanation may be that the two men did not remain in the potteries which they later owned but that after receiving their training

[1] P. Mesienus signed only 3 times, his three *liberti* 21 times. The one slave uses the form *Rufio Mesieni*, and it therefore is probable that *P. Mess Helen* who signs twice was a fourth *libertus* rather than a slave. Apparently in a small establishment the slaves had obtained their freedom and were carrying on the business with greater activity after the death or withdrawal of their patron.

[2] Oxé (p. 134) regards the name of the owner *Rasini* as identical with *L. Rasini Pisanus* or *Pisaurensis* (C.I.L. II, 6257[160]). Chase (*op. cit.*, p. 20) differentiates between the two on the basis of the style of their signed work, dating Pisanus much later.

[3] Dragendorff, *op. cit.*, p. 54; Oxé, p. 138. The other potters sign invariably in the form (Cocco) *Naevi*.

[4] Oxé (p. 130, n. 1) reads *Gaius* or preferably *Gaus* (*a*). If *Caius* or *Gaius* is correct the man was himself a potter; if Gaus ( ), the *cognomen* may be genitive. U. Pasqui (*Not. d. Sr.* (1894) p. 121 no. 21) concludes from the signature (R)*asini Saufei* that Saufeius had been a slave or *socius* of Rasinius. It indicates rather the purchase of a slave of Rasinius by Saufeius. Cf. *Quartio Rasini Memmi* (C.I.L. XI, 6700[546] *et al.*).

and after being manumitted they set out on business enterprises of their own.

In the earliest group of Arretine potteries, therefore, nine owners were *ingenui*, two probably *liberti*. One free owner seems to have been a working potter, but among the employees there were no *ingenui*. Slave labor formed the body of the workmen, 123 out of 131. The proportion of employees of libertine status was 1 to 19.[1]

II. A second group of five potteries is roughly dated by Oxé from 30 B.C. on.[2]

---

[1] Support for the conditions in the small Arretine potteries is drawn from two other groups, the pre-Arretine potters, and the makers of Amphorae Calabriae (dated by Mommsen) in the last part of the republican period (C.I.L. IX, p. 613).

Pre-Arretine potteries

Owners	Workmen 27	
	Slaves 17	Libertus 1
Q. Arrius, Po Valley (Oxé, p. 127)	1	—
C. Arrius (C.I.L. III, 10186¹)	1	—
L. and C. Sarius, Po Valley, (Oxé, p. 127)	6	1
St. Rullius, Campania? (Oxé, p. 128)	2	—
C. Rullius (Oxé, p. 128).	7	—

Amphorae Calabriae.

Owners	Slaves 9	Liberti 0
M. Betilienus (Oxé, p. 126, C.I.L. IX, 6079¹²)	4	—
L. Malleolus (Oxé, p. 126)	2	—
A. Ovinius, (Oxé, p. 127; C.I.L. X, 8050³, ¹⁰)	3	—

The owners seem to be all freemen but no free labor appears. Twenty-six slaves and one *libertus* are employed.

[2] *Op. cit.*, p. 132. The equivocal signature of the type *Cn. Atei Hilarus* occurs in each of the five potteries and this increase in its use makes statistics on status difficult. In a few cases other tests have thrown light on the individual who uses the signature and made his identification as *libertus* or *ingenuus* possible or probable. *A. Sesti Pila* and *A. Vibius Scrofa* have *cognomina* indicating free status and therefore are probably owners of potteries. *L. Tetti Samia, L. Tetti Crito, A. Sesti Dama* and *M. Perenni Bargates* are pretty certainly of libertine status if we may judge from their *cognomina;* the frequency of Samia's signature (occurring 83 times) makes it probable that he owned his pottery. Though the form of the name *M. Perenni Tigran* ( ) does not preclude slave status for Tigranus, his slave *Bello Perenni* signs also in the form *Bello Tigrani* indicating the full name of his owner was actually *Perennius Tigranus*. The *cognomen* probably implies libertine status (Cf. C.I.L. VI, 27415, 35975). That Tigranus was owner of this pottery is indicated by the frequency with which his signature occurs (59 times. Cf. Oxé, p. 137).

Owner		Workmen 84	
	Slaves 68	Liberti 4	Possible *liberti*, i. e. using the *Cn Atei Hilarus* form of signatures, 12
M. Perennius Tigranus	17	1 Bargates	5
L. Tettius Samia	9	1 Crito	1
C. Annius	25	....	3
A. Sestius Pila	12	1 Dama	2
A. Vibius Scrofa	5	1 Venicus	1

Four of the potteries were of considerable size. The largest was owned by C. Annius, to all appearance a freeman; the signatures of twenty-five out of his twenty-eight workmen indicate slave status. The pottery of the *libertus*, L. Tettius Samia, shows one *libertus* employee to nine slaves; eleven signatures of this one *libertus* have been found, all outside Arretium, an indication, possibly, that he was in charge of a branch pottery. Samia was himself a potter[1] and the two *liberti* may have been partners. Seventeen slaves were employed by the *libertus*, Tigranus, of whom certainly one, possibly five, were manumitted.[2] A. Vibius Scrofa, a freeman, was himself a potter[3] in a small establishment of seven workmen; six of these were slaves including his *procurator* who owned a slave of his own;[4] the seventh is the only *libertus* actually designated as such in the signatures of this period.[5] A. Sestius Pila, another freeman, manumitted one out of his thirteen slaves.

Of the five potteries of the second period, therefore, three were owned by freemen, two by *liberti;* one freeman owner was himself a potter but free labor was absent; slaves formed

---

Assuming these conjectures to be correct, the above table of owners and workmen is made out.

[1] He signs *L. Tetti Samia.*

[2] It may be that the signatures consisting of the *nomina* alone, *M. Perenni, L. Tetti,* represent the patrons of the two *liberti,* Tigranus and Samia, earlier owners of the potteries under whom the *liberti* learned their art and whom they succeeded.

[3] He signs *A. Vibiu Scrofe* (C.I.L. XI, 6700⁷⁶⁶ᵃ), *A. Vibi figul.* (C.I.L. XI, 6700⁷⁶⁵), etc.

[4] See Oxé, pp. 136–7, who thinks he was manumitted.

[5] *A. Vibi A. l. Venici* (C.I.L. XIII, 10009²⁹⁴).

the working force, 68 out of 72. The proportion of *liberti* employed was 1 to 18.[1]

A pottery of the P. Mesienus type dated tentatively by Oxé in this period [2] remains to be mentioned. The signature *C. Sert (ori)* appears in connection with the *cognomina* Ocella and Proculus.[3] Apparently either a pottery owner with one or two workmen or two *liberti* working for themselves are indicated here. Several other potteries of the same type can be added from a study of the signatures.[4] An attempt on the part of a working potter to set up for himself may be indicated. The *libertus* element in such modest establishments was proportionally large.

III. The third group of potters is dated in the years after 20 B.C. The later signatures may be as late as the reign of Tiberius.

Owner	Slaves, 154	Liberti, 10	Workmen, 236 Possible *liberti*, i. e. using *Cn. Atei Hilarus* signature, 72
P. Cornelius	58	1, Potus	21
L. Iegidius Calvio	7	0	0
L. Nonius	6	0	1
T. Rufrenus	4	2, Rufio, Fronto	2
C. Sentius	5	1, Firmus	0
C. Tellius	11	0	0
C. Titius Nepos	17	1	4
L. Titius	26	2, Thyrsus, Jusculus	7
C. Cispius	8	1, Hilarus	33
C. Memmius	12	2, Mahes, Hilarus	4

[1] If not only the certain *liberti* but all persons signing in the form *Cn. Atei Hilarus* are reckoned as *liberti*, the proportion would rise to 1 in 5. Though on the basis of our present knowledge this increase in the number of *liberti* cannot be accepted, a high rate of manumission is not out of the question in itself. The industry required a skilled hand and considerable intelligence.

[2] *Op. cit.*, p. 138.

[3] *C. Sert Ocel, C. Sertori Procul;* Proculus also signs as a slave. Oxé (p. 138) regards the *cognomen* Ocella as indicative of free status (cf. C.I.L. IX, 5128) and, therefore, identifies *C. Sert Ocel* with the owner of the pottery. But in XI, 6700[237] the name is servile and in IX, 3542 it may well be libertine.

[4] Cf. the firms of working potters, L. Avillius Sura and C. Umbricius

The group is dominated by the name of P. Cornelius. He is named in the signatures of almost sixty slaves and details of the organization of his pottery would be of peculiar interest. The workman whose signature occurs most often, perhaps a foreman, is a *libertus;* the status of twenty-one other employees is hidden behind the form *Cn Atei Hilarus* which they use.[1] The small potteries of L. Iegidius Calvio, L. Nonius and C. Tellius on the other hand are represented entirely by slave signatures and that of C. Sentius includes only one *libertus.* T. Rufrenus manumitted certainly two, possibly all of his four workmen and we may see here another example of the small pottery managed and worked by a little group of freedmen. C. Cispius and L. Iegidius Calvio though apparently *ingenui* were working potters.[2]

In the third group, therefore, the potteries are owned by freemen; two owners are working potters; free labor among employees is absent; the workmen are largely slaves.[3]

In summing up the results of this brief study, attention is again drawn to the fact that only a small number of signatures is available and of that small number many do not fix the status of the signer and cannot be safely assigned to any one group. Two conclusions, however, can be drawn. First, there is no indication of the employment of free labor in any Arretine pottery. Apparently by the middle of the first century B.C. no field was open to Italian workmen in this

---

Philologus, signing *Philologus et Sura* or vice versa, and the firm of L. Gellius Quadratus (Oxé, p. 139), a working potter (C.I.L. XIII, 10009[211]), and L. Sempronius; Gellius employed two slaves and one slave or *libertus.*

[1] If we assume them to be *liberti*, the ratio of manumitted to unmanumitted slaves in the pottery would be more than 1 to 3. A similarly high proportion of *liberti* would be shown in the potteries of C. Titius Nepos and L. Titius (1 to 4) and of C. Cispius and C. Memmius (1 to 2).

[2] C.I.L. VI, 6700,[193], [323]; XIII, 10009,[79], etc. Volusinus of this period himself a potter (C.I.L. XI, 6700[821]) with 8 slaves has almost certainly the cognomen Nestor (cf. XV, 5790 and 5374, Oxé, p. 134), and if so, is a *libertus.*

[3] Certainly 154 out of 236 are slaves. The ratio of certain *liberti* to certain slaves is 1 to 16 but 1 to 3 if the 72 signatures of the *Cn Atei Hilarus* type are added to those of the certain *liberti.*

industry, although it demanded a relatively high type of workman and was carried on in a small town, not in a great emporium of cheap slave labor.[1] The workmen were all slaves or ex-slaves. The freeman appears through the whole period in the rôle of owner of the pottery, a place which he occupies fairly generally.[2] Second, manumission was frequent among the slave potters though its rate cannot be established. In potteries of the first period where the signatures are clear the proportion of *liberti* is slightly lower (1 to 19) than in the last two periods (1 to 18, 1 to 16); it is very much lower if we include among the *liberti* of the last two periods some or all of the users of the signature, *Cn Atei Hilarus*, (1 to 5 in the second, 1 to 3 in the third). Skillful workmen, either slaves or *liberti*, rose to positions of importance; *liberti* were in charge of branch potteries[3] and in several cases became owners of the potteries.

A brief study of the employment of labor in the two restricted fields, domestic and personal service and the finer kinds of manufacture, goes to show that in both the foreign and slave stock filled the labor market. It will be remembered that this was not the case on the estates discussed by Cato and Varro where, though the routine work was done by slaves it was supplemented at many points by the work of Italian freemen working independently as day or contract laborers. Many small farms, further, were carried on entirely by their owners without the assistance of slave labor. But in the range of labor employed by the professional man and in the potteries, the slave or freedman met little competition from the *ingenuus*. It is true that in both fields traces of a different condition of things can be found: a few free immigrants lived

---

[1] Cf. the scattering potteries in Puteoli, the Po Valley, and Calabria (p. 84, n. 1) where the same situation held.

[2] Four, possibly 5, owners of potteries were themselves potters.

[3] Oxé, *Die terra-sigillata Gefässe des Cn. Ateius*, Ann. Bonn. 101 (1897) pp. 22 ff.

by their professions in Rome; a number of the tradesmen were citizens and some of them may have been of native stock; some of the contractors both in town and country may have been freemen, and a few of the freeborn owners of potteries were themselves proficient in their art. But the rank and file of the workers studied were slaves and *liberti;* the *ingenui* and *peregrini* were the exceptions. The work entrusted to the slave or *libertus* was of various kinds and of every degree of responsibility. At the close of the first chapter the numerical preponderance of the foreign population was shown. It is well to carry in mind their complete domination of two fields covered in this study.

What was the relation between the foreigner as represented in the workers of the Roman *familiae* or the Arretine potteries and the body of *plebs, urbana* or *rustica?* Here again it was widely different from the relation of the foreign born agricultural laborer to the plebs. On the farms the laborer was in a blind alley. He seldom progressed from servile to libertine status but lived and died a slave, for manumission depended not only on the natural ability of the slave and his desire to free himself but on the nature of his employment. With the advantages, one or all, of less isolated, more stimulating lives, of greater opportunities for training or for the use of natural intelligence, and of personal relations with their owners, the slaves of the *familia urbana* or of the industrial plant ran a good chance of themselves becoming partial citizens and of seeing their sons full Roman citizens. The secretaries, stewards and gardeners and the potters passed over into the body of plebs in a steady stream. While it is impossible to ascertain the relative proportion of slaves and *liberti,* the large numbers of the *liberti* are striking. As fast as the responsibility placed on the individual worker increased, the proportion of *liberti* in the occupation rose until practically every individual might be included among them. The conditions shown here were certainly repeated elsewhere in the world of labor.

The increase of foreigners, the decrease of the native stock in Italy had by Cicero's day reached such a point that among the working classes in many occupations, skilled and unskilled, the foreigners held the field. The ease of manumission in the Republic effected a further result. Great numbers of the foreign workers passed from slave to libertine status. From such foreigners many a Roman citizen of the late Republic and the Empire must have been descended, and in their social and religious instincts lay the seed of many a growth which was to appear in imperial Rome.

VITA

I, Marion Edwards Park, was born in Andover, Massachusetts, on December 31, 1875. My parents were William Edwards Park and Sara Edwards Park. I was graduated at Bryn Mawr College in 1898 and attended graduate courses at Bryn Mawr College in 1912–14 and 1916–17 and at Johns Hopkins University in 1915–16. In 1902–06 I was instructor in the Classics in Colorado College, Colorado Springs, and in 1914–15 associate professor in the same college. I have attended the graduate seminaries of Professors Arthur L. Wheeler, Tenney Frank and Wilmer Cave Wright at Bryn Mawr College and of Professors Kirby Flower Smith and C. W. E. Miller at Johns Hopkins University. The doctor's examinations in my Major Subject Latin and my Minor Subject Greek were held in November 1916. Special acknowledgment is due to Professor Tenney Frank under whose direction I have written my dissertation.

OCCUPATIONS OF THE LOWER CLASSES
IN ROMAN SOCIETY

THE UNIVERSITY OF CHICAGO PRESS
CHICAGO, ILLINOIS

—

THE BAKER & TAYLOR COMPANY
NEW YORK

THE CAMBRIDGE UNIVERSITY PRESS
LONDON

THE MARUZEN-KABUSHIKI-KAISHA
TOKYO, OSAKA, KYOTO, FUKUOKA, SENDAI

THE COMMERCIAL PRESS, LIMITED
SHANGHAI

OCCUPATIONS OF
THE LOWER CLASSES IN
ROMAN SOCIETY

By

MIMA MAXEY

THE UNIVERSITY OF CHICAGO PRESS
CHICAGO · ILLINOIS

PREFACE

THE STUDY

The discussions given on the following pages are the result of a study of Justinian's _Digest_ undertaken to see what contribution it offers to our knowledge of the occupations of the
humble man in the Roman world. It arose from a conviction that
there was a large amount of incidental information in the citations of jurists there that offered illuminating,commentary on Roman life and that it had been little used in previous studies of
occupations.

The _Digest_ has proved to be a source rich in information
about the work that was done in the Roman world. This information
appears largely in adjudications in disputes over inheritances
and legacies and in suits of one sort or another. It is derived
also from illustrations that jurists add to make clear the point
that they are discussing. In addition to these sources, information may be gained from the background upon which some discussion
is imposed, a thing accepted and acknowledged in the ordinary situations of life. Since the information is given in such casual
fashion, one would expect it to vary in importance, and this in
fact happens. A large number of occupations are mentioned in a
quite colorless context. Frequently this casual mention is the
only occurrence of the particular occupation and we have almost
nothing in the light of which the nature of the work can be understood. On the other hand, just this mere mention sometimes indicates basic work of the world of the day, and the very paucity of
information shows how completely that business was woven into the
pattern of daily life. Other occupations are discussed in a fashion that affords some information. In some cases this is entirely
in accord with information gained from other sources. At times
additional information is gained, rounding out and strengthening
the outlines of the previously known picture. At times the new
information is such that it brings a virtual rewriting of the
story of that occupation in the light of this new contribution.
At times the new facts are entirely on a phase of the subject not

previously discussed, and so a new chapter is added on that subject.

Those occupations that required the investment of capital, business, and commerce in all its phases have been excluded from this discussion. Professions, government service, and service in the army also have been excluded. The occupations included, accordingly, are those dealing with the actual work necessary that the life of the day might go on, those dealing with food and its production, clothing, housing, certain amenities of life, and transportation of men and things.

The study has been made under the direction of Professor Gordon J. Laing. To him the author is deeply indebted for advice on procedure, searching criticism, and constant encouragement. To Professor Henry W. Prescott, who has read the manuscript and has been both generous and gracious in giving assistance, the author is likewise indebted.

TABLE OF CONTENTS

INTRODUCTION

THE ECONOMIC BACKGROUND

Any code of laws affords not only a background of law in the light of which specific situations can be judged and some indication of the underlying principles of justice that prevailed when and where it was pertinent, but also affords both a general picture of the social and economic situation and specific information about various phases of the world of that day. A study of Justinian's Digest yields a well rounded picture of the economic conditions prevailing in the Roman world from the time of the contributing jurists to that of Justinian, offering both specific information with regard to the occupations pursued and also general information about the structure of which they were a part. This latter information is in part presupposed - familiarly referred to as a situation of which every one was cognizant. In part it is indicated by specific facts that can be interpreted only in a particular setting and which, therefore, indirectly furnish evidence for that setting.

The information that the Digest gives, accordingly, presents the underlying economic situation. The world of the day had passed the period when all industry was done in the household for the household. There are, to be sure, many instances that show just that state of affairs (Scaevola, Dig. xxxiii. 7. 27), but in addition to that we find work done in the household for gain (e.g. Ulpian, Dig. xiv. 4. 1. 1; Ulpian, Dig. xxxiii. 7. 12. 12), and shops and other organized businesses of varying size existing solely as income-producing agencies (e.g. Scaevola, Dig. xxxvi. 1. 80 (78). 12; Ulpian, Dig. xiv. 3. 5. 9).

That the outstanding feature of this economic situation was slavery is well known. The extent to which the work of the world was done by slaves and the picture that the Digest presents of the prevalence of the ownership of slaves in large numbers and small, among the wealthy and among those that had little wealth, in the city and in the country, make it difficult to believe that the number of slaves was rapidly decreasing during the period cov-

-1-

ered by the jurists cited and that the ratio of slaves to free citizens was as low as historians compute it.

The ownership of slaves was found among masters of widely different economic status. Perhaps the most surprising master that is found is the colonus, the peasant farmer. The colonus himself was a hardworking freeman, who, when slave labor failed, became the tiller of the soil and performed the tasks formerly discharged by slaves. In the Digest we find a case in which he had a slave of his own and we judge that the slave had a long, hard day's work (Ulpian, Dig. ix. 2. 27. 9). The slave of a man of such status was probably one who knew hard labor with few features to ameliorate his lot.

In larger numbers than is true in the case of this man, so poor himself that he could own but one slave to alleviate his own toil, we find the owner with a number of slaves who rendered service in his home, either in the city or country (Alfenus Varus, Dig. L. 16. 203; Ulpian, Dig. xxxiii. 7. 8. 1). Slaves from a ménage of this sort apparently had the most pleasant relations with the master and we most frequently find manumission occurring among slaves of this kind.

In the luxurious praedium urbanum we find large retinues of slaves. They were certainly the property of men of great wealth, men rich enough to have more than one residence, leaving each manned even in their absence (Alfenus Varus, Dig. L. 16. 203). So impersonal was the relationship between master and slave that the slaves were considered part of the equipment of the property and were part of the legacy when it, with its equipment, passed to a legatee (Ulpian, Dig. xxxiii. 7. 12).

The praedium rusticum also was fully manned with slaves, and these slaves also were considered part of the equipment of the estate and not to be alienated from it when it was transferred with its equipment. These praedia, however, were economically quite a different thing from the luxurious residences maintained for the pleasure of the owner, and the justification for the retention of the slaves on the estate may be made on strictly economic grounds, for these praedia were really huge economic producing agencies (Ulpian, Dig. xxxiii. 7. 12). Their income was derived from various products. Those that are especially evident in the Digest are fish, fowl and larger game, and wool products. The slaves of such an estate were an essential part of the economic unit.

Slaves were found belonging to masters, also, who maintained commercial organizations that furnished either services or finished products to the community. Foremost among these were the bakers. They baked bread not only for the general public who preferred to buy from a baker rather than to operate their own ovens (Ulpian, Dig. xiv. 3. 5. 9), but also for government distribution through the annona (CIL VI. 1958). Those who furnished skilled services were the fullers, sarcinatores, operators of baths, and barbers.

In addition to owners who had slaves for the maintenance of their own business and for personal service, we find owners who let slaves of varying degrees of skill to others. The latter apparently preferred to hire specific services rather than to own their own slaves. The representation made by the owner as to the skill of the slave so let (Ulpian, Dig. ix. 2. 27. 34), and the contract under which he was let, for example, whether he was to work on a scaffold or not (Ulpian, Dig. xiii. 6. 5. 7), made cases of such sort frequently matters for adjudication.

In this world in which slavery played so large a part, we find in occupations of the humble not only slaves but some freedmen and a fairly large number of poor freemen. However, whatever the nature of the ownership of slaves, they are found fulfilling the basic needs of the world of their day. The more essential the service that life might go smoothly, the more fully we find slaves constituting the personnel of the occupation.

Slaves.--In every occupation concerned with food we find slaves serving. In most cases the slaves were kept to provide and serve food for the master and his family. In some instances of this sort a corps of slaves, trained or in training, was kept on each estate that service might be at hand when the master came (Alfenus Varus, Dig. L. 16. 203). In other instances the master took with him not only slaves to prepare and serve food but others to provide it, fishermen being an example (Scaevola, Dig. xxxiii. 7. 27). Such a retinue upon occasion travelled with the master even outside of Italy (Alfenus Varus, Dig. L. 16. 203). In addition to these slaves who prepared and served food for the master, on large rural estates there were found numbers of such slaves whose function was to prepare and serve food for the groups of slaves working on the estate. These slaves as well as those doing the work of the estate were regarded as part of the _instrumentum_ of the estate and when there was a transfer of the estate with its _instrumentum_ they went with it (Ulpian, _Dig_. xxxiii. 7. 12). The slaves and their functions on such estates often varied from those on the estate on which the master resided and also from one estate of this type to another. For example, some of these estates had a _pistor_ who probably served as both miller and baker (Ulpian, _Dig_. xxxiii. 7. 12. 5). Others had a separate miller, while the baking was done by women with no distinctive title (_Ibid_.). On others an ordinary farm laborer did the grinding for the women (Paulus, _Dig_. xxxiii. 7. 18. 5). Beside these slaves who served other slaves on large rural estates, there were slaves who were maintained for their contribution to the cash return from the estate, such as fishermen, fowlers, and hunters (Ulpian, _Dig_. xxxiii. 7. 12. 12). There is evidence of effective organization of such slaves in the person of a _praepositus piscatorum_ (Marcianus, _Dig_. xxxii. 65). Both these overseers and the slaves who did the work were part of the _instrumentum_ of these estates, inalienable from the estate when it was transferred with its _instrumentum_. Finally in the group concerned with food we find the slaves who worked in organized businesses, such as bakeries. There we find them performing various duties, some actually serving as bakers (Pomponius, _Dig_. xxxiii. 7. 15), others keeping fires going (Ulpian, _Dig_. xxxix. 2. 24. 7), others delivering bread and taking orders for future deliveries (Ulpian, _Dig_. xiv. 3. 5. 9). In short, slaves are found in every sort of place concerned with food supply and service.

The situation in regard to food is exactly duplicated by that concerned with clothing. We find spinners and weavers and menders producing and caring for the clothing for the household (Alfenus, _Dig_. xxxiii. 7. 16. 2; Gaius, _Dig_. xv. 1. 27). On large estates we find slaves provided for production of woolen cloth, first shepherds and shearers of sheep, women to keep the fire going for washing the wool after shearing and for the fullers, spinners, weavers, and fullers to dress the finished cloth - all part of the _instrumentum_ of such an estate (Ulpian, _Dig_. xxxiii. 7. 12. 6). The fulleries alone of such organizations, located near springs on the estate, were large enough to give rise to a complaint from the man on the neighboring estate because the water used in washing ran down on his land (Ulpian, _Dig_. xxxix. 3. 3).

In addition to these huge estates where the entire work was done
from raising the sheep to completing the cloth, we find very un-
pretentious business ventures in the hands of slaves, such as a
shoe shop. In one case a shoemaker was left to a person by will
with the explicit statement that he was to support the legatee by
his trade (Scaevola, Dig. xxxvi. 1. 80 (78). 12). In addition to
these little shops operated by a single slave, we find large establishments owned probably by a freeman with slaves doing the
work. Such were the establishments of fullers and menders (Paulus,
Dig. xlvii. 2. 83 (82)). In all these trades the work was sufficiently skilled to require apprenticeships. When the master was
absent for any extended travel, the shops would be left under one
of the slaves who served as procurator or institor (Ulpian, Dig.
xiv. 3. 5. 10), another illustration of the extent to which confidence was placed in slaves, a thing so apparent throughout the
Digest.

The field of personal service was so completely the field
of slaves that no case appears in which such service was performed
by a freeman. From this field came the largest number of freedmen in the fields considered because the slaves in that service
were close to the master, attracted his notice, and from the very
intimacy of their service often aroused feelings of affection or
gratitude. The nurse, the attendant of the schoolboy, the caretaker of the boy (Ulpian, Dig. xl. 2. 13), the valet (Ulpian, Dig.
xxxviii. 2. 14. 7), the nomenclator (Ulpian, Dig. xxxviii. 1. 7.
5), are repeatedly mentioned as freed either during the life of
the master or by will. In one case we are told that the master
freed a nomenclator with a contract that he would continue to
serve in that capacity after attaining his freedom (Venuleius,
Dig. xl. 12. 44). That situation probably prevailed in many cases
when the slave was freed during the lifetime of the master. In
lieu of freedom, the master sometimes made some humane provision
for a slave after his death. For example, one master left his
attendants (pedisequi) to care for a temple with an injunction to
his heir to give them a monthly allowance of food and a yearly
supply of clothing (Scaevola, Dig. xxxiv. 1. 17). All these instances occurred in the case of slaves whose service was rendered
directly to the master or members of his household.

A large number of slaves in domestic service were engaged
in caring for the house of the master, many of them serving in

highly specialized tasks in the luxurious villas. While many of
them had pleasant work, often in tasks that demanded skill and
training, their relationship with the master was a remote one.
They were regarded as part of the instrumentum of the estate and
were transferred with it when it with its equipment passed into
the hands of a new owner (Ulpian, Dig. xxxiii. 7. 12).

Some slaves in domestic service were kept on the large estates to care for the needs of the retinues of slaves there. Barbers serving slaves are particularly mentioned in this class (Ulpian, Dig. xxxiii. 7. 12. 5).

Another group of these slaves in service was attached not
to an estate, but to some sort of business such as an inn (Ulpian,
Dig. iv. 9. 1. 5) or bath (Paulus, Dig. xxxiii. 7. 13. 1) or bakery (Paulus, Dig. xxxiii. 7. 18. 1). One appeared serving as
steward in the cabin of a boat (Ulpian, Dig. iv. 9. 1. 3). The
lot of these slaves was often unspeakably hard. They, too, were
transferred not as individuals but as part of the instrumentum of
the place in which they served (Paulus, Dig. xxxiii. 7. 18. 1).
For the most part the patrons of the places where they served were
warned not to intrust their belongings to slaves of that sort,
though some of them, as the steward in the cabin and the baker's
delivery boy, were in positions of responsibility and were to be
trusted.

Work in the field of transportation was not preempted by
slaves. In the case of certain occupations it is difficult to ascertain the status of the workman and the evidence of inscriptions
and literary sources has to be sought before any assignment can be
made. Two occupations remain apparently exclusively filled by
slaves. One of these is that of the stable boy who was either in
the service of a private owner in city or country or who, in the
service of an inn, took care of the horses of travellers who pat-
ronized the inn (Alfenus, Dig. ix. 1. 5; xxxii. 60. 1). Another
is that of the muleteer, who appears in various capacities. In
many cases he was engaged in driving mules for his master. In
some instances his work was on the rural estate, in others in town.
In one case in town muleteers were driving loaded wagons up the
Capitoline Hill (Alfenus, Dig. ix. 2. 52. 2). It was probably a
muleteer who drove the sleeping carriage of the wife of the master
(Scaevola, Dig. xxxiv. 2. 13). In addition to these muleteers who
drove for their owners, others were let out by their owners to

drive other people's mules (Ulpian, Dig. ix. 2. 27. 34). This is
another instance of the acquiring of income by letting the services of slaves. A third sort of service is indicated in the case
of the muleteer engaged in commercial transportation of passengers
and their luggage. The muleteer in that case was an authorized
agent (institor) of the master, placed in charge of a business
(Labeo, Dig. xix. 2. 60. 8).

In agriculture the work was done for the most part by
slaves. The passages dealing with the work of slaves in agriculture give much information about the general situation of the
times. There were certainly small farms from which the master got
the produce to supply his own household. He may have lived on the
farm, or he may have lived in the city and used the farm only as
a source of supply. A slave with general functions is found working on such a small estate (Alfenus Varus, Dig. L. 16. 203). On
the other hand not only are there large numbers of slaves with
highly specialized tasks, regarded as part of the instrumentum of
the estate, a situation which in itself indicates the large domain, but there are many references to the saltus, the great
stretches of uncultivated grazing lands, on which were kept sheep
and which were guarded by more than one saltuarius (Ulpian, Dig.
xxxiii. 7. 12). The raising of swine, which we know was important
for meat supply, is referred to in a discussion as to ownership
when wolves have fallen upon the swine, the swine-herd was unable
to cope with the wolves, and the rescue was effected by a neighbor with dogs (Ulpian, Dig. xli. 1. 44).

The physical character of the agricultural land is indicated by repeated discussions of drainage on the one hand and irrigation on the other. The necessity for drainage indicates in
the first place reclamation of swamp land such as the Pomptine
Marshes. There are more references to the draining off of rain
water (Alfenus, Dig. xxxix. 3. 24. 2). These furnish evidence of
necessity for conservation of soil and crops during the rainy season and in the neighborhood of mountains. It is very evident, on
the other hand, that irrigation trenches were provided and maintained to tide over the season of heat and drought (Ulpian, Dig.
xliii. 20. 1. 11).

In addition to control of floods and drought, it is clear
that provision was made in every period for keeping up the fertil-
ity of the soil. Even on the estates that had extensive grazing

grounds to which stock was sent, animals were kept on that portion
of the land under cultivation solely for the upkeep of the land
itself and those animals with the slaves that cared for them were
part of the _instrumentum_ of the estate (Alfenus, _Dig_. xxxii. 60. 3).

Although agriculture was preeminently the business of the
Roman world and far the largest number of slaves were concerned
with it and with domestic service, there were other businesses in
which they were engaged. The business was owned as a rule by a
freeman. In many cases, if the owner did not manage it himself,
a freeman would do that too. Actual labor connected with the business and especially menial labor would be done by slaves. Work of
that sort in mills and bakeries, fulleries, mending establishments,
and about inns and shops has already been mentioned. There were
also bathing establishments with retinues of slave attendants (Ulpian, _Dig_. iii. 2. 4. 2). Barber shops had slaves serving both in
menial tasks and as barbers too in all probability (CIL XV. 7172).
The slave shoemaker with his little shop was previously mentioned.
A slave plasterer also appears (Ulpian, _Dig_. xiii. 6. 5. 7). It
is possible that he was merely a trained slave on an estate,
though he may equally well have been connected with an urban establishment.

Freedmen.--This very widespread service of the slave on
all sorts of estates, in urban businesses, in general and highly
specialized roles reveals how completely his labor was utilized
in meeting the basic needs of the world of the day. It is note-
worthy, too, that the tasks were performed by slaves rather than
freedmen. In a few cases we find slaves freed under contract to
continue serving their patron in the same capacity in which they
had served him when he was their master. Inscriptional evidence,
too, shows freedmen in these occupations. In the _Digest_, however,
in spite of the frequency of the granting of freedom both by will
and in the lifetime of the owner, one is impressed by the few instances in which freedmen appear in this sort of work. We are
forced to the conclusion that, on the whole, slaves were freed
because they had showed skill and ability in capacities higher in
the social scale than this sort of occupation, for example, professions or administration or commerce.

Freemen.--The small freeman, on the other hand, appears
in sufficiently large numbers to convince one that not all poor
freemen lived on the dole. One is impressed in many cases by in-

dications of extreme poverty, but the reasonable fairness of his
world impresses one too. We find many freemen who were fishermen
(Ulpian, Dig. ix. 2. 29. 3; Neratius, Dig. xxxxi. 1. 15). Three
kinds of evidence attest their poverty. In one case money was
advanced to a fisherman to buy equipment (Scaevola, Dig. xxii. 2.
5). In another case a person who had gone to the city to dispose
of the catch of a group of fishermen was directed to complete his
business and return at once without lingering in the city to participate in the dole there (Callistratus, Dig. L. 11. 2). The
third kind of evidence is concerned with the safeguarding of the
right of fishermen to build huts on the shore and retain the right
to them as long as they occupied them. This situation appears so
frequently and is discussed from so many angles that it must indicate that that sort of housing was usual, and if so the men must
have been poor (Marcianus, Dig. 1. 8. 6; Neratius, Dig. xxxxi. 1.
14).

The incident in regard to marketing fish in the city suggests some sort of commercial organization among the men. It is
possible that this was a collegium and the man who went was elected
as a representative of the group.

Freemen are found working as fowlers and hunters also
(Gaius, Dig. xxxxi. 1. 3. 1; Tryphoninus, Dig. vii. 1. 62). The
Digest reveals little about them as they appear for the most part
in suits for trespass. Such infringement of right is precisely
what one would expect in the case of a poor man living in a world
in which the land was owned by the wealthy and its game used as a
source of income for the rich owner.

A combination of the claim for right of domain on the part
of fishermen and the assumption of privileges on the land of the
rich is found in a kind of squatter sovereignty in the saltus.
One of the specific tasks of saltuarii was to preserve boundaries
intact (Pomponius, Dig. vii. 8. 16. 1). This meant to prevent
such preemption of homesites. The people who were guilty of such
infringement were, again, probably poor.

Divers were probably poor freemen. The discussion of the
work of divers reveals interesting situations in shipping. The
boats that plied the Mediterranean were apparently too large to
enter even the Tiber, to say nothing of the smaller streams flow-
ing into the Mediterranean. The result was that cargoes were
transferred at the mouth of the rivers into small vessels in which

they were transported to their destinations. In the course of
the transfer the smaller boats were often overturned and the cargo
went down (Callistratus, _Dig_. xiv. 2. 4; Ulpian, _Dig_. xix. 2. 13.
1, 2). It was from the rescue of goods of this sort chiefly that
divers got their income.

    Another freeman in about the same class as these was the
agricultural worker who worked on shares with the master, either
at tilling fields or raising stock. His share was apparently
larger than modern sharecroppers receive, but when he is mentioned
there is a connotation of poverty (Gaius, _Dig_. xix. 2. 25. 6).

    By and large, the freemen thus far discussed were working
at trades in which the capital outlay for equipment was not large,
skill was not particularly high, and to some extent luck determined results. Another group appears engaged in small businesses
involving some outlay for equipment and some skill. There was,
for example, the itinerant barber with his chair and razors, who
stopped and did business on the street, anywhere that patrons appeared. He was found not only in the city (Ulpian, _Dig_. ix. 2.
11), but in remote parts of the empire in places where poorer men
would be found in numbers (_Edict. Diocl_. vii. 22). There was also
the _plaustrarius_ (Ulpian, _Dig_. ix. 2. 27. 33), whose stock in
trade was his wagon and the animal or animals that drew it. His
skill lay in loading and driving. He hauled whatever the opportunity might offer. There was also the shoemaker with a shop as
well as his tools and materials for shoes and their repair. The
shop might be large enough to accommodate apprentices, also free-
born, who were learning the trade (Ulpian, _Dig_. ix. 2. 5. 3).

    In addition to these humble freemen, poor, with little
stock in trade, often with little skill, we find those in businesses that demanded more skill, more capital, or both. In trades
concerned with food we find bakers, who probably did not do the
actual work themselves but owned the business, with slave bakers
doing the work (Ulpian, _Dig_. xiv. 3. 5. 9; Paulus, _Dig_. xxvii. 1.
46). There was also the _pistrinarius_, who probably did not own
but managed a bakery (Ulpian, _Dig_. xvi. 3. 1. 9). In trades concerned with clothing, we find free fullers. While some of them
may have had small establishments in which they did the work, again
the situation was probably the same as in the case of the bakery.
The freeman would own and perhaps manage the business with slaves
doing the actual work (Ulpian, _Dig_. xiv. 3. 5. 7. 10). The build-

ing trades also contained freemen. Of these we may mention especially the superintendent of building (aedificator) (Venuleius, Dig. xlv. 1. 137. 3), the dresser of stones (lapidarius) (Tarruntenus Paternus, Dig. L. 6. 7 (6)), and the plasterer (Ulpian, Dig. ix. 2. 27. 35). The plasterer certainly did the actual work himself. It is possible, however, that his business would so expand that he would have slaves working under him also, either his own slaves, or those hired for a special piece of work. In transportation we find the cisiarius and carrucarius, who were certainly, at times at least, freemen (Ulpian, Dig. xix. 2. 13). It is possible that in this business, too, we may find the individual who drives his own cisium and the successful business man who has so enlarged his business as to have drivers working under him. We find the balneator also who had a small bathing establishment maintained by the fees paid by patrons (Ulpian, Dig. iii. 2. 4. 2; Edict. Diocl. vii. 76). Here, too, probably slaves did the necessary work about the place. We find inscriptions indicating that certain freemen were engaged in tasks that we should normally rate as service, for example, stratores and fossores (Ulpian, Dig. i. 16. 4. 1; Tarruntenus Paternus, Dig. L. 6. 7. (6)). The Digest states that such functions were performed in the army by soldiers, and inscriptions referring to freemen may indicate that type of military service, especially as many inscriptions expressly state that the man was a soldier.

Such in brief was the economic condition of the humble man in Rome in the period covered by the citations in the Digest. It was a society in which work was done both for the bare maintenance of the man and his family and for commercial profit on a larger scale. In a world in which the dominating feature was slavery, we naturally find many slaves in the occupations of the humble man. Of freedmen there is a surprisingly small number engaged in these activities. On the other hand there is a considerable number of freemen so occupied, poor, to be sure, but managing to maintain a fairly satisfactory existence.

CHAPTER I

OCCUPATIONS CONCERNED WITH FOOD

Many of the occupations in which we find the humble man
engaged in the Digest are concerned with food. Certain ones of
these deal with the acquisition and provision of food stuffs;
others are centered about an intermediate step in the preparation
of the raw material; others are concerned with provision of food
for a household or its conservation within the house; a final
group has to do with cooking and serving food.

Piscator.--Of the occupations concerned with the acquisition of food, that of the fisherman is mentioned most frequently
in the Digest. Piscatores were slaves,[1] freedmen,[2] freedwomen,[3]
and probably freemen in humble circumstances[4] who engaged in fishing as a business. While fishing as sport was probably common and
certainly had devotees of prominence,[5] the frequency with which
fishing as a serious occupation is mentioned in the Digest as well
as elsewhere is evidence that the demand for fish for sale was
great in the Roman world. It far outstripped the demand for fowl
and other game. The fact that fishing and hunting are expressly
mentioned as pursuits not justifying the giving of furloughs by
commanders of soldiers is evidence both of fondness for fish and
of the importance in the minds of the Romans of procuring an ade-
quate supply. Macer, the author of the opinion in the Digest,
quotes an earlier jurist, Paternus, as saying: "debere eum, qui
se meminerit armato praeesse, parcissime commeatum dare....ad opus
privatum piscatum venatum militem non mittere."[6] Men of wealth
took their own fishermen with them from place to place to supply
their own needs - "an servi piscatores, qui solebant in ministerio
testatoris esse et ubique eum sequi et urbicis rationibus expunge-
bantur nec mortis testatoris tempore in praediis legatis deprehensi
fuerant, legati esse videantur."[7] Such fishermen were regarded as

---

[1]Scaev. Dig. xxxiii. 7. 27.   [2]CIL VI. 29700.
[3]CIL VI. 9801.   [4]CIL VI. 9799.
[5]Suet. Aug. 83; Nero 30.   [6]Macer, Dig. xlix. 16. 12. 1.
[7]Scaev. Dig. xxxiii. 7. 27.

part of the retinue of personal attendants of the master. Pomponius, in making clear the utter loss of land inundated by river or sea, says that not even by fishing can right to such land be retained: "Si ager cuius usus fructus noster sit, flumine vel mari inundatus fuerit, amittitur usus fructus....ac ne piscando quidem retinere poterimus usum fructum."[1]

As to the organization of the business of fishing, fishermen were ordered to go to the city to dispose of their catch. They were not to linger about the city to participate in the dole there, but must dispose of their fish quickly and return to their work: "Si quis ipsos....piscatores deferre utensilia in civitatem iusserit, ut ipsi ea distrahant, destituetur annonae praebitio....: qui confestim ubi detulerint mercem, tradere eam et ad opera sua reverti debeant."[2] Whether they were selling to propolae, the regular dealers in fish, or were selling independently to the customer we do not know. We have indication of a distribution organization in a reference to a slave placed in charge of the actual slave fishermen. This person was not technically regarded as a negotiator as Marcianus tells us: "cubicularios vel obsonatores vel eos, qui piscatoribus praepositi sunt, non videri negotiationis appellatione contineri."[3] So great was the pressure on the market or so great the gambling spirit of the ancient Romans that contracts were made for the future catch of fishermen: "veluti cum futurum iactum retis a piscatore emimus....nam etiamsi nihil capit, nihilo minus emptor pretium praestare necesse habebit."[4] Fishermen were organized into collegia.[5] Frequency of inscriptions referring to these collegia leads one to believe that these were large organizations.

Fishing in streams and lakes was common.[6] In the Digest, however, salt water fishing is far more prominent.[7] There fishing in boats[8] and with dragnets - "everriculum (quod Graece σαγήνη dicitur)"[9] - was usual. The boats of the fishermen were apparently

---

[1]Pompon. Dig. vii. 4. 23.   [2]Call. Dig. L. 11. 2.

[3]Marcian. Dig. xxxii. 65.   [4]Ulp. Dig. xix. 1. 11. 18.

[5]CIL V. 7850; VI. 1872; 29701; 29702.

[6]Marcian. Dig. 1. 8. 4. 1; Proc. Dig. xviii. 1. 69; Ulp. Dig. xliii. 14. 1. 7; Idem, Dig. xlvii. 10. 13. 7.

[7]Ulp. Dig. xliii. 8. 2. 9.

[8]Dig. ix. 2. 29; xxxiii. 7. 17; xlix. 15. 2.

[9]Ulp. Dig. xlvii. 10. 13. 7.

frail, as one judges not only by the word applied to them, "nau-
cellas, quae piscium capiendorum causa comparatae sunt,"[1] but also
by the fact that if commandeered in time of war, they, with pleasure craft, did not have to be returned to their owners when the
war was over: "Navibus longis atque onerariis propter belli usum
postliminium est, non piscatoriis aut si quas actuarias voluptatis
causa paraverunt."[2]

Fishing boats fell into difficulties of various sorts.
One citation tells of a boat driven into the nets of other fishermen. If the fishermen were at fault, they had to make good the
loss of the nets but not the possible catch of fish. Ulpian's report of the case is as follows:

> Item Labeo scribit, si, cum vi ventorum navis impulsa es-
> set in funes anchorarum alterius et nautae funes praecidis-
> sent, si nullo alio modo....explicare se potuit, nullam ac-
> tionem dandam. Idemque Labeo et Proculus et circa retia pis-
> catorum in quae navis piscatorum inciderat, aestimarunt. Plane
> si culpa nautarum id factum esset, lege Aquilia agendum. Sed
> ubi damni iniuria agitur ob retia, non piscium, qui ideo capti
> non sunt, fieri aestimationem, cum incertum fuerit, an caperen-
> tur. Idemque et in venatoribus et in aucupibus probandum.[3]

In another citation the governor of a province was instructed to
take measures to prevent fishermen from luring vessels into danger
by showing a light on their boat at night that would be mistaken
for the light of a harbor - "Ne piscatores nocte lumine ostenso
fallant navigantes, quasi in portum aliquem delaturi, eoque modo
in periculum naves et qui in eis sunt deducant sibique execrandam
praedam parent, praesidis provinciae religiosa constantia effi-
ciat."[4] The suggestion is that such things had been done for the
resulting booty. This is the only derogatory remark about fishermen that appears in the Digest if we may consider another citation
a reference to the human weakness of the fisherman for good equipment rather than to any culpable tendency on the part of an individual to make inroads on another person's money. This citation
is: "Nec dubitabis, si piscatori erogaturo in apparatum plurimum
pecuniae dederim, ut, si cepisset, redderet."[5]

If this last citation refers to fishermen who were freemen, as it very well may, it suggests poverty on the part of the

---

[1]Marcian. Dig. xxxiii. 7. 17. 1.

[2]Marcell. Dig. xlix. 15. 2.   [3]Ulp. Dig. ix. 2. 29. 3.

[4]Ulp. Dig. xlvii. 9. 10.   [5]Scaev. Dig. xxii. 2. 5.

fishermen.[1] Of this hints are found elsewhere. One fishing in the sea was permitted to build a hut on the shore in which to live - "In mare piscantibus liberum est casam in litore ponere, in qua se recipiant."[2] Such a building was his only while it stood and was occupied by him. When he had left or it had fallen into decay, the spot was likewise available for the next person who took it over. Such building might require the consent of the praetor and could not be done to the disadvantage of another person. Opinions on this point were given by several jurists. Marcianus says: "In tantum, ut et soli domini constituantur qui ibi aedificant, sed quamdiu aedificium manet: alioquin aedificio dilapso quasi iure postliminii revertitur locus in pristinam causam, et si alius in eodem loco aedificaverit, eius fiet."[3] Neratius writes in the same tenor:

> Quod in litore quis aedificaverit, eius erit..... Illud videndum est, sublato aedificio, quod in litore positum erat, cuius condicionis is locus sit, hoc est utrum maneat eius cuius fuit aedificium, an rursus in pristinam causam reccidit perindeque publicus sit, ac si numquam in eo aedificatum fuisset. Quod propius est, ut existimari debeat.[4]

Papinianus's opinion is as follows:

> Praescriptio longae possessionis ad optinenda loca iuris gentium publica concedi non solet. Quod ita procedit, si quis, aedificio funditus diruto quod in litore posuerat (forte quod aut deposuerat aut dereliquerat aedificium), alterius postea eodem loco extructo, occupantis datam exceptionem opponat.[5]

Pomponius is the author of an opinion that aims at protecting the interests of the public: "Quamvis quod in litore publico vel in mari exstruerimus nostrum fiat, tamen decretum praetoris adhibendum est, ut id facere liceat: immo etiam manu prohibendus est, si cum incommodo ceterorum id faciat."[6] Building on a river bank in this fashion was not permitted as Neratius tells us: "Qui autem in ripa fluminis aedificat, non suum facit."[7] River banks, however, were at the disposal of fishermen for tying their boats to trees, for spreading their nets to dry, and for unloading the contents of their boats: "Riparum usus publicus est iure gentium sicut ipsius fluminis. Itaque navem ad eas appellere, funes ex

---

[1]For a discussion of poverty among fishermen see L. Bunsmann, De Piscatorum in Litteris Usu (Münster, 1910), pp. 20 ff. See also Verg. Aen. xii. 518 ff.

[2]Gaius, Dig. 1. 8. 5. [3]Marcian. Dig. i. 8. 6.

[4]Nerat. Dig. xli. 1. 14. [5]Papin. Dig. xli. 3. 45.

[6]Pompon. Dig. xli. 1. 50. [7]Nerat. Dig. xli. 1. 15.

arboribus ibi natis religare, retia siccare et ex mare reducere,
onus aliquid in his reponere cuilibet liberum est, sicuti per ip-
sum flumen navigare."[1]

As a rule fishing rights in the sea and in streams rated
as _publica_ were free to all. Even a slough which one had fished
for many years could not be preempted by him: "vel si quis, quod
in fluminis publici deverticulo solus pluribus annis piscatus sit,
alterum eodem iure prohibeat."[2] We find, however, in the transfer
of an estate explicit reservation of fishing rights off another
estate owned by the man who sold: "Venditor fundi Geroniani fundo
Botriano, quem retinebat, legem dederat, ne contra eum piscatio
thynnaria exerceatur."[3]

As to equipment of fishermen, the _Digest_ mentions only
boats,[4] the dragnet,[5] and the usual net, _rete_, which seems to have
been used as a dragnet also.[6] From other sources we know that
hooks[7] and lines, alone[8] and with poles,[9] were used. Larger fish
were speared.[10]

The _Digest_ mentions in one instance only a particular kind
of fish caught. This was the tunny,[11] a fish that stood high in
the esteem of the Romans.[12]

Venator.--Another group that served for the acquisition
of food was that of hunters. The _venator_ was a slave that hunted
on an estate - "Si in agro venationes sint, puto venatores quoque
et vestigatores et canes et cetera quae ad venationem sunt neces-
saria instrumento contineri."[13] The jurists offer clear evidence
that the business of the _venator_ was important. Such slaves were
in some cases responsible for the meat supply of the establishment
of the master as Paulus tells us in the _Sententiae_: "Venatores

---

[1]Gaius, _Dig_. i. 8. 5.

[2]Papin. _Dig_. xli. 3. 45. An apparently contradictory
statement with almost identical wording appears in Marcian. _Dig_.
xliv. 3. 7.

[3]Ulp. _Dig_. viii. 4. 13.

[4]Marcian. _Dig_. xxxiii. 7. 17; Marcell. _Dig_. xlix. 15. 2.

[5]Ulp. _Dig_. xlvii. 10. 13.   [6]Ulp. _Dig_. ix. 2. 29. 3.

[7]Ovid, _Ars Am_. i. 763.   [8]DS Fig. 5687.

[9]Plin. _N. H._ xvi. 172.   [10]Ovid, _loc. cit_.

[11]Ulp. _Dig_. viii. 4. 13.

[12]P. Rhode, "Thynnorum Captura," _Jahrbücher für Class_.
Phil. Sup. XVIII (1892), pp. 1-78.

[13]Ulp. _Dig_. xxxiii. 7. 12. 12.

servi vel aucupes an inter urbana ministeria contineantur dubium
remansit..... Tamen si instruendarum cotidianarum epularum gratia
habentur, debentur."[1] In some cases they contributed in marked
degree to the revenue of the estate - "maxime si ager et ex hoc
reditum habuit";[2] "nisi fructus fundi ex venationes constet";[3]
"quod etiam ad instrumenta pertinet, si quaestus fundi ex maxima
parte in venationibus consistat."[4] In the former case such slaves
belonged to the _familia urbana_ as the quotation from Paulus shows.
In the latter they certainly belonged to the _familia rustica_.
There is no doubt that _venatores_ were found among both the slaves
of the _villa urbana_ and the _villa rustica_ - "Venatores et aucupes
utrum in urbanis an in rusticis contineantur, potest dubitari:
sed dicendum est, ubi paterfamilias moraretur et hos alebat, ibi
eos numerari."[5]

In later times we find the term _venator_ applied to a freeman or freedman in a situation in which he is granted release from
more onerous obligations: "Quibusdam aliquam vacationem munerum
graviorum condicio tribuit..... In eodem numero haberi solent lani,
venatores, victimarii."[6] The very real contribution of the _vena-
tor_ to the food supply is in this case recognized, as in the case
of the slave _venatores_ in earlier times. The fact that inscriptions do not appear referring to these free hunters is an indication of humble social status and lack of organization among them.

Hunting is referred to by Sallust[7] as slaves' work. Although the evidence is perfectly good that the chase played no
mean part as gentlemen's sport,[8] any effort such as Von Kayser's
to brush aside the evidence that as a serious business it was
slaves' work is futile.[9] There is no evidence that the slaves attendant upon those participating in such sport were called _vena-
tores_. The one sure reference that we have calls them _famuli_.[10]
Evidence is lacking to prove that the _venatores_ were slaves that
cared for the game in a private game preserve, as Von Kayser
claims.[11] His assertion that the term _venatores_ included fowlers

---

[1]Paul. _Sent_. iii. 6. 71.   [2]Ulp. _Dig_. xxxiii. 7. 12. 12.
[3]Iulian. _Dig_. xxii. 1. 26.   [4]Paul. _Dig_. xxxiii. 7. 22.
[5]Paul. _Dig_. xxxii. 99. 1.   [6]Tarr. Pat. _Dig_. L. 6. 7.
[7]Sall. _Cat_. iv. 1.   [8]Verg. _Aen_. iv. 129 ff.

[9]B. von Kayser, _Jagd und Jagdrecht in Rom_ (Göttingen,
1894), p. 21.

[10]Nemes. _Cyn_. 298.   [11]Von Kayser, _op. cit._, p. 12.

and fishermen as well as hunters[1] is based on a far too literal interpretation of the passage cited from Pliny.[2] A reasonable interpretation of all evidence leads to exactly the opposite conclusion.

The Digest furnishes evidence that there was hunting on the part of freemen also, not for sport primarily, but for the game itself. Such evidence appears often in adjudications of right when trespass has occurred. Paulus says: "Qui foveas ursorum cervorumque capiendorum causa faciunt, si in itineribus fecerunt eoque aliquid decidit factumque deterius est, lege Aquilia obligati sunt: at si in aliis locis, ubi fieri solent, fecerunt, nihil tenentur."[3] Gaius states: "Nec interest quod ad feras bestias et volucres, utrum in suo fundo quisque capiat an in alieno. Plane qui in alienum fundum ingreditur venandi aucupandive gratia, potest a domino, si is providerit, iure prohiberi ne ingrederetur."[4] Evidence appears in decisions involving a fructuary and an owner also - "Usufructuarium venari in saltibus vel montibus possessionis probe dicitur: nec aprum aut cervum quem ceperit proprium domini capit."[5]

The Digest offers some details as to the equipment of hunters. Nets - "rete apraria";[6] snares - "In laqueum, quem venandi causa posueras, aper incidit";[7] pits;[8] and especially dogs[9] are mentioned. From other sources we can add finer meshed nets,[10] hunting spears,[11] and a quiver, which presupposes bows and arrows.[12]

Vestigator.--On estates on which hunting took place a slave called a vestigator appears.[13] He had the specialized task of locating in advance animals for the hunt,[14] and of blocking their escape from the area in which the hunt was to take place.[15] Columella used the word vestigator in referring to a person who

---

[1]Ibid., p. 10. [2]Plin. N. H. xvi. 1. 3.

[3]Paul. Dig. ix. 2. 28. [4]Gaius, Dig. xli. 1. 3. 1.

[5]Tryph. Dig. vii. 1. 62. See also Gaius, Dig. xli. 1. 5.

[6]Paul. Dig. xxxiii. 7. 22. [7]Proc. Dig. xli. 1. 55.

[8]Paul. Dig. ix. 2. 28. See Note 3.

[9]Ulp. Dig. xxxiii. 7. 12. 12. See Note 13, p. 16.

[10]Verg. Aen. iv. 131. [11]Ibid.

[12]Verg. Aen. iv. 138. [13]Ulp. Dig. xxxiii. 7. 12. 12.

[14]Apul. Met. viii. 4. (Oud. 513).

[15]Varro, L. L. v. 94; Apul. Met. viii. 4. (Oud. 513, 514); Serv. Aen. iv. 121.

tracked swarms of bees.[1] The word appears infrequently in Latin literature but the service rendered seems clear.

Auceps.--Another occupation that contributed to the food supply was that of the fowler. His role was probably less important than that of the fishermen and hunters, if we may so judge from the fact that he is less frequently referred to in the Digest. Aucupes appear in the Digest who were slaves serving as fowlers on estates - "Et si ab aucupio reditus fuit, aucupes et plagae et huius rei instrumentum."[2] The auceps is mentioned with hunters - "Venatores et aucupes utrum in urbanis an in rusticis contineantur, potest dubitari: sed dicendum est, ubi pater familias moraretur et eos alebat, ibi eos numerari."[3] - and with hunters and fishermen.[4] The fowler was expressly forbidden to trespass on other people's land if the owners were unwilling - "Divus Pius aucupibus ita rescripsit: ʼοὐκ ἔστιν εὔλογον ἀκόντων τῶν δεσποτῶν ὑμᾶς ἐν ἀλλοτρίοις χωρίοις ʼξεύειν.ʼ"[5] Such trespass was forbidden to hunters as well.[6] The further emphasis in the case of the fowler came, perhaps, because the temptation was greater in his case and escape relatively easier, at least easier than that of the hunter of larger game.

From other literary sources we learn that Antoninus Pius had his own hunters, fowlers, and fishermen, who kept his tables supplied with meat.[7] This is probably one case among many of the time, as the Digest indicates,[8] in which wealthy and thrifty owners of slaves thus supplied their own needs.

There are references that indicate that the consumption of fish and fowl rated as a luxury, the fare of the epicure as distinguished from that of the man of brawn. On this ground fowlers and fishermen were to be driven from the military camp while hunters of stags and boars were to be encouraged.[9] Whether slave fowlers and hunters are referred to or free ones, in either case the fighting caliber of the men is highly disparaged by the author of the panegyric on Theodosius: "Ut taceam infami saepe dilectu

---

[1]Col. ix. 8, 10.   [2]Ulp. Dig. xxxiii. 7. 12. 13.
[3]Paul. Dig. xxxii. 99. 1.
[4]Ulp. Dig. ix. 2. 29. 3. See Note 3, p. 14.
[5]Call. Dig. viii. 3. 16.   [6]Gaius, Dig. xli. 1. 3. 1.
[7]Capitol. Ant. Pius vii. 5.
[8]Paul. Dig. xxxii. 99. 1. See Note 3.   [9]Veg. Mil. 1. 7.

scriptos in provinciis aucipes ductasque sub signis venatorum co-
hortes militasse conviviis."[1]

By way of equipment for the fowler, the Digest mentions
nets only.[2] In addition to this, from other literary sources we
learn that he carried a pole, usually called harundo,[3] the best
of which came from Panormus.[4] This pole was called calamus[5] also, and ames and pertica aucupalis as well.[6] Sometimes the poles
had birdlime on them,[7] sometimes the birdlime was otherwise used.[8]
Nets (retia) were spread on forculae.[9]

Phasianarius.--Although pheasants were not raised for food
exclusively, they were used for food. We may accordingly include
among occupations that contributed to the food supply that of the
slave who cared for pheasants, the phasianarius: "Avibus legatis
anseres phasiani et gallinae et aviaria debebuntur: phasianarii
autem et pastores anserum non continentur."[10] He was found probably on large estates which had large numbers of slaves with highly
specialized functions. Martial's picture of the bounteous country
estate contains pheasants, for which there may have been such a
keeper.[11] While pheasants were commonly known,[12] they probably
were rated as luxuries both as food[13] and as stock for an aviary.[14]
In the tables of the Edict of Diocletian the price of pheasants is
high (one hundred denarii for hens running wild, the price doubled
for fattened birds), with males running twenty five per cent higher than hens.[15] Apparently the only mention of the phasianarius
outside of the Digest is the passage in the Sententiae of Paulus
which is the source of the citation.[16] Both passages say as to
the disposition of the keeper when the birds have been willed,

---

[1]Paneg. ii. 14. 3. W. Baehrens, XII Panegyrici Latini
(Leipzig, 1911).

[2]Ulp. Dig. xxxiii. 7. 12. 13. See Note 2, p. 19.

[3]Val. Flacc. vi. 262.   [4]Plin. N. H. xvi. 172.

[5]Mart. xiii. 68.

[6]Porph. on Hor. Epodes ii. 33; Festus, p. 19 L.

[7]Sil. Ital. vii. 674.   [8]Val. Flacc. vi. 263.

[9]See Note 6.   [10]Paul. Dig. xxxii. 66.

[11]Mart. iii. 58. 16.   [12]Mart. xiii. 72; Pallad. i. 29.

[13]Suet. Vit. 13.   [14]Lampr. Alex. 41. 7.

[15]Edict. Diocl. iv. 17, 18. See H. Blümner, Der Maximaltarif des Diocletian (Berlin, 1893), p. 76.

[16]Paul. Sent. iii. 6. 76.

that it is a question of the intention of the testator.

  Pistor.--Those occupations that appear in the Digest concerned with an intermediate step in manufacture of food are all
centered about the conversion of grain into bread, with milling
and baking. Martial makes clear the fact that the pistor was both
miller and baker:

A pistore, Cypere, non recedis:
et panem facis et facis farinam.[1]

In the Digest pistores appear as slaves: "Qui habebat Flaccum
fullonem et Philonicum'pistorem uxori Flaccum pistorem legaverat.
.... sin autem ignota nomina servorum essent, pistorem legatum videri."[2] In inscriptions freedmen also appear as pistores.[3] Among
these freedmen were the pistores candidarii, bakers of white
bread.[4] From the citations of the Digest it is clear that some
slaves of this class were found as part of the familia rustica, in
which case their work was to supply bread for the members of the
familia rustica - "pistorem et tonsorem qui rusticae familiae causa parati sunt."[5] Other pistores were members of the familia urbana.[6] Others were employed in a pistrinum from which bread was
sold: "ut ecce pistorio instrumento legato ita ipsi pistores inesse videri possunt, si pater familias pistrinum exercuit."[7] Cicero expressly states that the pistor was of the genus vulgare.[8]
This judgment the Digest reinforces by mentioning the pistor in
the same class as the tonsor.[9] The only hint that the Digest offers as to equipment of the pistor is the inclusion of the horses,
caballi, with the pistores when a pistrinum has passed to a new
owner by will: "et caballos, qui in pistrinis essent, et pistores."[10] These horses were undoubtedly used in grinding grain. A
passage in Paulus' Sententiae suggests that mules also were so
used.[11] It was customary to hire out trained pistores to others -
"Proinde si quis servos habuit proprios, sed quorum operas locabat
vel pistorias vel histrionicas vel alias similes."[12] Blümner

---

[1]Mart. viii. 16.
[3]CIL VI. 6219; 9802.
[5]Ulp. Dig. xxxiii. 7. 12. 5.
[7]Paul. Dig. xxxiii. 7. 18. 1.
[9]Ulp. Dig. xxxiii. 7. 12. 5.
[10]Pompon. Dig. xxxiii. 7. 15.
[11]Paul. Sent. iii. 6. 37. See Chap. III, Note 5, p. 48.
[12]Ulp. Dig. xxxii. 73. 3.

[2]Iavol. Dig. xxxiv. 5. 28.
[4]CIL XIV. 2302; XII. 4502.
[6]Paul. Sent. iii. 6. 72.
[8]Cic. Pro Rosc. Am. xlvi. 134.
See Note 5.

thinks that these _pistores_ were hired out to private individuals
or to proprietors of bakeries.[1] The _Edict_ of Diocletian fixed
the wages of such _pistores_ at fifty _denarii_ per day.[2]

The _Digest_ refers to another type of _pistor_ who seems to
have been an independent dealer in bread. This baker had a slave
who had a definite route for delivery of bread and regular patrons.
The wily slave collected in advance for deliveries, then ran away.
The judgment was that the baker must make good the orders if he
allowed sums of money to be given to the slave. Ulpian's words
are: "Si quis pistor servum suum solitus fuit in certum locum
mittere ad panem vendendum, deinde is pecunia accepta praesenti,
ut per dies singulos eis panem praestaret, conturbaverit, dubitari
non oportet, quin, si permisit ei ita dari summas, teneri debeat."[3]

The _pistores_ constituted one group that was permitted to
organize themselves into a _corpus_ or _collegium_ - "Item collegia
Romae certa sunt, quorum corpus....confirmatum est, veluti pistorum et quorundam aliorum."[4] Membership in the group might be held
by one who was at the head of a _pistrinum_ and such a person was
granted immunity from guardianship - "Qui in collegio pistorum
sunt, a tutelis excusantur, si modo per semet pistrinum exerceant.
Sed non alios puto excusandos quam qui intra numerum sunt."[5] Bakers in the city itself (_pistores urbici_) were excused from services as guardians even to sons of other members of the group -
"Urbici autem pistores a collegarum quoque filiorum tutelis excusantur."[6] Non-members did not have such immunity. We conclude,
accordingly, that the state was encouraging membership of the managers of bakeries in the union as well as permitting that of workers. The prominence of these _collegia_ and the importance of _pis-
tores_ as a whole undoubtedly grew out of the fact that the corn
dole in the later years of the empire was distributed in the form
of bread.[7]

Furnarius.--Another workman concerned in some fashion with
the baking of bread was the _furnarius_. The citation in the _Digest_
in which he appears reveals more about the legal mind than about
the _furnarius_ - "Praeterea si furni nomine damni infecti fuerit
cautum, deinde furnarii culpa damnum datum fuerit, non venire in

---

[1]Blümner, _op. cit._, p. 107.   [2]Edict. Diocl. vii. 12.
[3]Ulp. _Dig._ xiv. 3. 5. 9.   [4]Gaius, _Dig._ iii. 4. 1.
[5]Paul. _Dig._ xxvii. 1. 46.   [6]_Ibid_.   [7]CIL VI. 1958.

hanc stipulationem plerisque videtur."[1] It raises the question
whether loss occasioned through the fault of the furnarius can be
adjudicated with reference to a cautio damni infecti previously
given. The only light thrown on the furnarius is that he was actively connected with the operation of a furnus. The furnus was
certainly used for baking bread.[2] The furnarius appears in one
other case, clearly in connection with the baking of bread.[3] In
this second instance he seems to have been a freeman. Old editions of scholia on Juvenal mention a furnarius in connection with
the discussion of furnus.[4] In the Wessner edition furnarius[5] has
been replaced by mediastrini, a form that appears equivalent in
meaning to the more common mediastini.[6] Here reference is certainly to a slave. Inscriptions in which slaves and freedmen only
appear show a freedwoman called a furnaria,[7] as well as a furnarius.[8] In one case we find a doubling of roles, the same slave
serving as cellarius, in charge of the cella, the storeroom for
grain and wine, and as furnarius.[9]

Blümner[10] and Kapp[11] think that the word furnarius was a
late usage, applied to a person exactly equivalent to the earlier
pistor. The appearance of a freeman serving as furnarius, and
the fact that the same person served as both cellarius and furnarius are confirmatory evidence for this view. The alternative
possibility is that we have a late division of labor, the pistor,
the maker of bread, no longer serving as the baker of bread, a
function which had passed to the furnarius. In that case the
furnarius did the work which Thédenat with little ground for the
opinion assigns to the fornacator.[12]

Molitor.--Another occupation concerned with preparation
of grain was that of the molitor. The grain consumed by the familia rustica was ground on the estate - "Idem consultus de meta

---

[1]Ulp. Dig. xxxix. 2. 24. 7.   [2]Iuv. vii. 4 and scholium.
[3]Aug. Cont. Pet. ii. 83. 184.   [4]See Note 2.
[5]Kapp, TLL s. v. Furnarius.
[6]P. Wessner, Scholia in Iuvenalem Vetustiora (Leipzig,
1931), Iuv. vii. 4.
[7]CIL VIII. 24678.   [8]Ibid. and CIL VIII. 16921.
[9]CIL VI. 9253.
[10]H. Blümner, Technologie und Terminologie der Gewerbe und
Künste bei Griechen und Römern (Leipzig, 1875), I, p. 83.
[11]See Note 5.   [12]Thédenat, DS s. v. Furnus.

molendaria respondit, si rusticis eius fundi operariis moleretur, eam quoque deberi."[1] When that work was done by a special slave, not the ordinary slave of general functions, the molitor was the slave that ground that grain. He differed from the pistor in that he had nothing to do with the baking of the bread. Apparently the baking was done by women slaves in those ménages that had molitores. Ulpian says: "et mulieres quae panem coquant quaeque villam servent: item molitores, si ad usum rusticum parati sunt."[2] The inference of the passage is that such slaves were not found exclusively in the familia rustica. This interpretation of molitor as miller distinguished from baker is strengthened by the gloss molitur - ἀλέτης .[3]

Blümner, quoting the reference from Ulpian only, interprets the molitor as a proprietor of a mill at a time after milling and baking were differentiated.[4] The general context of the passage as well as the use of the words parati sunt indicate a slave of the establishment.

Marquardt considers that the molitor was in charge of a water mill.[5] No very secure evidence on this point appears. In an adjudication in regard to a meta molendaria Paulus qualifies his statement by saying: "si rusticis eius fundi operariis moleretur," probably implying again separation of milling and baking.[6] The only other occurrence of the word molendaria is in the expression asina molendaria in the same citation. The whole situation suggests that the molitor was a slave in charge of milling in a mill of the more usual type.

Pistrinarius.--The pistrinarius seems to have been a man that operated a pistrinum. He was able to make a contract for guarding a slave, who probably worked at the grinding of grain. For this guardianship he might receive pay. On the other hand he might pay the master for the services of the slave, assuming the obligation to guard him, or there might be an arrangement whereby the guarding was compensated for by the slave's labor. Finally the contract might involve the food of the slave only. Ulpian's

---

[1]Paul. Dig. xxxiii. 7. 18. 5.   [2]Ulp. Dig. xxxiii. 7. 12. 5.
[3]CGL II. 130. 26; III. 307. 1C.
[4]Blümner, Technologie, I, pp. 38, 39.
[5]J. Marquardt, Das Privatleben der Römer (Leipzig, 1886), p. 149.
[6]Paul. Dig. xxxiii. 7. 18. 5. See Note 1.

account of the situation is as follows:

> Si quis servum custodiendum coniecerit forte in pistri-
> num, si quidem merces intervenit custodiae, puto esse actio-
> nem adversus pistrinarium ex conducto: si vero mercedem ac-
> cipiebam ego pro hoc servo, quem in pistrinum accipiebat, ex
> locato me agere posse: quod si operae eius servi cum custo-
> dia pensabantur, quasi genus locati et conducti intervenit,
> sed quia pecunia non datur, praescriptis verbis datur actio:
> si vero nihil aliud quam cibaria praestabat nec de operis
> quicquam convenit, depositi actio est.[1]

All this seems to indicate that the pistrinarius was an independent manager of a pistrinum, though there is no indication as to
whether he was the owner or was managing for the owner. It seems
unlikely, accordingly, that he is to be identified with the molitor, an identification that Blümner implies, though he does not
assert it.[2]

Obsonator.--In addition to these occupational groups engaged in the supplying of food there appears a group within the
household who purchased, conserved, and served food. The obsonator appears in the Digest as a slave who did the marketing.
Freedmen who were obsonatores appear in inscriptions.[3] The jurist
who mentions the obsonator in the Digest is interested in making
it clear that he was not a negotiator although he bought in the
market.[4] Paulus states that such slaves belonged to the familia
urbana.[5] Those that appear in inscriptions were from the royal
households.[6] The context of literary references to the obsonator
leaves one with the impression that he bought dainties and more
luxurious foods.[7] This is in accord with Fournier's statement
that obsonium included all food except grain stuffs (far).[8] An
account of Hadrian's method of checking the work of obsonatores
leads one to believe that the obsonator did not always enjoy the
confidence of his master.[9]

Cellararius.--The Digest is explicit in its statement of
the status and function of the cellararius. He was a slave whose
appointment was made that he might keep accurate accounts: "cel-
lararium quoque, id est ideo praepositus, ut rationes salvae

---

[1]Ulp. Dig. xvi. 3. 1. 9.

[2]Blümner, Technologie, I, p. 39, note 1.

[3]CIL VI. 8945.   [4]Marcian. Dig. xxxii. 65. See Note 3, p.13.

[5]Paul. Sent. iii. 6. 72.   [6]CIL VI. 8946; 5353.

[7]Plaut. Mil. 667; Sen. Ep. 47. 8.

[8]Fournier, DS s. v. Cibaria, p. 1142.   [9]Spart. Had. 17. 4.

sint."[1] It seems safe to say that he was placed in charge of the
cellarium to keep track of its contents.

The word cellarium is first used by Scaevola, who says:
"Fortunio liberto meo ex domu mea, quam libertis dedi, diaetam,
in qua habitabam, item cellarium iunctum eidem diaetae ab herede
meo concedi volo."[2] Apparently, as he uses it, it means a room
attached to a suite, probably for provisions, and probably one
that can be locked. Servius uses the word in his comment on Aen.
I. 703, defining it as the storeroom for provisions to be used in
a few days as distinguished from penum, the storeroom for provisions that were to last for a longer time.[3] Isidore makes a like
distinction between cellarium and promptuarium.[4] The word appears
frequently in church Latin and in glosses, usually in the sense
of a storeroom for food and dishes for table service.[5]

The cellararius, then, was a slave not in charge of a general storeroom, cella, as was the cellarius, but in charge of a
particular storeroom, the cellarium. Paulus uses the word in a
context in which this interpretation fits perfectly, i.e. with
opsonatores and vestiarii.[6] The word appears in church Latin also in a similar sense.[7]

Cellarius.--The cellarius is mentioned in the Digest with
no information about him other than that he was a slave - "Nominatim videntur liberi esse iussi, qui vel ex artificio vel officio vel quolibet alio modo evidenter denotati essent, veluti 'dispensator meus,' 'cellarius meus,' 'cocus meus.'"[8] He was probably
originally in charge of the cella.[9] The cella in this sense was
a storeroom for grain,[10] oil, or wine.[11] There are instances of
the occurrence of cellarius which indicate a person in charge of
such a cella, as: "Ut cibus et potio sine fraude a cellariis
praebeatur."[12] and: "cellariis aliquid appendentibus aut metien-
tibus."[13] In view of the juxtaposition of dispensator and coquus,
it may be that the word here refers to such a person.

An instance occurs, however, in which it is evident that

---

[1]Ulp. Dig. xxxiii. 7. 12. 9.   [2]Scaev. Dig. xxxii. 41. 1.
[3]Serv. Aen. i. 703.   [4]Isid. Orig. xv. 5. 7.
[5]TLL s. v. Cellarius.   [6]Paul. Sent. iii. 6. 72.
[7]TLL s. v. Cellararius.   [8]Gaius, Dig. xl. 4. 24.
[9]CGL II. 451. 28.   [10]Ulp. Dig. xxxiii. 9. 3. 3.
[11]Cato R. R. iii. 2.   [12]Col. xi. 1. 19.   [13]Col. xii. 3.8.

the word is applied to one in charge of a storeroom for wine.[1]
One suspects when the word is found linked with the word coquus,
as here and elsewhere,[2] that that was the function of that particular cellarius.

A second interpretation, however, is possible, arising
from the appearance of the word in an epigram of Martial's that
reads in part as follows:

> hinc cellarius experitur artes
> ut condat vario vafer sapore
> in rutae folium Capelliana.
> sic inplet gabatas paropsidesque
> et leves scutulas cavasque lances.
> Hoc lautum vocat, hoc putat venustum
> unum ponere ferculis tot assem.[3]

This epigram clearly establishes the fact that the cellarius may
have been a butler in charge of a pantry, not one in charge of
wine only. As this function and the connection with dishes immediately suggest the cellararius, the problem promptly arises as
to the relationship between the two. Either we have here a level-
ling of words among the Romans themselves such as occurs in the
case of the same two words among German commentators or differentiation of the two functions occurred at a late date. Objection
to the latter view arises from the fact that Scaevola, who first
uses the word cellarium as distinguished from cella, is of about
the same period as Gaius, the author of the citation in which cellarius appears. The word cellararius is found later in citations
from Ulpian and Paulus.[4] One scribe at least who copied a scholium on Horace was acquainted with both words or copied what he
saw without being acquainted with it.[5]

Coquus.--The Digest refers to cooks frequently. All that
appear there were slaves. One was given as a legacy - "Igitur et
si ita servus legatus sit: 'Stichum cocum,' 'Stichum sutorem Ti-
Tio lego,' licet neque cocus neque sutor sit, ad legatarium per-
tinebit."[6] Another was freed by will.[7] Two jurists mention the
doubling of roles of slaves. In one citation the same people

---

[1]Plin. N. H. xix. 188.

[2]Col. xii. 4. 2; Sen. Ep. 122. 16.   [3]Mart. xi. 31. 15-21.

[4]Dig. xxxiii. 7. 12; Paul. Sent. iii. 6. 72.

[5]Sch. Hor. Sat. ii. 2. 16. (O. Keller. Pseudoacronis
Scholia in Horatium Vetustiora (Leipzig, 1902)).

[6]Gaius, Dig. xxxv. 1. 17. 1.   [7]Gaius, Dig. xl. 4. 24.

served as cooks, litter bearers, and weavers - "Si unus servus
plura artificia sciat et alii coci legati fuerunt, alii textores,
alii lecticarii, ei cedere servum dicendum est, cui legati sunt
in quo artificio plerumque versabatur."[1] In the other case they
were cooks and litter bearers - "Servis lecticariis legatis si
idem lecticarius sit et cocus, accedet legato."[2] The cook was
included among the slaves attached to the personal service of the
master - "Et sibi videre eos demum usus sui causa patrem familias
habere, qui ad eius corpus tuendum atque ipsius cultum praepositi
destinatique essent, quo in genere iunctores, cubicularii, coci,
ministratores."[3] The last citation dealing with cooks is concerned with the representation made by the man who wold a cook. If
the cook was recommended as excellent, the jurist ruled that that
must mean excellent in his art. If, however, he was presented
merely as a cook, even if he was a very ordinary cook, no misrep-
resentation could be charged to the person who sold him. Gaius's
words are: "Venditor, qui optimum cocum esse dixerit, optimum in
eo artificio praestare debet: qui vero simpliciter cocum esse
dixerit, satis facere videtur, etiamsi mediocrem cocum praestet."[4]
Paulus says that cooks were included in the familia urbana.[5] The
Digest makes no such statement, but lends support to it by including in the familia rustica women whose function was to cook food
other than bread for the slaves, "quae pulmentaria rusticis coquant,"[6] and even women to bake bread, "Mulieres quae panem coquant."[7]

On the whole this picture of the cook agrees with that
drawn from literary sources. Livy tells us that slaves who served
as cooks were known early, were not highly regarded, and were
cheap. Subsequently cooking was regarded as an art and cooks were
expensive.[8] This new attitude rather clearly indicates the coming of the gourmet, the sort of person that would inspire such a
book as that of Apicius.[9] On the other hand, it is the first
step toward the coming of the gourmand and the innumerable ill-
nesses that Seneca charges to cooks.[10] This remark of Seneca's

---

[1]Marcian. Dig. xxxii. 65. 2.   [2]Paul. Dig. xxxii. 99. 4.
[3]Alf. Var. Dig. L. 16. 203.   [4]Gaius, Dig. xxi. 1. 18. 1.
[5]Paul. Sent. iii. 6. 72.   [6]Ulp. Dig. xxxiii. 7. 12. 5.
[7]Ibid.   [8]Liv. xxxix. 6. 9.
[9]Apicius, De Re Coquinaria.   [10]Sen. Ep. 95. 23.

and one citation from the _Digest_ indicate that one household might have many cooks.[1] This state of affairs is even more clearly indicated by references to the _archimageiros_.[2]

Pliny tells us that the baking in earlier times was done in the house, but finally passed into the hands of _pistores_.[3] Not only was this true in the city, but the great estates in the country had their own slave bakers.[4] However, the _Digest_ makes it clear that in some rural situations the old custom persisted and women still did the baking as well as the cooking.[5]

There is one type of cook of whom the _Digest_ gives no hint, the cook that could be hired for special occasions by those that had no cook or by those that had cooks inadequate for some particular event.[6] These cooks are met frequently in comedy,[7] where they furnish highly comic embellishment.[8] We find a reference to _coqui publici_ as late as the time of Julianus.[9] A _collegium_ of cooks appears, probably a burial association.[10]

Numerous references to the kitchen equipment used by the cook appear. The _Digest_ lists the following: _caccabi_, _patinae_, _aenum quod supra focum pandet_, _urcei_.[11] Isidore adds _ollae_, _patellae_, _cucumae_, _lebetae_, _sartagines_, _tripedes_, _molae_, _cribra_, _rutabula_.[12] Anthimus adds the _spatula_.[13]

Ministrator.--The slave who served at the table was called _ministrator_ as Seneca tells us.[14] Petronius mentions especially his serving wine.[15] The only information that the _Digest_ gives about the _ministrator_ is the fact that he was attached to the personal service of the master.[16] The _ministratores_ were young, handsome,[17] of uniform size, and well-groomed.[18] Their hair was carefully cared for.[19] Inscriptions show that they served in the

---

[1]See Note 1, p. 28.   [2]Iuv. ix. 109; CIL VI. 7458.

[3]Plin. _N. H._ xviii. 107, 108.

[4]See Note 7, p. 28. See also _Pistor_.

[5]See Notes 6 and 7, p. 28.

[6]Plin. _N. H._ xviii. 108; Paul. Fest. p. 173 M; 176 L.

[7]Plaut. _Aul._ 280.   [8]Plaut. _Pseud._ 790 ff.

[9]Cassiod. _Hist._ vi. 11.   [10]CIL. VI. 7458.

[11]Paul. _Dig._ xxxiii. 7. 18. 3.   [12]Isid. _Orig._ xx. 8.

[13]Anthim. 35.   [14]Sen. _Ep._ 95. 24.   [15]Petr. 31.

[16]Alf. Var. _Dig._ L. 16. 203. See Note 3, p. 28.

[17]Cic. _De. Fin._ ii. 8. 23.   [18]Sen. _Ep._ 119. 13.

[19]Ambr. _Ep._ 69. 7.

royal households and that many were freed.[1] It may be that these
ministratores were trained in a paedagogium.[2] There was a collegium of ministratores.[3] An inscription appears of a person called
a frumento ministratorum, probably a slave who cared for the food
of the rather large retinue of ministratores.[4]

---

[1]CIL VI. 8915 ff.; 9641 ff.
[2]See Chapter III, Note
[3]CIL VI. 8914.   [4]CIL VI. 8924 - 8926.

CHAPTER II

OCCUPATIONS CONCERNED WITH CLOTHING

Another group of occupations in which we find humbler folk engaged is centered about clothing. Certain of these are concerned with the conversion of raw material into shape that can be used for clothing, i.e. spinning and weaving. One occupation only appears in the Digest that had to do with the conversion of material into wearable form, that of the shoemaker. A larger number appear concerned with the upkeep of the garment after it had been made and worn.

Lanipendia.--In spinning, the work seems to have been portioned out by a lanipendia to the women who did the spinning. In the Digest she appears only when a man's wife is compared to a lanipendia. A garment was made for a woman out of her husband's wool under her supervision. We are told that she was, as it were, a lanipendia and managed the work for her husband. Pomponius says: "Sed si vir lana sua vestimentum mulieri confecerit, quamvis id uxori confectum fuerit et uxoris cura, tamen viri esse neque impedire, quod in ea re uxor tamquam lanipendia fuerit et viri negotium procurarit."[1] This clearly indicates that a lanipendia had supervision over the spinning, weaving, and making of the garment. In inscriptions a lanipenda appears, a slave or freedwoman, who, we assume, had the same function.[2] The masculine form lanipendus also is found there.[3] An old scholium on Juvenal, not recognized by Wessner, defines libraria as lanipendia.[4] Wessner recognizes a scholium that contains the word, but throws no light on the meaning.[5] The work of portioning out the work for spinners is mentioned frequently with no reference to the person who portioned it out.[6] The ball of wool also, which constituted the portion, is mentioned frequently.[7]

---

[1]Pompon. Dig. xxiv. 1. 31.   [2]CIL VI. 9496-9498.
[3]CIL VI. 3976; 8870.   [4]Iuv. vi. 476.
[5]Sch. Iuv. vi. 497.   [6]Prop. iv. 7. 41; Iust. i. 3. 2.
[7]Varro. R. R. ii. 11. 9; Hor. Ep. i. 13. 14; Ov. Met. vi

19.

Lanifica.--The actual spinners were known as lanificae.
Those that appear in the Digest were slave women kept to clothe
the slaves of the familia rustica - "Item lanificas quae familiam
rusticam vestiunt."[1] They were not considered part of the instrumentum of the estate.[2] They were, however, included in a legacy
of the estate and its instrumenta on the ground that they were
part of the equipment that the man who had lived there had provided for the estate. The opinion of Alfenus is as follows:

> Consultus de mulieribus lanificis an instrumento contine-
> rentur, respondit non quidem esse instrumenti fundi, sed quo-
> niam ipse pater familias, qui legasset, in eo fundo habitas-
> set, dubitari non oportere, quin et ancillae et ceterae res,
> quibus pater familias in eo fundo esset instructus, omnes le-
> gatae viderentur.[3]

Paulus also says that maids who made clothing for the rustic slaves
went with the instrumentum.[4]

Both Petronius[5] and Tibullus[6] make it clear that the poorest slaves and those least highly regarded were put at the spinning. In contrast with this attitude, skill in spinning was reckoned as one of the very highest and most commendable qualities of
the Roman matron[7] and Minerva herself is called lanifica.[8]

Textor.--Weavers, all of whom were slaves, appear several
times in the Digest. Both men and women served as weavers -
"textores meos omnes....lego";[9] "ut textorum et textricum cibaria
diceret contineri."[10] In no case is a single weaver left in a
legacy, an indication that when wool was dealt with it was in considerable quantity. One woman weaver appears in a citation in
which we are told that even she might have the right of actio in
peculio - "maxime si qua sarcinatrix aut textrix erit aut aliquod
artificium vulgare exerceat, datur propter eam actio."[11] Weavers
are mentioned in conjunction with fullers,[12] with the repairer of
garments,[13] and by implication are classed as servi vulgares.[14]
Weavers are mentioned among the slaves that had more than one
service to perform, serving as cooks and litter bearers as well

---

[1]Ulp. Dig. xxxiii. 7. 12. 5.   [2]See Note 6, p. 34.
[3]Alf. Dig. xxxiii. 7. 16. 2.   [4]Paul. Sent. iii. 6. 37.
[5]Petr. 132.   [6]Tib. iv. 10. 3.
[7]Auson. Par. ii. 4; xvi. 4.   [8]Ov. Met. vi. 6; 23.
[9]Pompon. Dig. xxx. 36.   [10]Ulp. Dig. xxxiii. 9. 3. 6.
[11]Gaius, Dig. xv. 1. 27.   [12]See Note 3, p. 33.
[13]See Note 11.   [14]Ibid.

as weavers.[1] So important were weavers in the ordinary work of the Roman ménage that the question was raised whether they were included in the class of slaves acquired for the master's own service. Alfenus says: "Itemque de servis eadem ratione quaeri, qui eorum usus sui causa parati essent? Utrum textores...."[2] They were not considered part of the stock in trade of a mercator - "Licet mercis appellatio angustior sit, ut neque ad servos fullones vel sarcinatores vel textores.... pertineat."[3]

The social rating of the weaver in Latin literature quite corresponds to the statement of the Digest that the weaver was of the ordo vulgaris.[4] Martial classes him with the shoemakers and with fullers,[5] in the latter agreeing with Ulpian. One weaver appears, however, who had served as triumvir, quaestor, and tribune.[6] He may have held these offices in a burial association, though Waltzing does not mention an association of weavers.

Ulpian, in passing judgment on what constitutes instrumentum, mentions stages of weaving and refers to the warp and woof.[7] The Digest offers nothing further on the process of weaving.

Sutor.--The only workman appearing in the Digest who produced articles ready to wear was the shoemaker. Shoemakers appear who were slaves.[8] Paulus includes a sutor among the slaves necessary in a villa rustica.[9] In one case the sutor was a verna, a slave born in the house, a class that usually received better treatment than other slaves. In this case the sutor was willed to a foster child with the intention that the slave should support the new owner. The small shoe shop operated by a slave for his master is here clearly indicated. The words of Scaevola are: "Hoc amplius 'eidem alumno meo hominem Caletanum et vernam sutorem, qui eum artificio suo mercede data alere poterit.'"[10] Not all shoemakers were slaves, however, as the Digest makes clear. In one case we are expressly told that a shoemaker had a freeborn apprentice. This apprentice proved so unsatisfactory a pupil that the sutor lost his temper, threw a last at him, and put out his eye:

---

[1]Marcian. Dig. xxxii. 65. See Chapter I, Note 1, p. 28.
[2]Alf. Var. Dig. L. 16. 203.   [3]Ulp. Dig. xiv. 4. 1. 1.
[4]Suet. Gram. 23; Iuv. ix. 30; Mart. iv. 19. 1.
[5]Mart. xii. 59. 6.   [6]CIL VI. 9290.   [7]Dig. xxxiv. 2. 22.
[8]Gaius, Dig. xxxv. 1. 17. 1. See Chapter I, Note 6, p.27.
[9]Paul. Sent. iii. 6. 37.   [10]Scaev. Dig. xxxvi. 1. 80 (78). 12.

"Sutor.... puero discenti ingenuo filio familias, parum bene facienti quod demonstraverit, forma calcei cervicem percussit, ut oculus puero perfunderetur."[1] The status of the _sutor_ is not clear, but in subsequently recounting this or a similar incident Ulpian says that the father of the boy could bring a suit _ex locato_ - "ex locato esse actionem patri eius."[2] The _sutor_ in that case was probably a freedman, or possibly even a freeman. It is interesting to note in passing that the jurists hasten to support the principle of discipline for apprentices, criticizing only the severity. Ulpian says: "quamvis enim magistris levis castigatio concessa sit, tamen hunc modum non tenuisse."[3] Paulus adds by way of comment on the incident: "praeceptoris enim nimia saevitia culpae adsignatur."[4]

Sutores were one group whose rights and duties were specifically defined in the _Lex Metalli Vipascensis_.[5]

Fullo.--The information about fullers that appears in the _Digest_ offers little as to the process of the industry, but much about the business. In one citation we find reference to slaves on an estate serving as fullers - "lanificae et lanae et tonsores et fullones et focariae non agri sunt instrumentum sed instrumenti."[6] They are of the _genus vulgare_, mentioned along with the shearers of sheep and spinners, and are classed as _instrumentum instrumenti_. These fullers the context clearly marks as those who dressed the newly woven lengths of woolen cloth.[7] As early as the time of Varro these fullers were found on estates, yet even then not all estates had them; some utilized the services of neighboring fullers.[8]

The fuller that maintains a business of his own is the usual figure appearing in the _Digest_. Though he was paid for expert service he was nevertheless held responsible for the safeguarding of goods entrusted to him - "Nam et fullo et sarcinator non pro custodia sed pro arte mercedem accipiunt, et tamen custodiae nomine ex locato tenentur."[9] The recovery of a garment from

---

[1] Ulp. _Dig._ ix. 2. 5. 3. [2] Ulp. _Dig._ xix. 2. 13. 4.
[3] _Ibid._ [4] Paul. _Dig._ ix. 2. 6.
[5] CIL II. 5181. 32-37. [6] Ulp. _Dig._ xxxiii. 7. 12. 6.
[7] Ulp. _Dig._ xlvii. 2. 12; Paul. _Sent._ ii. 31. 29.
[8] Varro _R. R._ i. 16. 4.
[9] Gaius, _Dig._ iv. 9. 5. See also Gaius, _Dig._ xix. 5. 22.

a fuller is cited as an illustration of the statement that a suit
ex locato may be brought for the recovery of the identical thing
in question as opposed to the value of the thing - "Respondit rerum locatarum duo genera esse, ut aut idem redderetur (sicuti cum
vestimenta fulloni curanda locarentur) aut eiusdem generis redderetur."[1] If, however, a fuller lost a garment and made restitu-
tion to its owner, the owner had no further action against the
fuller - "Si fullo aut sarcinator vestimenta perdiderit eoque nomine domino satisfecerit, necesse est domino vindicationem eorum
et condictionem cedere."[2] If a fuller undertook the work on a
garment, then passed it on to another person to do and the garment was stolen from the second person, the original contractor
was held responsible - "Si ego tibi poliendum vestimentum loca-
vero, tu vero inscio aut invito me commodaveris Titio et Titio
furtum factum sit...."[3] If the garment was stolen from the fuller's, the owner could sue the fuller ex locato or he could bring
action against the thief at the fuller's expense:

> Vestimenta tua fullo perdidit et habes unde petas nec re-
> petere vis: agis nihilo minus ex locato cum fullone, sed
> iudicem aestimaturum, an possis adversus furem magis agere et
> ab eo tuas res consequi fullonis videlicet sumptibus: sed si
> hoc tibi impossibile esse perspexerit, tunc fullonem quidem
> tibi condemnabit, tuas autem actiones te ei praestare compel-
> let.[4]

In fact, he could even choose whether he would sue the fuller ex
locato or for theft, but he could not sue him on both charges:

> Fullo actione locati de domino liberatus est: negat eum
> furti recte acturum Labeo. Item si furti egisset, priusquam
> ex locato cum eo ageretur et, antequam de furto iudicaretur,
> locati actione liberatus esset, et fur ab eo absolvi debet.
> Quod si nihil eorum ante accidisset, furem ei condemnari opor-
> tere.[5]

The law took cognizance of the plight of the fuller also.
If garments were let to him to wash, were lost, and paid for by
the fuller, then subsequently found by the master, it is granted
implicitly that the fuller could get his money. The question is
raised only on what ground he may bring suit - "Si fullo vestimenta lavanda conduxerit, deinde amissis eis domino pretium ex
locato conventus praestiterit posteaque dominus invenerit vestimenta, qua actione debeat consequi pretium quod dedit?"[6] As a

---

[1]Alf. Dig. xix. 2. 31. [2]Gaius, Dig. xix. 2. 25. 8.
[3]Ulp. Dig. xlvii. 2. 48. 4. [4]Labeo, Dig. xix. 2. 60. 2.
[5]Iavol. Dig. xlvii. 2. 91. [6]Ulp. Dig. xii. 7. 2.

rule, when garments were stolen from a fuller, he brought action
against the thief. If he was insolvent, however, the owner of
the garment might bring action - "Itaque fullo, qui curanda po-
liendave vestimenta accepit, semper agit: praestare enim custodiam debet. Si autem solvendo non est, ad dominum actio redit."[1]
A fuller had the right to action for damages "si quadrupes pauperiem fecisse dicatur" as well as the owner of the garments, on
the ground that he was responsible for goods entrusted to his
care - "Haec actio non solum domino, sed etiam ei cuius interest
competit, veluti ei cui res commodata est, item fulloni, quia eo
quod tenentur damnum videntur pati."[2]

  Goods left with fullers were not only lost or stolen, but
various other accidents befell them. If mice gnawed holes in
them, the fuller was liable for a suit ex locato and the jurist
sententiously adds that he should have guarded against this - "Si
fullo vestimenta polienda acceperit eaque mures roserint, ex locato tenetur, quia debuit ab hac re cavere."[3] If _pallia_ were ex-
changed, i.e. a garment delivered to a person other than the owner, who in turn received a _pallium_ not his own, the fuller was
responsible ex locato even if he had committed the error unwitting-
ly - "Et si pallium fullo permutaverit et alii alterius dederit,
ex locato actione tenebitur, etiamsi ignarus fecerit."[4] While it
is possible that this occurred through delivery to the slave of
the owner at the fuller's, it may possibly indicate that there existed a delivery service from the fuller's.[5] If the fuller wore a
garment sent to him to be cleaned, he was liable for action for
theft - "Fullo et sarcinator, qui polienda vel sarcienda vestimenta accepit, si forte his utatur, ex contrectatione eorum furtum
fecisse videtur, quia non in eam causam ab eo videntur accepta."[6]
The jurist adds the reason for his opinion: he did not receive
the garment for that purpose.

  The quarters of the fuller seem to have been located in
any spot that he could find to his advantage. In one case a fullery was established in the neighborhood of a spring that rose on
an estate. The water from the fullery was permitted to run off

---

[1]Ulp. _Dig._ xlvii. 2. 12. [2]Paul. _Dig._ ix. 1. 2.
[3]Ulp. _Dig._ xix. 2. 13. 6. [4]_Ibid._
[5]See Chapter I, Note 3, p. 22.
[6]Paul. _Dig._ xlvii. 2. 83 (82).

on the land of a neighbor, who brought action aquae pluviae arcendae, but the man that built the fullery was not subject to judgment on that ground - "Apud Trebatium relatum est eum, in cuius fundo aqua oritur, fullonicas circa fontem instituisse et ex his aquam in fundum vicini immittere coepisse: ait ergo non teneri eum aquae pluviae arcendae actione."[1] Another citation concerning the drying of clothes in the street in front of a fuller's shop locates the shop on a used thoroughfare - "Ἐπιμελείσθωσαν δὲ καὶ ὅπως πρὸ τῶν ἐργαστηρίων μηδὲν προκείμενον ᾖ, πλὴν ἐὰν κναφεὺς ἱμάτια ψύγῃ."[2] When the use of a house had been granted to a person, the jurist ruled that the fructuary was under moral obligation not to start a fullery in it - "Meritoria illic facere fructuarius non debet..... Quod autem dicit meritoria non facturum ita accipe quae vulgo deversoria vel fullonica appellant."[3] These last citations indicate that a fullery, while it was a public nuisance to some extent, was at the same time a necessary and profitable institution.

One citation appears that makes clear the fact that fullers had apprentices and that they conducted a rather pretentious establishment. A fuller departing for foreign travel left a person in charge of his fullery and apprentices. One of the latter took in garments, then fled, taking the garments with him. The jurist ruled that if the person in charge had been left as procurator, the fuller was not liable, but if as institor, he was. Ulpian says:

Item fullonum et sarcinatorum praepositus (institor appellatur)..... Sed et cum fullo peregre proficiscens rogasset, ut discipulis suis, quibus tabernam instructam tradiderat, imperaret, post cuius profectionem vestimenta discipulus accepisset et fugisset, fullonem non teneri, si quasi procurator fuit relictus: sin vero quasi institor teneri.[4]

A later citation expressly states, however, that goods passing through the hands of fullers can not be classed as goods of trade (merx), but adds the opinion that, like other kinds of business, that of the fuller was subject to tax. The opinion reads: "....dominus....ex hoc ědicto in tributum vocatur. Licet mercis appellatio angustior sit, ut neque ad servos fullones....pertineat,.... ad omnes negotiationes porrigendum edictum."[5] This citation indi-

---

[1] Ulp. Dig. xxxix. 3. 3.   [2] (Papin.), Dig. xliii. 10. 1. 4.
[3] Ulp. Dig. vii. 1. 13. 8.   [4] Ulp. Dig. xiv. 3. 5. 7, 10.
[5] Ulp. Dig. xiv. 4. 1.

cates that slaves operated fulleries, we assume either for the master or as a venture of their own involving their peculium.

Sarcinator.--Another occupation concerned with the upkeep of clothes was that of the sarcinator. The Digest makes clear that some sarcinatores were slaves.[1] Inscriptions show freedmen also.[2] Freemen may have plied the trade, but proof that they did so is lacking. There is no sure evidence that the sarcinator worked in the house of the master. It is clear that his work was usually done outside of the home.[3] The actual work may have been done by slaves,[4] and seems to have been done at times, at least, in an establishment of some size with an institor at the head of it.[5] People engaged in this business, however, were not classified as those engaged in trade.[6] Sarcinatores were held responsible for garments left with them whether they were doing the work gratis or received pay for it,[7] although technically they received the money in return for skilled labor, not for guarding the garment.[8] If they used the garments left with them, they were judged guilty of theft.[9] They made reparation for lost garments.[10]

The context of the passages in which the sarcinator appears in the Digest agrees with the explicit statements of other sources that he repaired garments.[11] Not a great deal can be learned about the process. The mending seems at times to have been clearly patching with pieces of goods - "nam et sarcinatores concipere dicuntur vestimenta cum e diverso coniungunt et adsuunt."[12] The extreme variety of the work is indicated by the specifications and price range appearing in the Edict of Diocletian.[13]

Sarcinatrix.--The sarcinatrix that appears in the Digest

---

[1]Ibid. See Note 3, p. 33.   [2]Or. 7274.
[3]Gaius, Dig. xix. 2. 25. 8. See Note 2, p. 35.
[4]See Note 3, p. 33.
[5]Ulp. Dig. xiv. 3. 5. 7, 10. See Note 4, p. 37.
[6]See Note 3, p. 33.   [7]Gaius, Dig. xix. 5. 22.
[8]Gaius, Dig. iv. 9. 5. See Note 9, p. 34.
[9]Paul. Dig. xlvii. 2. 83 (82). See Note 6, p. 36.
[10]Gaius, Dig. xix. 2. 25. 8. See Note 2, p. 35.
[11]Lucil. apud Non. p. 175. 33; Gaius, Inst. iii. 143.
[12]Serv. Aen. xii. 13.
[13]Edict. Diocl. vii. 48 ff.

was a slave.[1] She was working in the house of the master and
seems to have belonged to the class of slaves known as _vulgares_.
The context of the passage is in harmony with the explicit statement of Nonius that the _sarcinatrix_ repaired garments.[2] Not a
great deal can be learned about the process of the work of the
sarcinatrix. We know that she used a needle.[3] She used something
that was known as _machina_ - "homines rusticos in vindemia incon-
dita cantare, sarcinatrices in machinis."[4] What these _machinae_
were we do not know. The _sarcinatrix_ may have used some sort of
hoop for stretching the garment or even used small looms to weave
in parts. Inscriptions show slaves[5] and freedwomen[6] only working
as _sarcinatrices_.

---

[1]Gaius, _Dig_. xv. 1. 27. See Note 11, p. 32.
[2]Non. p. 56. 23.   [3]Fest. p. 8 L.   [4]See Note 2.
[5]CIL VI. 9039 b.   [6]CIL VI. 9037; 9038.

CHAPTER III

OCCUPATIONS CONCERNED WITH SERVICE FOR THE HOUSEHOLD

A very large number of humble folk was engaged in the
service of the household. Some of these were concerned with the
care of the house itself. Some served in the upkeep of the premises. Certain ones were engaged in the personal service and care
of members of the family. Others, though members of the staff of
house servants, rendered their service chiefly outside of the
house.

Scoparius.--One of the humblest members of the group who
attended to the house itself was the scoparius - "Quibusdam in
regionibus accedunt instrumento, si villa cultior est, veluti atrienses scoparii."[1] This reference of Ulpian's in the Digest furnishes our only information about the scoparius, who was obviously
the wielder of a broom, scopae.[2] He was a slave, found apparently
in a villa of the better sort. The context suggests that he was
associated with the atriensis, possibly subordinate to him, though
this is by no means a certain deduction from the allocation of the
words. If the words qui verrunt describe the work of a scoparius
as they very well may, there is evidence in one of Cicero's para-
doxes that a slave performing the work that a scoparius would
naturally perform was subordinate to an atriensis.[3] Our inference
is that when a scoparius appears we are dealing with a ménage that
had a large number of slaves with highly specialized functions.

In other cases were sweeping is done it is done either by
slaves to whom no title is given,[4] or by a slave other than the
scoparius, as in the case in the Cena Trimalchionis.[5] Whether
Trimalchio had missed the acme of elegance in failing to have a

---

[1] Ulp. Dig. xxxiii. 7. 8. 1.

[2] The word appears with this meaning in church Latin. See
C. D. Du Cange, Glossarium Mediae et Infimae Latinitatis (Paris,
1840), s. v.

[3] Cic. Par. v. 37.

[4] Plaut. Asin. 424 ff.; Stich. 347; 351; 375.

[5] Petr. 34.

scoparius, or whether it was more impressive to have a slave of
higher order performing the task of sweeping up fallen dishes it
is impossible to say. The facts that the function is referred to
without the use of the word in earlier Latin and that the word appears in later Latin only lead to the conclusion, however, that
the word was not in use in earlier times.

A freedman scoparius who seems to have served in a temple
of Isis and who lived to the age of eighty appears in an inscription from Syracuse.[1]

Atriarius.--Another slave engaged in menial work in the
house was the atriarius. The citation in the Digest in which the
word appears furnishes our chief information about atriarii. They
were slaves of the lower ranks, classed with the focarii. In this
case at least they were connected with a caupona or stabulum, and
are expressly mentioned as those to whom valuables may not be intrusted by patrons of the place. Ulpian's words are: "Caupones
autem et stabularios aeque eos accipiemus, qui cauponam vel stabulum exercent, institoresve eorum. Ceterum si qui opera mediastini
fungitur, non continetur, ut puta atriarii et focarii et his similes."[2]

The only other occurrence of the word appears in the records of a collegium found at Antium as a restoration in an era-
sure.[3] The condition of the inscription makes it impossible to
draw any inference as to the person so named though the reading
seems to be granted as correct. He appears in a company, in part
slaves, in part freedmen, of widely differing occupations. They
may have been the highly specialized slaves of a wealthy villa,
possibly a villa of the emperor's, or they may have been drawn
from various sources into a single burial society.

It is impossible to prove that the atriarii were not slaves
working under the atriensis and doing the heavy work,[4] as is the
view of Chapot,[5] Habel,[6] and Marquardt.[7] From any data that we
have at present, however, it is quite impossible to prove that

---

[1]CIL X. 7129.   [2]Ulp. Dig. iv. 9. 1. 5.

[3]CIL X. 6638. C 2. 6.   [4]See Note 3, p. 40.

[5]DS s. v. Servi, p. 1275.   [6]PW s. v. Atriarius.

[7]Privatleben, p. 142, n. 3. Marquardt considers the scoparius and atriarius identical. There is no evidence that this
is true. Both words seem to be late usages. That fact would
suggest that the functions differed.

they were.

    Atriensis.--The atriensis himself is found in three cita-
tions in the Digest. In the first, one from Ulpian, the transfer
of a slave by a fructuary from a group of musical entertainers to
the position of atriensis is considered an abuse of privileges -
"Si....vel de symphonia atriensem vel de palaestra stercorandis
latrinis praeponat, abuti videbitur proprietate."[1] The context
clearly indicates that the work of the atriensis was degrading for
a trained musician. In certain regions if the villa was of the
better sort the atrienses were considered part of the instrumentum
of the fundus.[2] Atrienses, then, seem to have been slaves of specialized function, found on estates where there were many slaves.
In another citation, one from Alfenus, the question was raised
whether atrienses were to be considered as part of the group of
slaves attached to the personal service of the master - "Itemque
de servis eadem ratione quaeri, qui eorum usus sui causa parati
essent? Utrum....atrienses."[3]

    From other literary sources it is clear that three sorts
of atriensis were known. In the Asinaria of Plautus an atriensis
seems to be imposing both mentally and physically, one who manages
the house, buys and sells, takes in and pays out money.[4] Servius,
referring to this atriensis, says "servum atriensem, in tota familia plurimum posse."[5] Cicero says that atrienses were servants
of better position,[6] and suggests that they should be younger men
and suitably dressed.[7] If we may interpret Suetonius' cella Pala-
tini atriensis as the storeroom of the atriensis attached to the
palace on the Palatine - an interpretation by no means certain -
that sort of atriensis, the keeper of the storeroom, was still
found at the time of Caligula.[8]

    A second sort of atriensis is that occurring in glosses as
οἰκοφύλαξ, ianitor, ostiarius.[9] As early as the time of Plautus
an atriensis appears sub ianua.[10] In Apuleius atrienses appear
with ianitores.[11] While not identified with them, they are thought

---

[1]Ulp. Dig. vii. 1. 15. 1.

[2]Ulp. Dig. xxxiii. 7. 8. 1. See Note 1, p. 40.

[3]Alf. Var. Dig. L. 16. 203. [4]Plaut. Asin. 350-1; 420 ff.

[5]Serv. Aen. ix. 645. [6]See Note 3, p. 40. [7]Pis. 67.

[8]Suet. Cal. 57. 2. [9]CGL III. 305. 9; V. 441. 54.

[10]Cas. 462. [11]Mund. 26.

of in the same connection. A scholium on Juvenal refers to the same sort of service.[1]

The third sort, probably referred to by the gloss _atria habens_,[2] is first found in Columella's account of the work of the _vilica_ in the country, who must keep after the _atrienses_ to get them to set forth the dishes, and wipe and keep shining and free from rust things made of iron.[3] This type of slave is probably referred to again by Pliny as part of the expense of a pretentious estate.[4] Phaedrus' fable of the elegant _atriensis_ surely deals with one of this sort.[5] To this class all the _atrienses_ of the _Digest_ who have been previously discussed probably belonged, as well as most of those in the inscriptions.[6] Inscriptions dealing with _atrienses_ are colorless for the most part, but one died at the age of twenty,[7] and another was _ex hortis_,[8] both suggesting this type of slave.

Supellecticarius.--Another person in the service of the household was the _supellecticarius_, who appears in the _Digest_ as a slave - "Idem Celsus eodem libro ait etiam supellecticarios et ceteros hoc genus servos contineri id est ministeria."[9] - and who surely cared for the furnishings (_supellex_) of the house. _Supellex_ included furniture, and vessels of silver, bronze, glass and terra cotta.[10] One of the duties of the _supellecticarius_ may very well have been the keeping of the inventory of the _supellex_ to which Varro refers.[11] In inscriptions _supellecticarii_ appear who were freedmen.[12] The titles a _supellectile_[13] and _ad supellectilem_[14] were used apparently as equivalent to _supellecticarius_. In-

---

[1]Schol. Iuv. vii. 7. [2]CGL II. 568. 40.

[3]Col. xii. 3. 9. Though for the most part the _atriensis_ appears in the _villa urbana_ as Ruggiero says (Ettore de Ruggiero, _Dizionario Epigrafico_ (Roma, 1895), _s. v._) in this case he is clearly part of the _familia rustica_.

[4]Plin. _Ep._ iii. 19. 3. [5]Phaed. ii. 5. 11.

[6]Any distinction between _atriensis_ and _atriarius_ in the abbreviations _atr_ and _atri_ usual in inscriptions seems quite impossible. A safer procedure is to assume that the humbler ones were _atrienses_ of this last sort.

[7]CIL VI. 9199. [8]CIL VI. 6241.

[9]Ulp. _Dig._ xxxiii. 7. 12. 31.

[10]Paul. _Dig._ xxxiii. 10. 3; xxxiii. 7. 18.

[11]Varro _R. R._ 1. 22. 6. [12]CIL VI. 4035.

[13]CIL VI. 3719; 4035. [14]CIL VI. 9049.

scriptions that permit the drawing of any inference lead one to
the conclusion that a slave with such functions would be found in
the mansions of the rich only.[1] One inscription mentions a person called a supellectile and also atrienses.[2] It is probably
true that the supellecticarius was subordinate to the atriensis.[3]
This inscription, however, offers no evidence to that effect. Another inscription has been used to show that a woman served as
supellecticarius.[4] The inscription is difficult to interpret but
its appearance as given by Gori indicates that the supellecticarius
was a man.[5]

      Ostiarius.--The slave that guarded the door, the ostiarius,
is mentioned twice in the Digest as belonging to the instrumentum
of an estate. In one case he is associated with the muleteer -
"item ostiarium mulionemque."[6] In the other case he appears with
the landscape gardiner, the caretaker of the diaeta, and the water
boy - "ostiarii autem inquit, vel topiarii diaetarii aquarii."[7]
This variation of companions gives a fair picture of the ostiarius
as we piece it together from references in literature. A purchased slave,[8] in some cases chained to his post in the vestibule,[9]
his companion a dog,[10] harsh and arrogant, one before whom guests
cowered but whom they disdained,[11] he was a necessary and valuable
guardian of the door.[12] This picture persists from the days of
the Republic to the time of Nero, and presents a slave whose lot
was hardly enviable. A less unpleasant picture of the ostiarius
appears in inscriptions of slaves[13] and freedmen[14] of the imperial
house whose lot was evidently easier, since they had even an organization with decurio[15] and scribe[16] of their own. With these

---

[1]CIL VI. 3719; 8654.   [2]CIL X. 6638 C.

[3]Cf. W. E. Waters, Petronius, Cena Trimalchionis (Chicago,
1924), p. 70.

[4]CIL VI. 9049 = 33758. Bormann questions the authenticity
of this inscription.

[5]A. F. Gorius, Monumentum Libertorum et Servorum Liviae
Augustae (Florence, 1727), p. 160. This appears in CIL VI. 9049.

[6]Ulp. Dig. xxxiii. 7. 12. 9.   [7]Idem, xxxiii. 7. 12. 42.

[8]Sen. De. Ir. iii. 37. 2.

[9]Suet. De Clar. Rhet. iii; Ov. Am. i. 6. 1.

[10]See Note 8.   [11]Sen. De Const. Sap. xiv.1.

[12]Varro R. R. i. 13. 2.   [13]CIL VI. 3995 ff.

[14]CIL VI. 8961; 8962.   [15]CIL VI. 8962.   [16]CIL VI. 8961.

ostiarii we may class those of the later reference of Ulpian.
Here too belongs the ostiarius of Petronius,[1] who, when freed
from his own peculiar duties in the efficient household of Trimalchio, employed his time shelling peas. To what extent such ex-
traneous duties were provided for the ostiarius and other specialized slaves we have little means of judging.

Cubicularius.--Another person who served in the house was
the cubicularius. He was usually a slave and was in the personal
service of the master as a citation from Alfenus shows.[2] A citation from Ulpian shows that the cubicularius was in particularly
close touch with the master. Ulpian's words are as follows:

> Si patris mortem defendere necesse habuerit, an dicendum
> sit hic quoque ei succurrendum, si libertum paternum propter
> hoc accusavit, medicum forte patris aut cubicularium aut quem
> alium, qui circa patrem fuerat? Et puto succurrendum, si af-
> fectione et periculo paternae substantiae ducente necesse
> habuit accusationem vel calumniosam instituere.[3]

This last citation shows also that freedmen served as cubicularii.[4]

The Digest gives little information as to the service rendered by cubicularii, but it evidently included the purchase of
things for the use of the master, for, with obsonatores and slaves
placed in charge of fishermen, they are excepted from the number
of those who would be included under the caption of people engaged
in trade.[5] Charisius tells us that the function of the cubicularius was the guarding of the bedroom.[6] Paulus includes cubicularii
among the slaves of the familia urbana,[7] though it is perfectly
clear that the cubicularius upon occasion went where his master
went,[8] even when that involved foreign travel.[9] The cubicularius
seems to have been trusted to a very high degree, not only being
permitted to listen in at secret conferences,[10] but even chosen

---

[1]Petr. 28. 8.

[2]Alf. Var. Dig. L. 16. 203. See Chapter I, Note 3, p.28.

[3]Ulp. Dig. xxxviii. 2. 14. 7.

[4]Inscriptional evidence shows that both slaves and freedmen served as cubicularii (CIL VI. 8777-8; 8782-3; 8789; 8794).
Freedmen only seem to have been called a cubiculo.

[5]Marcian. Dig. xxxii. 65. See Chapter I, Note 3, p. 13.

[6]Char. Gramm. 1. 76.   [7]Paul. Sent. iii. 6. 72.

[8]Amm. xxvii. 10. 11.   [9]Suet. Iul. 4.

[10]Suet. Tib. 21.

to carry out designs of the master that could be entrusted to no
one else.[1] We find cubicularii constituting the jury that tried
a dispensator in the house of Trimalchio.[2] The effect of this position of preference on the cubicularii themselves was threefold
as was to be expected. In certain cases they were held responsible for the advantage that their position gave them and were tor-
tured to exact confession if anything went wrong with the master.[3]
In the Digest we find that this occurred even in the case of a
freedman.[4] In other cases the cubicularius was impressed with the
importance of his position and showed it by a lofty manner,[5] which
proved particularly irritating inasmuch as he seems to have been
the person through whom admission to the presence of the master
was arranged.[6] In this last function he may have proved not only
haughty but venal.[7] Finally cases occurred in which cubicularii
became so tyrannical even over the masters themselves that the
masters asserted their power and disposed of the cubicularii involved.[8] In a late period in the imperial palace when the regi-
mentation was great, cubicularii were subject to a grand chamber-
lain, praepositus sacri cubiculi, subsequently to the master of
the offices.[9]

Cubicularii seem to have served women as well as men.[10]
In royal households they were so numerous that they were divided
into stationes.[11] A slave called supra cubicularios had the oversight and direction of these cubicularii.[12] A freedman called a
frumento cubiculariorum appears, who probably provided food for

---

[1]Suet. Ner. 38.   [2]Petr. 53.   [3]Quint. Decl. 328.

[4]Ulp. Dig. xxxviii. 2. 14. 7. See Note 3, p. 45.

[5]See Note 11, p. 44.   [6]Cic. Att. vi. 2. 5.

[7]Cic. Ver. iii. 4. 8.   [8]Lampr. Com. xv. 1, 2.

[9]A. E. R. Boak, The Master of the Offices in the Later Roman and Byzantine Empires (New York, 1919), pp. 27, 40.

[10]Apul. Met. x. 28 (Oud. 732); Porph. Hor. Car. 1. 37. 9.

[11]CIL VI. 8774; 8775. Marquardt (Privatleben, p. 144)
thinks that these stationes consisted of those on night duty and
of those on day service. Friedländer once thought that the basis
of assignment was nearness to the person of the emperor (1st ed.
Leipzig, 1881, p. 100). In subsequent editions, including the
revision by Wissowa, the statement is made that the basis of assignment is not clear (L. Friedländer and G. Wissowa, Darstellungen aus der Sittengeschichte Roms, (Leipzig, 1919), p. 59). There
is no evidence on which to base an opinion. The fact that inscriptions refer chiefly to members of the Statio Prima leads one
to believe that membership in that statio was a higher honor.

[12]CIL VI. 8766.

them.[1] Another freedman called ab aegris cubiculariorum is found
in an inscription.[2] There was a collegium of cubicularii, probably a burial association.[3]

    Diaetarius.--Another slave who served about the house was
the diaetarius. Ulpian in listing the contents of the instrumentum of an estate says: "Ostiarii autem....vel topiarii diaetarii
aquarii domui, tantum deservientes continebuntur."[4] No evidence
as to the duties of the diaetarius appears, but it is clear that
he was in charge of a diaeta. In the usual usage a diaeta was a
room[5] or an apartment[6] in a house, either upstairs[7] or down,[8] or
a room or rooms built in the garden apart from the house.[9] The
context of the passage in which diaetarius appears, since it is
flanked on one side by topiarius and on the other by aquarius,
suggests that the diaetarius that the jurist had in mind may have
been in charge of a room or rooms in the garden. Paulus, however,
using not diaetarius to be sure, but its equivalent zetarius, offers a context that suggests a slave in charge of an apartment.[10]

    The word diaeta is used to denote the cabin of a ship al-
so.[11] In the Digest there is reference to a diaetarius connected
with that sort of diaeta. Ulpian states expressly that his function was that of guardianship, that he was a person to whom one
could entrust his belongings with the expectation of their being
kept safely, and that he was appointed by the manager (exercitor)
of the ship. Ulpian's words are as follows:

> Et sunt quidam in navibus, qui custodiae gratia navibus
> praeponuntur, ut ναυφύλακες et diaetarii. Si quis igitur
> ex his receperit, puto in exercitorem dandam actionem, quia
> is, qui eos huiusmodi officio praeponit, committi eis permit-
> tit, quamquam ipse navicularius vel magister id faciat, quod
> χειρέμβολον appellant.[12]

    Focarius.--The focarius was another slave of the house-
hold. He appears but once in the Digest.[13] There focarii are

---

[1]CIL VI. 8771-2.   [2]CIL VI. 8770.

[3]CIL VI. 8771; 8767.   [4]Ulp. Dig. xxxiii. 7. 12. 42.

[5]Plin. Ep. ii. 17. 12.   [6]Plin. Ep. v. 6. 31.

[7]Dig. xxxix. 5. 32.   [8]See Note 5.

[9]Dig. xxx. 43. 1; Stat. Silv. ii. 2. 83.

[10]Paul. Sent. iii. 6. 58.   [11]Petr. 115.

[12]Ulp. Dig. iv. 9. 1. 3.

[13]Idem, Dig. iv. 9. 1. 5. See Note 2, p. 41.

classed as <u>mediastini</u>, slaves whose duties were menial, and as slaves working in inns were especially excepted from responsibility for belongings of patrons. We judge that there was a <u>collegium</u> of <u>focarii</u> from a reference to <u>Genius collegi (f)ocariorum</u>.[1] There is no evidence as to the duties of the <u>focarius</u>, but one assumes from the word itself and the evidence above that he had the care of the hearth, carried wood and kept the fires going.

 <u>Focaria</u>.--The <u>focaria</u> is mentioned more frequently than the <u>focarius</u> both in the <u>Digest</u> and elsewhere. In one citation, with the <u>vilica</u>, she is mentioned as belonging to the <u>instrumentum</u> of an estate - "item focariam et vilicam, si modo aliquo officio virum adiuvet."[2] In a second case she is mentioned among workers who shared in the preparation of wool.[3] In this case she may have kept the fires going for washing the wool and for the fullers. In both these cases we are dealing with a slave on an estate. The <u>focaria</u>, however, like the <u>focarius</u>, is expressly mentioned in the transfer of an inn, a bakery, or shops connected with them - "'quae tabernarum exercendarum instruendarum pistrini cauponae causa facta parataque sunt, do lego,' his verbis Servius respondit et caballos, qui in pistrinis essent, et pistores, et in cauponio institores et focariam mercesque....legatas videri."[4] Paulus lists the <u>focaria</u> as part of the <u>instrumentum</u> of a bakery - "conservandorum fructuum causa comparata instrumento cedunt, veluti dolia....pistores, asini, focariae."[5] The common function in these various situations may have been keeping up fires and she may have carried wood for that purpose.

 The word <u>focaria</u> appears in the <u>Vulgate</u> equivalent to μαχειρίσσα which appears in the <u>Septuagint</u>, and is rendered <u>cook</u> in the English versions.[6] Express mention of cooks by Ulpian almost immediately before the first mention of the <u>focaria</u> offers some evidence against the possibility of such interpretation here,

---

[1] W. Brambach, <u>Corpus Inscriptionum Rhenanarum</u> (Elberfeldae, 1867), 2041 add.

[2] Ulp. <u>Dig</u>. xxxiii. 7. 12. 5.

[3] <u>Idem</u>, <u>Dig</u>. xxxiii. 7. 12. 6. See Chapter II, Note 6, p. 34.

[4] Pompon. <u>Dig</u>. xxxiii. 7. 15. [5] Paul. <u>Sent</u>. iii. 6. 37.

[6] I Kings 8: 13. The word <u>cook</u> appears in English versions from Coverdale (1535) to and including the American revision by Smith (1931).

though it is hardly conclusive.[1] The word appears in the <u>Codex</u>
of Justinian[2] and in inscriptions[3] with the meaning <u>soldier's</u>
<u>concubine</u>.

<u>Fornacarius Servus</u>.--In the one case in which the <u>forni-</u>
<u>carius</u> (<u>sic</u>) <u>servus</u> appears, he is the slave of a peasant farmer.
He fell asleep at the furnace. The fire, unwatched, set fire to
the villa and it burned. He did not necessarily lay the fire,
but served as guardian of it. The judgment of the jurist is that
he should have put out the fire or should have provided such protection that it could not spread, if he was to yield to a natural
human weakness. Not having done so, he was responsible for the
burning of the farm-house. Ulpian's words are as follows:

> Si fornicarius servus coloni ad fornacem obdormisset et
> villa fuerit exusta, Neratius scribit ex locato conventum
> praestare debere, si neglegens in eligendis ministeriis fuit:
> ceterum si alius ignem subiecerit fornaci, alius neglegenter
> custodierit, an tenebitur qui subiecerit? Nam qui custodit,
> nihil fecit, qui recte ignem subiecit, non peccavit: quid
> ergo est? Puto utilem competere actionem tam in eum qui ad
> fornacem obdormivit quam in eum qui neglegenter custodit, nec
> quisquam dixerit in eo qui obdormivit, rem eum humanam et
> naturalem passum, cum deberet vel ignem extinguere vel ita
> munire, ne evagetur.[4]

Beyond this we know nothing of the <u>fornacarius</u> <u>servus</u> or his work.
Was his yielding to sleep indication of night work, of long hours
of monotonous and unexacting labor, or of warmth and quiet after
hard work out of doors, such as one would expect from a single
slave of a poor man? Of this there is no hint. Likewise nothing
is known as to what sort of <u>fornax</u> he was supposed to watch. It
may have been one for heating the bath of the villa as Mau thinks.[5]
If so, one wonders that the slave of the <u>colonus</u> was watching it
and feels that normally some one other than a <u>colonus</u> would be in
charge of a villa pretentious enough to have a bath. On the other
hand this slave may have been the wood gatherer for the furnace
used for baking bread, as the <u>focarius</u> was for the stove of the
house, as Marquardt thinks.[6] The word <u>fornax</u> appears with reference to that type of furnace[7] and this with certain drawings of

---

[1]See Note 2, p. 48.   [2]<u>Cod</u>. <u>Iust</u>. v. 16. 2.

[3]CIL XI. 39. See also Or. 2671.

[4]Ulp. <u>Dig</u>. ix. 2. 27. 9.   [5]A. Mau, PW <u>s</u>. <u>v</u>. <u>Fornax</u>.

[6]Marquardt, <u>Privatleben</u>, p. 146, note 4.

[7]Lact. i. 20. 35; Ov. <u>Fasti</u> ii. 523-6; vi. 313-4; 349,350.

such a furnace[1] lend credence to this latter view.

Aquarius.--In addition to these attendants who served in the house, workmen appear in the Digest whose service was rendered outside of the house. One of these was the aquarius. He appears once only in the Digest.[2] In that passage he is clearly a slave and is classed among slaves whose work was specialized and of a less unpleasant type. All of them were probably workers in a pleasure garden and this aquarius may have been a water boy who used sprinkling jars of the type that are found surviving.[3] Paulus refers to an aquarius of this same sort in a like context when he says: "Domo cum omni iure suo sicut instructa est legata urbana familia, item artifices et vestiarii et zetarii et aquarii itidem domui servientes legato cedunt."[4]

While this legal evidence presents a rather clear and simple picture, on the whole it is rather difficult to ascertain either the functions or the status of an aquarius. Though the word does not appear in Plautus, very menial functions are outlined for a person who might well be called an aquarius. The description is as follows:

> dabitur tibi amphora una et una semita,
> fons unus, unum ahenum et octo dolia:
> quae nisi erunt semper plena, ego te implebo flagris.
> ita te aggerunda curvom aqua faciam probe
> ut postilena possit ex te fieri.[5]

In the time of Cicero a slave who did the sprinkling, but again is not called aquarius is listed as under the direction of the atriensis.[6] Juvenal also gives the aquarius a very low rating, the aquarius in this case being either a hired freeman or a hired slave.[7] No hint of the function of the aquarius is given in Juvenal. These cases are all apparently aquarii of the city. The Digest itself gives evidence that in the country, too, there may have been work quite as humble and as onerous, though here again the person who did the work is not named - "vas aenum, in quo sapa coqueretur et defrutum fiat et aqua ad bibendum lavandamque familiam paratur."[8]

---

[1]DS s. v. Furnus.

[2]Ulp. Dig. xxxiii. 7. 12. 42.   See Note 7, p. 44.

[3]DS Fig. 7012, s. v. Topiarius.   [4]Paul. Sent. iii. 6. 58.

[5]Plaut. Cas. 121-125.   [6]See Note 3, p. 40.

[7]Iuv. vi. 332.   [8]Ulp. Dig. xxxiii. 7. 12. 10.

On the estates in the country and probably also in the
imperial palaces there seem to have been slaves serving as aquarii
who had a higher status and less menial duties than those just
discussed, possibly attending to the connections with aqueducts
and the entire province of water supply rather than serving as
mere water carriers.[1] To this class the aquarii mentioned by Ulpian and Paulus may possibly have belonged. The freemen who patrolled the aqueducts and controlled the tapping of aqueducts in
their assigned territory also were called aquarii.[2] Even these
aquarii were rated by Caelius among tabernarii as dregs of society.[3]

The Edict of Diocletian fixed the wages of the aquarius
at twenty five denarii per day when working.[4] Whether this aquarius was the man who patrolled the aqueducts or one working on a
private estate is not clear. The business at least was that of
a freeman or a slave hired out by his master.

Topiarius.--Another workman who rendered service outside
the house was the topiarius, who served as landscape gardener -
"topiarium enim ornandi....fundi magis quam colendi paratum esse."[5] Topiarii were usually slaves - "instrumento fundi saltuarium et topiarios."[6] Freedmen, however, appear in inscriptions
who were topiarii.[7] The topiarius potted and watered plants -
"Dolia fictilia, item plumbea, quibus terra adgesta est, et in
his viridiaria posita aedium esse Labeo Trebatius putant";[8] "Si
etiam viridiaria sint, topiarii."[9] He planted and landscaped
pleasure gardens,[10] protected plants from pests and parasites,
trimmed trees and bushes into shapes of animals, and trained
vines.[11] The necessity for apprenticeship, the fact that he was
a skilled workman, and the pleasant nature of the work may have
placed the topiarius among slaves of higher rank. Evidence of
this is lacking, however, inasmuch as the passage from Cicero[12]
cited by La Faye[13] as evidence is an interpolation rejected in

---

[1]CIL VI. 7973; 8653.   [2]Frontin. De Aq. ix.

[3]Cic. Ad. Fam. viii. 6. 4.   [4]Edict. Diocl. vii. 31.

[5]Alf. Dig. xxxii. 60. 3.   [6]Marcian. Dig. xxxiii. 7. 17. 2.

[7]CIL VI. 4360; 7300.   [8]Iavol. Dig. xxxiii. 7. 26.

[9]Ulp. Dig. xxxiii. 7. 8. 1.   [10]Col. x.

[11]Plin. N. H. xvi. 76; Firm. Math. viii. 10. 6.

[12]See Note 3, p. 40.   [13]La Faye, DS s. v. Hortulanus.

later texts. The watering of plants was in some cases probably done by a water boy, the aquarius.[1] The topiarius had other slaves learning the business from him.[2]

The word topiarius appears in the time of Cicero.[3] It occurs more often in the time of the empire, usually in connection with temple gardens, the imperial gardens, and the villas of the wealthy.[4]

Ornatrix.--The group of occupations just discussed is concerned chiefly with the care of the house. Another group appears consisting of people who primarily rendered personal service to those dwelling in the house. One of these is the ornatrix who probably served as lady's maid. The ornatrix that appears in the Digest was a slave. Marcianus makes clear that she was a trained servant and says that no slave in training could reach a point of proficiency such as to justify her being classed among skilled ornatrices in two months or less. He adds, however, that some jurists granted that slaves in training for a shorter time should be classed as ornatrices in the matter of legacies. Marcianus says: "Ornatricibus legatis Celsus scripsit eas, quae duos tantum menses apud magistrum fuerunt, legato non cedere, alii et has cedere, ne necesse sit nullam cedere, cum omnes adhuc discere possint et omne artificium incrementum recipit."[5] In Suetonius we find reference to a freedwoman who served as ornatrix.[6]

We have some evidence as to the actual work of the ornatrix. The word acus is defined by Festus as "qua sarcinatrix vel etiam ornatrix utitur."[7] A note in Servius's comment on the Aeneid which says: "nam calamistrum est acus maior, quae calefacta et adhibita intorquet capillos"[8] leads us to interpret the acus to which Festus refers as a curling iron. The curling iron, then, of which we have examples and illustrations, was one thing that she used.[9] There is good evidence also for the use of the acus crinalis,[10] which Ulpian mentions cum margarita.[11] This was the

---

[1]Ulp. Dig. xxxiii. 7. 12. 9. See Note 6, p. 44.

[2]CIL V. 5316. [3]Cic. Ad Q. F. iii. 1. 5.

[4]CIL X. 1744; VI. 9082. [5]Marcian. Dig. xxxii. 65. 3.

[6]Suet. Claud. 40. [7]Paul. ex Fest. p. 8 L.

[8]Serv. Aen. xii. 100.

[9]DS Fig. 992, s.v. Calamistrum; Gori, Insc. Etr. I. p.10. The latter appears with illustration indicated in CIL XI. 1471.

[10]Apul. Met. viii. 13. [11]Ulp. Dig. xxxiv. 2. 25. 10.

property of the mistress to be sure but surely used by the _ornatrix_ in performing the functions of her trade. A tombstone of an _ornatrix_ has on one side a comb, on the other a hairpin.[1] From all this we infer that she was chiefly a hairdresser. In that capacity the _ornatrix_ called _ornatrix puerorum_ probably served.[2] But she did more than dress hair. A scene from the _Mostellaria_ in which the word _ornatrix_ does not appear presents a slave who may have been an _ornatrix_.[3] In that scene bleaches, rouge, and creams are noted.[4] A scholium on Juvenal mentions _ornatrices_ as though their presence in the service of the mistress was to be taken for granted.[5]

Nutrix.--Another person in personal service was the _nutrix_. Usually the _nutrix_ that appears in the _Digest_ is a slave as in the following citations: "Stichus nutricis meae nepos liber esto";[6] "Si minor annis viginti manumittit, huius modi solent causae manumissionis recipi....";[7] "si educator, si paedagogus ipsius, si nutrix....dummodo non minor annis decem et octo sit."[8] In one case two _nutrices_ appear who have the names of freewomen and have legacies willed to them. The word may be used here as the feminine of _nutritor_,[9] in which case they were really foster mothers of the child, or they may have been slave nurses who had been set free. The passage is as follows:

> Qui Semproniam ex parte decima et Maeviam ex parte decima, alumnum ex reliquis partibus instituerat heredes, curatorem alumno dedit, cum iure facere putaret: et curatoris fidei commisit ne pateretur fundum venire, sed cum Sempronia et Maevia nutricibus suis frueretur reditu eius.[10]

One citation makes it clear that the _nutrix_ fed children from her own breast:

> Ad nutricia quoque officium praesidis vel praetoris devenit: namque nutrices ob alimoniam infantium apud praesides quod sibi debetur petunt. Sed nutricia eo usque producemus quoad infantes uberibus aluntur: ceterum post haec cessant partes praetoris vel praesidis.[11]

---

[1]CIL VI. 9727.   [2]CIL X. 1941.

[3]Plaut. _Most_. 157 ff.

[4]On the use of cosmetics see O. Wilner, "Roman Beauty Culture," _C. J._ XXVII (1931), pp. 26-38.

[5]Sch. Iuv. vi. 477.   [6]Scaev. _Dig_. xxxiv. 1. 20.

[7]Ulp. _Dig_. xl. 2. 11.   [8]_Ibid_. 13.

[9]Scaev. _Dig_. xxxiii. 7. 27.   [10]_Idem_, _Dig_. xxxiii. 2. 34. 1.

[11]Ulp. _Dig_. L. 13. 1. 14.

Nurses were supplied to the children of dotal maidservants and
any expense incurred in providing them was rightly charged to the
dowry. Paulus's word are: "Si quid in pueros ex ancillis dotali-
bus natos maritus impenderit aut in doctrinam aut alimenta, non
servatur marito....sed illud servatur quod nutrici datum est ad
educendum."[1] An allowance for maintenance for a nurse was judged
a prior claim against an owner - "Qui iam testato conventus a Pro-
cula nutrice Thetidis in solvendis alimentis respondit non se habere, unde alimenta eiusdem exsolvat, sed debere eam patri suo
restituere Lucio Titio....Seiae Proculae solutis alimentis."[2] The
nutrix of one's infancy served also when one was grown.[3] The
nurse is listed in a context that connotes a close tie of affection even when the child that she had nursed had become a man.[4]
In another case the nurse seems to have pressed claims for the
welfare of the child that she had cared for in infancy.[5]

This picture of the nurse drawn from the Digest is, on
the whole, the same as that drawn from literature. The relegation
of the child to the ministrations of a nurse instead of those of
its own mother is adversely commented on by more than one Roman
writer.[6] As an institution of Roman life, however, the nutrix
was accepted.[7] She continued to serve her charge far beyond the
age of childhood.[8] The nurse of Domitian cared for his body even
after his murder.[9] The nurse was retained and regarded with affection,[10] and her presence was a mark of honor to such an extent
that Juvenal pictures Ogulnia as hiring a nurse with other things
that would mark her as a woman of means and honor.[11]

As to the actual services of the nurse, we find that she
sang to children,[12] that she told them stories,[13] that she cons-
ciously influenced their ideas and conduct.[14] She fed them[15] and
taught them to eat, even putting in their mouths food that she

---

[1]Paul. Dig. xxiv. 1. 28. 1.   [2]Idem, Dig. xli. 7. 8.
[3]See Note 2 and Note 8, p. 53.   [4]See Note 8, p. 53.
[5]See Note 2.   [6]Tac. Ger.xx; Dial. 29; Gell. xii. 1.
[7]Cic. Tusc. iii. 1. 2; Quint. Inst. i. 1. 11.
[8]Liv. iii. 44. 7; Apul. Met. viii. 10.
[9]Suet. Dom. 17.   [10]Aen. iv. 632-3.
[11]Iuv. vi. 354.   [12]Pers. Sat. iii. 18.
[13]Tib. 1. 3. 85; Lucr.v. 230.   [14]Iuv. xiv. 208.
[15]Macr. Sat. v. 11. 15.

had chewed for them.[1] Greek sources picture her as pacifying the
child by striking the stone over which the child had stumbled,[2]
and Galen states with approval that a nurse may put a restless
child to sleep by nursing it, by moving it - the ancient version
of rocking it, one judges - or by singing to it.[3] Quintilian
pleads for excellence of diction as well as excellence of character in the nurse.[4]

Educator.--Personal service was rendered by the educator
also. He appears once in the Digest, in a list of slaves that a
master less than twenty years old may manumit.[5] Virtually the
same list appears in a like situation in the Institutes and in it
the educator again is found.[6] Gaius in a similar situation gives
a very brief list, which contains the paedagogus but not the educator.[7] No hint as to the function of the educator is given other
than the fact that he appears with the paedagogus and nutrix and
set apart from the alumnus. The word appears in inscriptions and
in the works of Latin authors also opposed to alumnus.[8] An inscription referring to Nicomedes, who is called educator in the
life of Verus,[9] uses the word nutritor to identify his service.[10]
This is evidence that the word is equivalent to nutritor.[11] This
idea is further suggested by the appearance of the word educator
with the verb nutrio.[12] This evidence leaves the impression that
slave educatores were responsible for the general care of the
child. In this they are to be differentiated from paedagogi, who
were responsible for attending the boy and assisting in his formal
training.[13] Free-born educatores are mentioned who were foster

---

[1]Cic. De Orat. ii. 162.   [2]Epict. Diss. iii. 194.

[3]Galen, De San. Tuend. i. 8 (Kühn, Vol. VI).

[4]Quint. Inst. i. 1. 11.

[5]Ulp. Dig. xl. 2. 13. See Note 8, p. 53.

[6]Inst. i. 6. 5.   [7]Gaius, Inst. i. 19; 39.

[8]CIL VI. 15983; 16844; Tert. Adv. Marc. i. 23.

[9]Capitol. Ver. ii. 9.   [10]CIL VI. 1598.

[11]See also W. M. Lindsay, Glossaria Latina (Paris, 1926),
II Abav. ED. 12.

[12]Lact. Inst. ii. 11. 9.

[13]This differentiation of paedagogus and educator is made
in spite of Furneaux's note (H. Furneaux, The Annals of Tacitus
(Oxford, 1907), xi. 1. 2 et al.) on the basis of Inst. I. 6. 5.
....paedagogum, nutricem, educatorem.

fathers of the boy.[1] All passages which offer any evidence at
all indicate that the _educator_ was held high in the esteem and affection of the man whom he had served.[2]

     Paedagogus.--Another member of the group that rendered
personal service was the _paedagogus_. He appears in the _Digest_ as
the personal attendant of Roman boys. He was considered so important a part of a Roman household that objection was raised to
freeing one who was to be manumitted in accordance with a will on
the ground that the heir's need of him was so great that it was
not expedient for him to be deprived of his services - "Gaii Cas-
sii non est recepta sententia existimantis et heredi et legatario
remittendam interdum proprii servi manumittendi necessitatem, si
vel usus tam necessarius esset ut eo carere non expediret, veluti
dispensatoris paedagogive liberorum."[3] The _paedagogus_ was one of
the slaves that a youth between the ages of eighteen and twenty
was permitted to free.[4] Apparently _paedagogi_ attended not only
children but the women of the household upon occasion. They are
expressly mentioned as one class of such _comites_ by Ulpian, who
says: "Inter comites utique paedagogi erunt."[5]

     Roman literature gives an even stronger picture of the
general prevalence and prominence of the _paedagogus_ in Roman life.
In spite of the statement of Plutarch,[6] corroborated by Tacitus,[7]
that bad slaves were chosen for the office though they should be
upright ones only, on the whole the impression that we gain of
the _paedagogus_ is favorable. He accompanied the boys to school
and listened in on the lessons that they learned there.[8] He went
to the theater[9] and to the tribunal[10] with his charges. So closely were _paedagogi_ identified with their charges that they were
slain with them in a general slaughter.[11] When a single boy was
murdered, his _paedagogus_ too lost his life in his effort to pro-

---

[1]Tac. _An._ xv. 62; Capitol. _Ver._ 11. 9; Val. Max. 11. 2. 9.
[2]Cic. _Planc._ 81; Sen. _Ben._ iii. 17. 4; CIL II. 4319.
[3]Maecian. _Dig._ xl. 5. 35.
[4]Ulp. _Dig._ xl. 2. 13. See Note 8, p. 53.
[5]_Idem_, _Dig._ xlvii. 10. 15. 16.
[6]Plut. _De Lib. Ed._ vii.   [7]Tac. _Dial. de Orat._ xxix.
[8]Suet. _De Gram._ 23.   [9]Suet. _Oct._ 44.
[10]Quint. _Inst._ vi. 1. 41.   [11]Suet. _Ner._ 36.

tect his charge.[1] The _paedagogus_ continued to serve his charge
at times far beyond the usual period of childhood.[2]

The methods whereby the _paedagogus_ trained the child in
the way he should go were often open to censure. He scolded,[3] he
tweaked ears,[4] he pinched,[5] he used the ferule,[6] he went about
with vinegary aspect,[7] he sometimes carelessly failed to hold the
youth to right performance, then punished him for his lapses.[8] In
spite of this array of pedagogical sins, which are ascribed in
their entirety to no single _paedagogus_, the _paedagogus_ performed
a function in the field of the inculcation of manners and morals
that met the approval of Seneca, who was no mean judge of moral
training.[9] As a final exhibit of the _paedagogus_ at his best we
may cite the inscription that has been found on the tombstone of
one _paedagogus_, an inscription which despite any granted charge
of smugness and complacency must be granted also a standard of
moral value worth inculcating into Roman youth. The pertinent
part of the inscription is as follows:

> vixi quam diu potui sine lite
> sine rixa sine controversia
> sine aere alieno amicis fidem
> bonam praestiti peculio
> pauper animo divitissimus[10]

The _paedagogus_[11] who was in charge of a _paedagogium_ does
not appear in the _Digest_. Reference is made there, however, to
the _paedagogium_.[12]

---

[1]App. _B. C._ iv. 30.   [2]Suet. _Claud._ 2.

[3]Plut. _Cat. Maior_, 20; Suet. _Ner._ 36.   [4]Plut. _loc. cit._

[5]See Note 10, p. 56.   [6]Mart. x. 62.

[7]Suet. _Ner._ 37.   [8]Quint. _Inst._ 1. 3. 15.

[9]Sen. _Ep._ 94. 8, 9; 25. 6; 89. 13; 60. 1.

[10]CIL VI. 8012.

[11]CIL VI. 8968-75. A _subpaedagogus_ appears in CIL VI. 8976,
a _praeceptor puerorum_ in CIL VI. 8978.

[12]Ulpian says that if an estate was willed with its equipment there were included the _paedagogia_, training schools which
the master had there that there might be attendants in the dining
room when he came - "ea paedagogia, quae ibi habebat, ut, cum ibi
venisset, praesto essent in triclinio." (_Dig._ xxxiii. 7. 12. 32).
Paulus includes among necessary expenses _doctrina puerorum_ (_Dig._
L. 16. 79. 1). The statements of the _Digest_ admit of the view,
at least, that _paedagogia_ existed that were institutions of a well
ordered house to keep things functioning smoothly. In literature
the picture of the _paedagogium_ consisting of _delicati_ is far more
prominent. Probably both sorts existed, the kind depending not
on the time, but on the master that maintained it.

Capsarius.--The capsarius also was engaged in personal
service. He appears in the Digest in three very different capacities, which will be discussed in turn.

One type of capsarius appears who is accurately defined
in the Digest as a slave who carried books, in this case, the context makes clear, the books of a schoolboy - "si....vel capsarius
(id est qui portat libros)."[1] In two other cases in Latin literature such a capsarius appears.[2] A gloss καμπτροφόρος indicates the same sort of service.[3]

The second sort of capsarius was a slave of a bath who
for a fee guarded the clothes of the bathers. Paulus's words concerning this capsarius are: "Adversus capsarios quoque, qui mercede servanda in balineis vestimenta suscipiunt, iudex est consti-
tutus, ut, si quid in servandis vestimentis fraudulenter admise-
rint, ipse cognoscat."[4] While the Digest does not expressly say
that he was a slave, one infers from the context that he was. Inscriptions show capsarii who were slaves,[5] one who was a freedman,[6] and one freeman.[7] It is impossible to judge, however, what
sort of capsarius each was, and inscriptions are few. A gloss
for capsarius gives as its equivalent εἱματοφύλαξ.[8] The fee
of the capsarius according to the Edict of Diocletian was two denarii per person.[9] That is a relatively high fee and may have
been set that a responsible person might be placed in charge of
the service. The citation from the Digest relates that a special
judge had been given cognizance of capsarii to prevent fraudulent
practices in the guarding of clothes. Numerous references in
literary sources make it clear that the clothes intrusted to the
slaves were stolen.[10] In some cases the capsarius was not a bath
slave at all, but one from the establishment of the master.[11]
Even he seems to have stolen garments left in his charge.[12]

The last type of capsarius was not a slave at all, but
was in the army. Of these capsarii Tarruntenus Paternus says:

---

[1]Ulp. Dig. xl. 2. 13.

[2]Suet. Ner. 36; Aug. in Ps. xl. 14. The name does not appear, but the function is indicated in Iuv. x. 117.

[3]CGL III. 199. 16.   [4]Paul. Dig. 1. 15. 3. 5.

[5]CIL VI. 6245.   [6]CIL VI. 7368.   [7]CIL V. 3158.

[8]CGL III. 307. 60.   [9]Edict. Diocl. vii. 75.

[10]Petr. 92. 7; Dig. xlvii. 17; Tert. De Fug. xiii.

[11]Petr. 30.   [12]Ibid.

"Quibusdam aliquam vacationem munerum graviorum condicio tribuit,
ut sunt....capsarii."[1] Inscriptions appear which indicate that
the capsarius was actually a soldier.[2] What his duties were we
do not know, but they seem to have required some skill, as we find
apprentices mentioned in an inscription.[3]

Nomenclator.--Another person whose service was distinctly
personal was the nomenclator. The jurists that mention him in
the Digest were especially interested in the fact that his was a
service that youth could render. In one case the young person
was a slave - "Potest tamen et impubes operas dare, veluti si no-
menculator sit vel histrio."[4] In the other case he was a freedman
- "Dabitur et in impuberem (libertum), cum adoleverit, operarum
actio: sed interdum et quamdiu impubes est....si forte....vel no-
menculator."[5] This matter of youth is mentioned by Pliny also.[6]
Seneca mentions a little old fellow who served as nomenclator who
failed to remember names and substituted others.[7] The reason for
the use of younger persons for the work is thus made clear, the
necessity for a good memory. The point is emphasized repeatedly
by Latin authors.[8] Failure to remember seems to have been fairly
common,[9] and the substitution of another name to cover the failure
was the usual remedy.[10]

The services that the nomenclator rendered were various.
He was expected to know the names of the people the master would
meet.[11] He whispered information to the master,[12] and nudged him
by way of warning when he was expected to recognize someone.[13] He
was sent upon occasion to seek out a person that his master wanted.[14] In large establishments he alone knew the names of all the
slaves.[15] He gave information about food at dinners.[16] He ren-

---

[1]Tarr. Pat. Dig. L. 6. 7 (6).   [2]CIL XIII. 5623.

[3]CIL VIII. 2553. This interpretation seems valid rather
than that of L. Renier, Inscriptions romains de l'Algierie (Paris,
1855-1886), n. 63.

[4]Venul. Dig. xl. 12. 44. 2.   [5]Ulp. Dig. xxxviii. 1. 7.5.

[6]Plin. Ep. ii. 14. 6.   [7]Sen. Ep. 27. 5.

[8]Sen. Ben. vi. 33. 4; Plin. N. H. xxix. 19.

[9]Macr. Sat. ii. 4. 15.   [10]Sen. Ben. i. 3. 10.

[11]Cic. Att. iv. 1. 5; Hor. Ep. i. 6. 49.

[12]Sen. De Brev. Vit. xiv. 4.   [13]Hor. Ep. i. 6. 49-51.

[14]Quint. Inst. vi. 3. 93.   [15]Plin. N. H. xxxiii. 6. 26.

[16]Petr. 47. 8.

dered service at the salutatio[1] as well as when the master was away from the house.[2] In some cases he reached a position so influential that he admitted or refused to admit visitors[3] and dispensed invitations to dinner.[4] Some nomenclators treated guests with haughty disdain.[5] Others even received bribes from them.[6] In this picture of progression from service to domination, it is a relief to find that not all masters were so dominated by the nomenclator. We are told, for example, that Hadrian gave names without his assistance and even corrected the nomenclator.[7]

Most nomenclators served men of prominence in the state, men of wealth, or members of the imperial family. One case appears, however, in which a nomenclator was the slave of a woman.[8]

Tonsor.--Another group that rendered personal service within the house was the slaves who served as barbers. Barbers on the whole, however, operated outside the home and are discussed, accordingly, among those that ply their trade apart from the household.

Cursor.--In addition to groups of people who rendered service within or about the house directly concerned with the upkeep and care of the house and premises and to those who served the occupants of the house, we find a group whose field of service was entirely out of the house. One member of this group was the cursor. He appears once only in the Digest, and we learn then that he was a slave and, in some instances at least, a slave born on the premises. Paulus says: "Si alii vernae, alii cursores legati sunt, si quidam et vernae et cursores sint, cursoribus cedent: semper enim species generi derogat."[9] Glosses indicate that there were two types of cursores, those who were literally runners, who carried messages or letters speedily, defined by the word ταχυ-δρόμος,[10] and those who served as attendants of the master, pedisequi according to the gloss.[11] Cursores of the former kind appear at all periods of Roman history. Such messengers appear in

[1]Sen. Ep. 19. 11. [2]Cic. Att. iv. 1. 5.

[3]Sen. De Tran. An. xii. 6. [4]See Note 1.

[5]See Note 11, p. 44.

[6]Lucian. De Merc. Cond. 10; Amm. xiv. 6. 15.

[7]Spart. Had. 20. 9. [8]Suet. Oct. 19.

[9]Paul. Dig. xxxii. 99. 5. [10]CGL II. 452. 19.

[11]CGL V. 283. 10.

comedy,[1] and are common in imperial times.[2] The special sandals whose price is listed in the <u>Edict</u> of Diocletian were probably for this type of <u>cursor</u>.[3] The <u>cursores</u> who received training in the house of Trimalchio may have been of this type,[4] though inscriptions referring to an <u>exercitator</u>[5] and <u>doctor cursorum</u>,[6] who seem to have been trainers of <u>cursores</u> in attendance upon the master, suggest that type of <u>cursor</u> there also.

The <u>cursores</u> who appear as escorts of emperors or private citizens are found in imperial times. Usually they were mounted,[7] were themselves splendidly arrayed,[8] and on horses handsomely caparisoned.[9] As a rule a large number of <u>cursores</u> preceded the master,[10] but cases occur from which one may judge that a single attendant rode ahead.[11] The <u>collegium</u> of <u>cursores</u> and Numidians rather certainly consisted of <u>cursores</u> of this type.[12]

A <u>cursor ludi magni</u>[13] and <u>cursor factionis prasinae et supra cursores</u>[14] seem to have been <u>venatores</u>, possibly mounted,[15] who fought with beasts in the arena. It is possible that the <u>cursores</u> to whom, with the <u>venatores</u>, the little pig willed his ankle-bones were <u>cursores</u> of this type,[16] though they are usually interpreted as runners of the first type.[17]

<u>Pedisequus</u>.--Another attendant of the master's when he went forth from the house was the <u>pedisequus</u>.[18] <u>Pedisequi</u>, who

---

[1]Plaut. <u>Poen</u>. 546.

[2]Suet. <u>Ner</u>. 49; <u>Tit</u>. 9; Apul. <u>Met</u>. x. 5 (Oud. 688).

[3]<u>Edict</u>. Diocl. ix. 14. See Blümner, <u>Maximaltarif</u>, p. 128.

[4]Petr. 29. 7.   [5]CIL VIII. 12622; 12905.

[6]CIL VIII. 12904.   [7]Suet. <u>Ner</u>. 30.

[8]Mart. iii. 47. 13.   [9]See Note 7.

[10]Sen. <u>Ep</u>. 87. 9; 123. 7.

[11]Mart. xii. 24; Lampr. <u>Alex</u>. 42. 2.

[12]CIL VIII. 12905 and Note 10. Mommsen offers an entirely different interpretation. See CIL VIII. Sup. 1, p. 1337.

[13]CIL VI. 10165.   [14]CIL VI. 33944; 33950.

[15]Sen. <u>Ep</u>. 87. 9.   [16]<u>Testamentum Porcelli</u>.

[17]See TLL <u>s</u>. <u>v</u>. <u>Cursor</u>.

[18]That the <u>pedisequus</u> himself went on foot is clear. When the master travelled outside the city he was attended by <u>cursores</u> (See <u>Cursor</u>). Chapot (DS <u>s</u>. <u>v</u>. <u>Servi</u>, p. 1276) thinks that the <u>pedisequus</u> attended him in the city whether he walked or went by litter. In favor of this opinion is the fact that the <u>pedisequa</u> surely accompanied the mistress when in her litter (See <u>Pedisequa</u>).

both in the Digest and in other references to them[1] appear in
groups and never as a single individual, were slaves who were disposed of by will in cases reported in the Digest. Papinianus mentions them in the following words: "Idem in familia erit sive....
legaverit ac postea servorum officia vel ministeria mutaverit.
Eadem sunt lecticariis aut pedisequis legatis."[2] One testator who
left his attendants to care for a temple requested the heir to
give them a monthly allowance of provisions and a yearly allowance
of clothing - "peto fideique tuae committo, des praestes in memoriam meam pedisequis meis, quos ad curam templi reliqui, singulis
menstrua cibaria et annua vestiaria certa."[3] This seems to have
been a humane provision for slaves to whom the master was attached. The pedisequus as a rule, however, does not seem to have been
rated very highly by the Roman world. In the Poenulus it is suggested that pedisequi rushed to the wine shop while the plays went
on.[4] When Nepos mentions the fact that Atticus had all his slaves
trained to read aloud and transcribe, we are told that even pedisequi were so trained, the implication being that this was a surprising achievement.[5]

     Pedisequa.--The pedisequa also served outside the house.
The pedisequae that appear in the Digest were slaves, and we find
that several of them served one mistress - "Titia servis quibusdam
et ancillis nominatim directas libertates dedit, deinde ita scripsit: 'et pedisequas omnes, quarum nomina in rationibus meis
scripta sunt, liberas esse volo.'"[6] In a passage in the Andria
likewise we find several pedisequae accompanying their mistress.
Their function is there clear. They were the personal attendants
of the mistress when she went forth from the house.[7] In Plautus,
on the other hand, we find but one attendant accompanying the mistress,[8] and that in one case an old woman, the girl's nurse.[9]

     The duties of the pedisequa may be listed by Ovid in the

---

Marquardt (Privatleben, p. 147), however, thinks that the pedisequus was in attendance only when the master went on foot. The
Digest's "lecticariis aut pedisequis legatis" admits of either
interpretation.

    [1]Plaut. Aul. 501; Poen. 41; Nep. Att. 13.
    [2]Papin. Dig. xxxi. 65.   [3]Scaev. Dig. xxxiv. 1. 17.
    [4]Plaut. Poen. 41.   [5]Nep. Att. 13.
    [6]Scaev. Dig. xl. 4. 59.   [7]Ter. And. 123.
    [8]Plaut. As. 183.   [9]Idem, Aul. 807.

Ars Amatoria, though the name does not appear.[1] The services
there mentioned are the carrying of the parasol for the girl, making way for the litter in a crowd, drawing out the stool for her
to step up to a couch, taking off and putting on her sandals. The
last thing mentioned, holding her mirror, suggests the ornatrix
rather than the pedisequa.

Lecticarius.--Another important service rendered outside
the house was that of the lecticarius, who was the litter bearer -
"Item legato continentur mancipia, puta lecticarii, qui solam mat-
rem familias portabant."[2] The lecticarii that appear in the Digest were slaves - "Eadem sunt lecticariis aut pedisequis legatis."[3] Cicero classes them as vulgares.[4] The Digest makes clear
the fact that in legacies they went in sets rather than as individuals - "Itemque quadrigae aut lecticariorum stipulatio una
est."[5] The number constituting a set here was eight - "Si ita
legatum sit: 'lecticarios octo aut pro his in homines singulos
certam pecuniam, utrum legatarius volet.'"[6] This number corresponds with that of the carriers whom Catullus reported purchased
in Asia Minor.[7] From other Latin authors we learn that sets of
six also were used.[8] There were legacies, however, in which individuals were consigned by will, as a citation from Marcianus
makes clear.[9] This was probably true when the number of slaves
was so small that one served in several capacities or when the
number was so large that there were slaves in training, who served
as understudies for several slaves whose work differed. The lecticarius of this sort appears in the citation quoted as cook,
weaver, or litter carrier. In another citation he appears as cook
and litter bearer.[10] This doubling of roles of slaves may be the
explanation of the manuscript reading lecticarius in the Cena Trimalchionis, and a strong argument for the retention of the original reading.[11] If this is the key to the situation, the employment of the lecticarius in such fashion was a mark both of the

---

[1]Ov. Ars Am. ii. 209 ff.   [2]Ulp. Dig. xxxii. 49.
[3]Papin. Dig. xxxi. 65.   [4]Cic. Pro Rosc. Am. xlvi. 134.
[5]Ulp. Dig. xlv. 1. 29.   [6]Pompon. Dig. xxx. 8. 2.
[7]Catull. x. 20.   [8]Mart. ii. 81; vi. 77. 4.
[9]Marcian. Dig. xxxii. 65. 2. See Chapter I, Note 1, p. 28.
[10]Paul. Dig. xxxii. 99. 4. See Chapter I, Note 2, p. 28.
[11]Petr. 34. 3.

wealth of the establishment and of the economical and efficient administration elsewhere stressed.

One citation previously quoted mentions bearers who carried the mistress of the house only.[1] Lamer mentions this as proof of the fact that these carriers were in a position of responsibility and trust.[2] The fact that his litter bearers defended Caligula at the time of his murder is further fortification for this position.[3] Marquardt[4] and Girard,[5] however, consider the mistress's having her own bearers an indication that often a house would have many lecticae with carriers for each. This opinion is reinforced by inscriptions referring to a slave supra lecticarios[6] or praepositus lecticariorum.[7]

The last citation that we have to consider mentions the matter of livery for carriers, in this case again the carriers of the wife - "Idem quaesiit, an....vestis, quam ancillis vel lecticariis eiusdem uxoris suae comparaverat vel fecerat, praestanda esset."[8] From other sources we learn what sort of livery was worn. Some wore a paenula and were trapped out like soldiers.[9] Others were clad in red.[10]

The litter seems to have been used outside of the city as well as within it.[11]

There existed across the Tiber the so-called castra lecticariorum.[12] What it was is not clear. Lamer insists that it was the place where the lecticarii stayed who served officials such as the tabellarii.[13] Marquardt thinks that there were lecticae for hire that may have been kept there.[14] The military or imperial connection that one expects from the use of the word castra is not apparent in either case.

---

[1]Dig. xxxii. 49. See Note 2, p. 63.

[2]PW s. v. Lectica, p. 1097.   [3]Suet. Cal. 58.

[4]Marquardt, Privatleben, p. 149.

[5]DS s. v. Lectica, p. 1004.   [6]CIL VI. 5198.

[7]CIL VI. 8875.   [8]Scaev. Dig. xxxiv. 2.13.

[9]Sen. De Ben. iii. 28. 5.   [10]Mart. ix. 22. 9.

[11]Sen. Ep. 31. 10.

[12]L. Preller, Die Regionen der Stadt Rom (Jena, 1846), pp. 218-9.

[13]PW s. v. Lectica, pp. 1093-4.

[14]Privatleben, p. 737.

A _collegium_ _lecticariorum_ appears in inscriptions,[1] which Liebenam[2] and Waltzing[3] think was a burial association.

Evidence does not appear that the word was used to denote a maker of _lecticae_.[4]

Tabellarius.--Another service rendered outside of the house was that of the _tabellarius_, who appears in one citation in the _Digest_. He was presumably a slave who was sent by his master with a letter. He was given a letter in reply. The writer disclaimed all responsibility for the letter after it was given to the _tabellarius_. The words of Paulus are: "Immo contra: nam si miseris ad me tabellarium tuum et ego rescribendi causa litteras tibi misero, simul atque tabellario tuo tradidero, tuae fient."[5] This is clearly an instance of the _tabellarius_ maintained in the private service of well-to-do citizens,[6] or of those that had messages of importance to send.[7] The use of the _tabellarius_ on the return trip to carry the reply to the letter was usual.[8] The fact that responsibility for the letter was disclaimed reminds us that the difficulty of finding reliable carriers was always prominent when the subject was mentioned.[9]

In addition to these carriers for private individuals, we find carriers attached to certain groups of people in certain businesses, most prominently the _publicani_, who seem to have had a particularly efficient service.[10] These _tabellarii_ were used by private individuals who wished to send letters in the direction in which they were going.[11] For those who did not have their own carriers or did not find those of others that they could use, there seems to have been a group of carriers serving for hire.[12]

---

[1]CIL VI. 6218.

[2]W. Liebenam, _Zur Geschichte und Organisation des Römische Vereinswesens_ (Leipzig, 1890), p. 130.

[3]J. P. Waltzing, _Étude Historique sur les Corporations Professionnelles chez les Romains_ (Louvain, 1895), IV, p. 157.

[4]Blümner (_Technologie_, II, p. 327, n. 4) says that the word was always used for carriers. Humbert (DS _s. v. Arcarii_) and Girard (DS _s. v. Lectica_, p. 1004) consider it used for makers of _lecticae_ as well. The _lectarius_ and _faber lectarius_ (CIL VI. 9503; 7882; 7988) were entirely different people, the makers of _lectus_.

[5]Paul. _Dig._ xli. 1. 65.   [6]Cic. _Fam._ viii. 8. 10.
[7]Cic. _Ad Q. F._ ii. 12. 3.   [8]Cic. _Fam._ xv. 17. 1.
[9]Cic. _Att._ v. 17. 1; Plin. _Ep._ ii. 12; viii. 3.
[10]Cic. _Att._ v. 16. 1.   [11]Cic. _Att._ v. 15. 3.
[12]Cic. _Att._ viii. 14.

Quite apart from this service privately maintained by and for private individuals and those in business, there is indisputable evidence of a state service existing from very early times.[1] This service was maintained and augmented by various emperors.[2] A castra tabellariorum across the Tiber may have been the quarters of tabellarii in the service of the state.[3] The use of the word castra, however, suggests military tabellarii, and it is known that not only were there slaves[4] and freedmen[5] in the service of the government, but freemen, soldiers, who carried military dispatches.[6]

The tabellarius may have travelled on foot upon occasion,[7] he may have used a litter in the city,[8] but our most certain evidence shows that he travelled by some sort of vehicle.[9] The tabellarii in the service of the state had regular stations for the changing of horses.[10] They wore the petasus,[11] and carried some sort of tessera[12] or diploma[13] for identification.

A collegium of tabellarii existed, in this case probably a burial association.[14]

---

[1]Strabo v. 4. 13; CIL I. 551 (1863); 638 (1893).

[2]Suet. Aug. 49; CIL X. 1741.

[3]H. Jordan, Topographie der Stadt Rom (Berlin, 1871), II, p. 574.

[4]CIL VI. 6342.   [5]CIL VI. 9915.

[6]Dio Cass. lxxviii. 14.

[7]Cic. Att. ix. 7. 1; Fam. xv. 17. 1.

[8]Lamer, PW s. v. Lectica.   [9]Petr. 79. 6.

[10]CIL I. 551 (1863); 638 (1893).   [11]Cic. Fam. xv. 17. 1.

[12]See Note 5.

[13]Plin. Ep. x. 64 (14). (M. Schuster, Teubner, 1933).

[14]CIL III. 6077; VIII. 1878; XII. 4449.

CHAPTER IV

OCCUPATIONS CONCERNED WITH TRANSPORTATION

Another group of occupations that required the service of humbler men was that centered about transportation. Some of these people were in the service of the individual traveller. Others belonged to groups that served the travelling public. Certain ones were engaged in the transportation of things of one kind or another.

Agaso.--One group of persons concerned with transportation was that of the agasones. The agasones that appear in the Digest were slaves. The Digest implies that the agaso belonged to the familia urbana, but certainly not to that portion of it that rendered personal service to the master. The words of Alfenus are: "Servis et ancillis urbanis legatis agasonem mulionem legato non contineri respondi: eos enim solos in eo numero haberi, quos pater familias circum se ipse sui cultus causa haberet."[1] Another citation implies that he did not belong to the familia rustica - "Agasonem enim missum in villam a patre familias non pertinere ad fundi legatum Mucius ait, quia non idcirco illo erat missus, ut ibi esset."[2] In another citation a tale is told of an agaso that had his leg broken by the kick of a mule when he led a horse into an inn - "Agaso cum in tabernam equum deduceret, mulam equus olfecit, mula calcem reiecit et crus agasoni fregit: consulebatur, possetne cum domino mulae agi, quod ea pauperiem fecisset. Respondi posse."[3] It is clear, then, that the agaso was a slave that cared for horses. As he is associated with a mulio in the first citation, we assume that his service somewhat corresponded to that of the mulio. We assume from the first two passages quoted above that he was the caretaker of horses of his master. Most literary references support this assumption.[4] One literary reference admits of the interpretation that he was a groom con-

---

[1]Alf. Dig. xxxii. 60. 1.   [2]Ulp. Dig. xxviii. 5. 35. 3.
[3]Alf. Dig. ix. 1. 5.
[4]Paul. Fest. 23 L; Porph. on Hor. Sat. ii. 8. 72; Serv. Aen. iii. 470.

nected with a stable, and has been so interpreted. Curtius in
recounting the training of certain young men says: "acceptos ab
agasonibus equos, cum rex ascensurus esset, admovebant."[1] So interpreted, this reference lends support to the theory that the
agaso mentioned in the passage last quoted from the Digest was a
hostler connected with the inn. A gloss states clearly that agasones had the care of horses.[2] Our conclusion is that the agaso
had the care of horses, that he might be in the service of a master either in the villa urbana or in a villa rustica, or that he
might be connected with a stable for the service of travellers.

Strator.--Stratores also served travellers. The stratores that appear in the Digest were freemen - "Quibusdam aliquam
vacationem munerum graviorum condicio tribuit, ut sunt....lapi-
darii....stratores."[3] Freemen appear in inscriptions[4] also, though
both slaves[5] and freedmen[6] are found there. The strator served
emperors[7] and other officials of the state.[8] Proconsuls, however,
were forbidden to have their own stratores, but soldiers performed
the duties of stratores for them - "Nemo proconsulum stratores
suos habere potest, sed vice eorum milites ministerio in provinciis funguntur."[9] The word itself leads one to believe that the
duties of the strator included the saddling of the horse and probably that would be a term sufficiently elastic to include everything necessary to prepare the horse for riding. The actual accounts of the work of the strator, however, deal with assisting
the emperor or general to mount.[10]

Military stratores appear in large numbers.[11] In later
times the functions of these military stratores were enlarged to
include trying out and approving horses purchased for military
purposes.[12] Later a strator appears in the Codex of Theodosian
who seems to have had the task of guarding prisoners.[13] He also
was attached to the army, if he was the same person referred to
by Symmachus, who wrote at about the same period.[14]

Iunctor.--The appearance of the iunctor in the Digest,

---

[1]Curt. viii. 6. 4.   [2]CGL V. 583. 7.
[3]Tarr. Pat. Dig. L. 6. 7 (6).   [4]CIL X. 7580.
[5]CIL VI. 6352.   [6]CIL VI. 4888.   [7]Amm. xxx. 5. 19.
[8]Eph. Ep. IV. pp. 406-7.   [9]Ulp. Dig. 1. 16. 4. 1.
[10]Spart. Car. vii. 2.   [11]CIL II. 4114.   See also note 8.
[12]Amm. xxix. 3. 5.   [13]Cod. Theod. ix. 3. 1.
[14]Symm. Ep. x. 38 (Seeck).

apparently the sole appearance of the word in Latin literature,
gives no information as to the work of the iunctor. The question
is raised as to what slaves a Roman dwelling in Sicily may bring
or send back to Rome duty free. The decision of the jurist was
that those slaves that the master had for his own use might be
brought in. He further defined such slaves as the slaves that he
had for the care and protection of his own body, illustrating his
definition by a list headed by iunctores and containing valets,
cooks, waiters at the table, and others (alii). The words of Alfenus are as follows: "Et sibi videri eos demum usus sui causa
patrem familias habere, qui ad eius corpus tuendum atque ipsius
cultum praepositi destinatique essent, quo in genere iunctores,
cubicularii, coci, ministratores."[1] This definition of intimate
personal service has driven commentators away from the interpretation of iunctores as yokers of animals, which is attested by
glosses[2] and by two inscriptions,[3] and which fits perfectly into
the situation of the passage cited but for the definition immediately preceding. That the definition represents a narrower use
of the term than even the usual juristic usage is showed by a
passage from Ulpian - "item iumentorum, quae dominici usus causa
parata sunt."[4] Quintilian mentions further as tax free such
things as may be classed as instrumenta itineris.[5] That class
might very well include such iunctores. We may have here, then,
parts of two categories brought together, an assimilation that is
possibly not the work of the jurist that originally defined suo
usu.

The interpretation dresser of wounds given by certain
commentators[6] has no basis other than the fact that it is in harmony with the definition and that the verb iungo is used in con-

---

[1] Alf. Var. Dig. L. 16. 203.

[2] CGL III. 367. 31; 74. 48; 173. 58; 241. 5.

[3] CIL VI. 31338a; 31369. See Waltzing, Corporations, IV,
p. 26, n. 63 and III, p. 313; also K. Sittl, Archiv für Lateinische
Lexikographie, I (1884), p. 318. Georges (K. E. Georges,
Ausführliches Lateinisch-Deutsches Handwörterbuch (Hanover und
Leipzig, 1918)) agrees with this interpretation.

[4] Ulp. Dig. xxxiii. 9. 3.

[5] Quint. Declam. ccclix. See also R. L. V. Cagnat, Étude
Historique sur les Impôts Indirects (Paris, 1882), p. 106.

[6] E. g. H. Meyer-Lübke, Romanisches Etymologisches Wörterbuch (Heidelberg, 1911), s. v. Iunctor.

nection with the dressing of wounds. That connection, however, is not such as to leave one feeling that the case is clear. In one case a salve serves as an astringent that draws the edges of a wound together;[1] in another the taking of the stitches draws the edges together.[2] When a personal subject appears, we are told that doctors draw the edges together by sewing.[3] In the one literary reference that is not a technical treatise on medicine the text is uncertain. The emendation to iungere seems fairly certain, however, and gives the reading "vulnera doctum iungere."[4] In short, this review of the evidence seems to indicate that iungo is not a highly technical word in medicine, and that the medicus, not a special iunctor, would perform the functions indicated.

Victorius emended the passage in the Digest by substituting unctor, a word that occurs frequently and fits into the definition of personal service. The appearance of unctor and unctura in glosses, defining ζευγτής and ζεῦξις respectively,[5] shows that there was confusion in the words iunctor and unctor and lends some support to the idea.

The conclusion to which the evidence leads one is that it is possible to retain the reading of the text and the normal interpretation of the word, although there is no very certain evidence as to who this iunctor was nor what his functions were.

Cisiarius.--In addition to this group just discussed, a group is found who served the public for hire. One of these is the cisiarius. He appears in inscriptions as a slave,[6] or as a freedman[7] as a rule. He was the driver of the light two-wheeled cisium, the vehicle that was used for rapid transportation by the Romans.[8] It was sometimes drawn by three mules.[9] In the citation in the Digest a case is given in which the driver, in his haste to pass others, overturned his vehicle and shook up or killed a slave. The jurist's decision was that he was liable for action ex locato, which makes it clear that he had rented out the services

---

[1]Scrib. Comp. 206.   [2]Cels. v. 26. 23.   [3]Cels. vii. 17. L.
[4]Stat. Theb. x. 733.   [5]CGL II. 322. 3.   [6]CIL X. 6342.
[7]CIL I. 1129 (1863); 1446 (1893); xiv. 2874.
[8]Verg. App. Cat. x. 3; Cic. Phil. ii. 31.
[9]Auson. Ep. iv. 6 (R. Pieper, Ausonii Opuscula [Leipzig, 1886]). That the animals used were mules is assumed on the basis of Capitol. Max. xxx. 6. A vehicle that is probably a cisium appears in reliefs. In one case it is drawn by two horses (See DS s.v. cisium), in others by one horse (See A. Mau, PW s.v. cisium).

of his vehicle and of himself as driver. The jurist adds that he
should have exercised reasonable self-restraint in driving. Ulpian's words are: "Item quaeritur, si cisiarius, id est carucarius, dum ceteros transire contendit, cisium evertit et servum quas-
savit vel occidit. Puto ex locato esse in eum actionem: tempera-
re enim debuit."[1]

Barring this citation, the word appears in inscriptions
only. There groups of drivers appear, indicating either that the
drivers were banded together into a collegium as is suggested by
the words Cisiariei Praenestinei which appear in an inscription,[2]
or that there were established locations for them corresponding
to cab-stands as is suggested by "....ab ianu ad gisiarios por-
ta(e) Stellatinae...."[3] One inscription has been used in an effort to prove that the cisiarius was a maker of cisia.[4] The inscription reads as follows:

> L. Tampius L f Peccio
> cisiar vivos fecit sibi et
> Maximae Oppiae C f
> uxori et Q. Oppio C f
> vivit[5]

The cisiarius in this case is a freeman. The entire inscription
impresses one as belonging to a greater personage than the ordinary driver of a cisium. That he was the owner of cisia with
slave drivers doing the work is at least as fair a guess as that
he was the maker of cisia. The only thing that we can be sure
of is that the cisiarius drove the cisium.

Carrucarius.--The word carucarius (sic) appears once in
the Digest, there thrown in parenthetically in explanation of the
word cisiarius.[6] One suspects that this is a marginal note that
got into the text, written perhaps at a time when the carruca was
better known than the cisium. The carrucarius was probably really
the driver of the carruca. The carruca, a four-wheeled carriage,
was drawn by mules - "Quaesitum est, si mula talis sit, ut trans-
iungi non possit, an sana sit. Et ait Pomponius sanam esse:
plerasque denique carrucarias tales esse, ut non possint trans-
iungi."[7] The drivers were called muliones carrucarii by Capito-
linus.[8]

---

[1]Ulp. Dig. xix. 2. 13.　　[2]CIL XIV. 2874.
[3]CIL X. 4660.　　[4]E. g. by Orelli, 4163.
[5]CIL XI. 6215.　[6]Ulp. Dig. xix. 2. 13. See Note 1.
[7]Idem, Dig. xxi. 1. 38. 8.　[8]Capitol. Max. xxx. 6.

Mulio.--Of the groups engaged in transportation the one
that appears most frequently in the Digest is that of the muliones, the drivers of mules. The Digest is rather illuminating with
regard to the troubles of muleteers. If his mules ran away and
injured another man's slave, the muleteer was responsible whether
the accident was due to lack of skill in handling mules or to lack
of strength. Apropos of the mention of lack of strength, Gaius
adds that no one should undertake a task in which he knew or should
know that his lack of strength would jeopardize another. Gaius's
words are as follows:

> Mulionemque quoque, si per imperitiam impetum mularum re-
> tinere non potuerit, si eae alienum hominem obtriverint, vulgo
> dicitur culpae nomine teneri.   Idem dicitur et si propter in-
> firmitatem sustinere mularum impetum non potuerit: nec vide-
> tur iniquum, si infirmitas culpae adnumeretur, cum affectare
> quisque non debeat, in quo vel intellegit vel intellegere de-
> bet infirmitatem suam alii periculosam futuram.[1]

If a man had hired out a slave to drive a mule, the slave
fastened the mule to his thumb by a halter, and the mule broke
away in such fashion as to tear out the slave's thumb and go head
over heels himself, the master of the slave was liable for the
injury to the mule if he had let out an unskilled slave as skilled.
If, however, the slave was not at fault, both the master of the
slave and the owner of the mule could look for damages to the person that had caused the trouble. Ulpian reports the incident
thus:

> Si quis servum conductum ad mulum regendum commendaverit
> et mulum ille ad pollicem suum eum alligaverit de loro et mu-
> lus eruperit sic, ut et pollicem avelleret servo et se prae-
> cipitaret, Mela scribit, si pro perito imperitus locatus sit,
> ex conducto agendum cum domino ob mulum ruptum vel debilita-
> tum, sed si ictu aut terrore mulus turbatus sit, tum dominum
> eius, id est muli, et servi cum eo qui turbavit habiturum le-
> gis Aquiliae actionem.[2]

An incident is told of two loaded wagons (plaustra) that
were being drawn up the Capitoline Hill. The muleteers of the
first, to help the struggling mules, got behind their wagon and
pushed. It began to slip back and they jumped aside with the result that it hit the second wagon and the latter ran over a slave
boy. The jurist's decision as to responsibility takes into consideration all possible reasons for the first wagon's getting out
of control. Alfenus says:

---

[1]Gaius, Dig. ix. 2. 8. 1.   [2]Ulp. Dig. ix. 2. 27. 34.

In clivo Capitolino duo plostra onusta mulae ducebant:
prioris plostri muliones conversum plostrum sublevabant, quo
facile mulae ducerent: inter superius plostrum cessim ire
coepit et cum muliones, qui inter duo plostra fuerunt, e medio
exissent, posterius plostrum a priore percussum retro redierat
et puerum cuiusdam obtriverat.[1]

In another citation mention is made of a slave muleteer
who had been hired by an owner of mules. He was so careless of
the mules that one died. Labeo's decision as to responsibility
was that if the slave had hired himself to the owner of the mules
the loss must be paid from his peculium, but if the master of the
slave had picked out for hire a slave that would cause such a loss
he was responsible. Labeo's statement is as follows:

Servum meum mulionem conduxisti: neglegentia eius mulus
tuus perit. Si ipse locasset, ex peculio dumtaxat et in rem
versum damnum tibi praestaturum, dico: sin autem ipse eum
locassem, non ultra me tibi praestaturum, quam dolum malum
et culpam meam abesse: quod si sine definitione personae
mulionem a me conduxisti et ego eum tibi dedissem, cuius neglegentia iumentum perierit, illam quoque culpam me tibi praestaturum aio, quod eum elegissem, qui eius modi damno te ad-
ficeret.[2]

Labeo tells us that the mulio who had rented out a carriage to carry luggage was responsible for the toll when a bridge
was crossed if he knew that such a thing was likely to happen -
"Vehiculum conduxisti, ut onus tuum portaret et secum iter faceret: id cum pontem transiret, redemptor eius pontis portorium ab
eo exigebat..... Puto, si mulio non ignoravit ea se transiturum,
cum vehiculum locaret, mulionem praestare debere."[3]

These incidents and the well-known story of the muleteer
Sabinus and his struggle with mud,[4] and Suetonius' account of a
muleteer's stopping to shoe a mule,[5] are all that we know about
the actual work of the muleteer.

The material quoted from the Digest makes it clear that
muleteers of three classes were found. There was the muleteer
that was actually in the service of his own master, driving and
attending to the master's mules whatever the particular job might
be.[6] Such muleteers might be reckoned in the familia urbana or
in the familia rustica - "Muliones de urbano ministerio sunt, nisi propter opus rurestre testator eos destinatos habebat."[7] They

---

[1]Alf. Dig. ix. 2. 52. 2.   [2]Labeo, Dig. xix. 2. 60. 7.
[3]Ibid. 8.   [4]Verg. App. Cat. x.   [5]Suet. Vesp. 23.
[6]Ulp. Dig. xxxiii. 7. 12. 9. See Chapter III, Note 6,p.44.
[7]Paul. Dig. xxxii. 99. 2.

were never personal attendants of the master.[1] There were also
muleteers that were let out by their masters to drive other men's
mules. In addition to these there was a group, probably no more
highly skilled but more responsible, who, in addition to doing
the actual driving, contracted for the service of themselves and
animals in transporting luggage or men and luggage. There is no
evidence that these muleteers owned their own mules. That they
drove and did business for others, is indicated by the classifica-
tion of muleteers as _institores_ - "Sed et muliones quis proprie
institores appellet."[2]

Knowledge as to the various capacities in which muleteers
served is derived partly from the _Digest_, partly from literary
sources. Muleteers drove the carriages of royalty,[3] transported
the city dweller in his travels,[4] even going to the most distant
places in charge of the same animals,[5] transported supplies of
provincial governors,[6] served with armies,[7] served in the ordinary
work of the farm,[8] served in bakeries.[9] The _carruca dormitoria_,
the sleeping car of the day, in one case at least kept for the
use of the wife, was drawn by mules - "Quaesitum est, an carrucha
dormitoria cum mulis, cum semper uxor usa est, ei debeatur."[10]
From this we may infer the service of a muleteer. With the outstanding exception of C. Ventidius Bassus (and Sabinus, if the
two are not one)[11] we have no certain record of a muleteer who was
not a slave.[12] There were, however, associations of muleteers.[13]

The _Edict_ of Diocletian fixed the wages of a muleteer
hired to another at twenty five _denarii_ per day plus his living.[14]
From the same document we find that the boots of the muleteer, as
those of the farmer, cost twenty per cent more than the boots of

---

[1]Alf. _Dig_. xxxii. 60. 1. See Note 1, p. 67.

[2]Ulp. _Dig_. xiv. 3. 5. 5.

[3]Varro _L_. _L_. v. 159; Suet. _Ner_. 30.

[4]Paul. _Dig_. xxxii. 99. 2. See Note 7, p.73. _Idem_, _Sent_.
iii. 6. 72.

[5]Sen. _Apoc_. vi. 1. (See Friedländer's note.)

[6]Gell. xv. 4. 3.

[7]Caes. _B_. _G_. vii. 45; Frontin. _De Mil_. ii. 4. 5.

[8]See Note 7, p. 73.   [9]Plin. _N_. _H_. vii. 43, 44. 135.

[10]Scaev. _Dig_. xxxiv. 2. 13.   [11]See Note 4, p. 73.

[12]See Note 5, p. 73.   [13]CIL IV. 97; 113.

[14]_Edict_. _Diocl_. vii. 19.

the soldier,[1] and that he had a lash with a wooden handle valued at sixteen denarii.[2]

Plaustrarius.--Another worker engaged in transportation who appears in the Digest is the plaustrarius. He was a driver of a wagon. If a stone fell from his wagon and did some damage, provided this happened because he had loaded his wagon badly and the load slipped on that account, he was liable. Ulpian says: "Si ex plostro lapis ceciderit et quid ruperit vel fregerit, Aquiliae actione plostrarium teneri placet, si male composuit lapides et ideo lapsi sunt."[3] No evidence appears on which an opinion can be based as to whether he was a slave, a freedman, or a freeman.

The word plostrarius or plaustrarius appears rarely. It is found in one inscription so mutilated that it is impossible to gain any information from it about the person involved.[4] One intact inscription remains in which lignari plostrari have advertised their support for a candidate for the aedileship.[5] This expression has always been interpreted to mean makers of wagons, and has served as support for the interpretation of the word plaustrarius as wagon-maker.[6] Other wall inscriptions appear, however, in which lignarii make known political preferences.[7] The fact that lignarii do thus appear as a politically conscious group, and the fact that other inscriptions occur in which two or more groups that we know were separate groups with separate functions appear in juxtaposition with no connecting conjunction,[8] make possible the interpretation, that here we have two groups of people involved, dealers in wood,[9] and the drivers of the wagons in which the wood was hauled. It is possible that the word plaustrarius was used as the equivalent of wagon maker, but there is no evidence that makes that interpretation inevitable in any ex-

---

[1]Ibid. ix. 5a.   [2]Ibid. x. 18.

[3]Ulp. Dig. ix. 2. 27. 33.   [4]CIL X. 3989.

[5]CIL IV. 485.

[6]Blümner, Technologie II, 325; La Faye, DS s. v. Plaustrarius; Liebenam, Vereinswesens, pp. 35-6; Marquardt, Privatleben, p. 728; Waltzing, Corporations, IV. p. 96.

[7]CIL IV. 951; 960.

[8]CIL VI. 29702 (Corpus Piscator)um urinatorum; CIL V. 2071 Collegiorum Fab Cent Dendr: Ibid. 5128 Coll. Fabr Cent Dend; Ibid. 5446 Centuria Centonar Dolabrar Scalar(i)or.

[9]CIL XIV. 278. See also Waltzing, Corp. II, pp. 55, 125.

tant case.[1] The meaning driver of a wagon is clear from the passage quoted from the _Digest_.

---

[1]The reading _claustrariorum_ in Lampr. **Alex**. **Sev**. 24. 5 is accepted.

CHAPTER V

OCCUPATIONS CONCERNED WITH AGRICULTURE

Another group of occupations in which service was rendered
by the more humble man is those concerned with agriculture. Many
of these had to do with the soil and crops of grain or other produce of the soil itself. Others were concerned with the raising
of stock.

Politor.--One of the persons that appears in the Digest
in connection with land is the politor. There he is clearly concerned with raising crops on the estate - "Si in coeunda socie-
tate, inquit, artem operamve pollicitus est alter, veluti cum pe-
cus in commune pascendum aut agrum politori damus in commune quae-
rendis fructibus, nimirum ibi etiam culpa praestanda est: pretium
enim operae artis est velamentum."[1] Today we should probably call
him a share cropper, though the amount returned to the landlord,
one ninth to one fifth, was less than that given by the modern
share cropper.[2] The passage quoted from the Digest admits of the
interpretation that he also took sheep out to graze. This sort
of laborer, called colonus partiarius,[3] appears in the Codex, and
we are there told that he received a share of the increase of the
flocks.[4] He prospered or suffered loss in the same proportion as
the owner of the land.[5] This same politor seems to have been the
person who hired his services to neighbors by the day.[6] As part
of such service he may have been the free laborer trusted with
the guarding of the oil press.[7]

Other politores that do not appear in the Digest are
known. Blümner[8] is of the opinion that there was one that put
the finish on walls, and that he is referred to in an inscrip-

_____

[1]Ulp. Dig. xvii. 2. 52. 2.   [2]Cato R. R. 136.
[3]Ibid. 136-7.   [4]Cod. Iust. ii. 3. 9 (8).
[5]Gaius, Dig. xix. 2. 25. 6. ....alioquin partiarius colonus quasi societatis iure et damnum et lucrum cum domino fundi
partitur.
[6]Cato R. R. v. 4.   [7]Ibid. xiii.
[8]Blümner, Technologie, III, p. 181.

tion[1] in a list of slaves with an _atriensis_ and a _topiarius_ close
on the list. The inscription as a whole, however, suggests a person doing general service outside the house, a slave _politor_ of
the sort suggested in the _Digest_ and by Cato.[2] Another slave _poli-
tor_ possibly of either sort appears in an inscription[3] published
later. The use of the verb _polio_ in describing the process of
finishing newly woven cloth is not to be questioned,[4] but the _Di-
gest_ makes it clear that the ordinary fuller, not a _politor_, did
the work.[5] The person that dressed precious stones certainly was
called a _politor_.[6] The common element in all these various occupations in which the _politor_ appears seems to be that of putting a
finish on something.[7] The single exception is the keeper of flocks,
who probably continued to bear the name _dresser of the soil_ when
the raising of stock had supplanted the original function.

    Operarius.--Another humble workman, at times certainly
connected with agriculture, was the _operarius_. He seems to have
been a slave of general rather than specific function, who helped
with any sort of work. He was of sufficient importance that any
action of his was binding on the master if the master had said
that he was responsible. As to this Ulpian says: "Plane si ad-
firmaverit mihi recte me credere operariis suis, non institoria
sed ex locato tenebitur."[8] In one citation he appears as a slave
cultivating the fields from which the produce came on which the
master lived - "Itemque de servis eadem ratione quaeri, qui eorum
usus sui causa parati essent? Utrum....operarii quoque rustici,
qui agrorum colendorum causa haberentur, ex quibus agris pater familias fructus caperet, quibus se toleraret."[9] It was the ruling

---

[1] CIL I. p. 327. C 2. 17 (1863); p. 247. C 42. 17 (1893);
X. 6638 C.

[2] See Note 6, p. 77.   [3] CIL VI. 37818.

[4] Gaius, _Dig_. xix. 5. 22; Ulp. _Dig_. xlvii. 2. 12; 48. 4.

[5] Ulp. _Dig_. xlvii. 2. 12.

[6] Firm. _Math_. iv. 14. 20 (Kroll-Skutsch).

[7] Fronto, _De Diff_. _Voc_. (A. Mai, Frankfurt, 1816, p. 476).
A. Walde und J. B. Hofmann, _Lateinisches Etymologisches Wörter-
buch_, 2nd ed. Heidelberg, 1910. Keil (H. Keil, _Commentarius in
Catonis De Agricultura_, Leipzig, 1894) II. 1. pp. 139 f. gives
satisfactory evidence that the word _polio_ was used with reference
to land. My conclusion as to the work of the _politor_ differs
from Keil's both because of the evidence of the _Digest_ and from
the fact that Cato (_R.R_. v. 4) places the _politor_ in a category
of workmen of general and not narrowly specialized function.

[8] Ulp. _Dig_. xiv. 3. 5. 10.   [9] Alf. Var. _Dig_. L. 16. 203.

of the jurist that that did not bring him into the class of slaves
maintained for the personal service of the master. In a second
citation we are told that if such a slave did the actual work of
grinding the grain, the millstone was included in the instrumentum
of the fundus - "Idem (Scaevola) consultus de meta molendaria respondit, si rusticis eius fundi operariis moleretur, eam quoque deberi."[1] Cato allowed five operarii for the cultivation of an olive orchard of two hundred forty jugera,[2] ten for one hundred jugera of vines.[3] The wages of an operarius according to the Edict
of Diocletian were twenty five denarii per day with his living.[4]
We have no way of knowing whether this operarius was a free laborer or a slave hired out by his master. The wage is the lowest
listed, the same as that of a camel driver. In literature the word
is used in a sense equivalent to our yokel.[5] It may have a like
significance in an inscription of the year 212 A.D.[6]

Fossor.--Another slave who served on a rural estate was
the fossor - "Pastores quoque et fossores ad legatarium pertinere."[7] The word itself indicates that he dug trenches (fossae).
The sort of trench dug is not indicated at this point in the Digest, but the context indicates that the reference is to a slave
performing the ordinary work of the estate. From Columella we
learn that the slave that dug furrows (sulci) between rows of
vines and trees, not plowing them, but digging by his own labor,
was called a fossor.[8] This is probably the most usual work that
a fossor would do. The Digest, however, mentions two other types
of work that may have been done by the fossor. One is the digging of ditches for drainage, to carry off surplus water from
rains. Paulus mentions this, saying: "Apud Labeonem proponitur
fossa vetus esse agrorum siccandorum causa nec memoriam extare,
quando facta est. Hanc inferior vicinus non purgabat."[9] Alfenus
says: "Sed et si fossas fecisset, ex quibus aqua pluvia posset
nocere, arbitrum, si appareat futurum, ut aqua pluvia noceret,
cogere oportere fossas eum explere et, nisi faceret, condemnare."[10]
These drainage ditches were of so great importance in agricultural

---

[1]Paul. Dig. xxxiii. 7. 18. 5.   [2]Cato R. R. x. 1.
[3]Ibid. xi. 1.   [4]Edict. Diocl. vii. 1a.
[5]Cic. Tusc. v.36. 104; Fam. viii. 1.2.   [6]Or. 2608.
[7]Paul. Dig. xxxiii. 7. 18. 8.   [8]Col. iii. 13. 3.
[9]Paul. Dig. xxxix. 3. 2. 1.   [10]Alf. Dig. xxxix. 3. 24.2.

life that the _Digest_ makes rather close specifications about
them. They were to be made for drainage only, not for collecting
water. They could be made only if the fields could not otherwise
be sowed. They had to be straight trenches with no curve. Ulpian's specifications are as follows:

> Sed et fossas agrorum siccandorum causa factas Mucius ait
> fundi colendi causa fieri, non tamen oportere corrivandae aquae
> causa fieri....sed et si quis arare et serere possit etiam
> sine sulcis aquariis, teneri eum, si quid ex his, licet agri
> colendi causa videatur fecisse: quod si aliter serere non pos-
> sit, nisi sulcos aquarios fecerit, non teneri. Ofilius autem
> ait sulcos agri colendi causa directos ita, ut in unam pergant
> partem, ius esse facere..... Sulcos tamen aquarios, qui ἕλικες
> appellantur, si quis faciat, aquae pluviae actione eum teneri
> ait.[1]

The other type of work that may have been done by the _fossor_ is
the digging of irrigation ditches. Ulpian refers to these when
he says: "Si fossa manu facta sit, per quam fluit publicum flumen, nihilo minus publica fit,"[2] and: "Illud quaeritur, utrum ea
tantum aqua his interdictis contineatur, quae ad agrum irrigandum
pertinet."[3] No instance appears in the _Digest_ of the elaborate
underground trenches for drainage that Michon discusses in his
article on _fossores_.[4]

Either there were _fossores_ who were not slaves, or contracts were made for digging ditches for which the actual labor
was done by slaves working under the contractor. At least ditches
were dug by contract. With regard to this Ulpian says: "Idem
puto et si quis faciendum aliquid stipulatus sit, ut puta....fos-
sam fodiri,"[5] and: "Inter artifices longa differentia est et in-
genii et naturae et doctrinae et institutionis. Ideo si....quis
promiserit....fossamve faciendam (a se)....fideiussor ipse....
fossam fodiens....non liberabit reum."[6]

A _fossor_ who served in the army[7] does not appear in the
Digest under the name _fossor_, but may be indicated by the expression "qui fossam faciunt."[8] Whether this indicates that the digging of the ordinary _fossa_ had become specialized work or whether
fossa here is equivalent to _cuniculum_ can not be determined from
the context. Possibly the latter is the better interpretation.

---

[1] Ulp. Dig. xxxix. 3. 1. 4, 5, 9.   [2] Idem, Dig. xliii. 12. 1. 8.
[3] Idem, Dig. xliii. 20. 1. 11.   [4] Michon, DS s.v. Fossor.
[5] Ulp. Dig. xlv. 1. 72.   [6] Idem, Dig. xlvi. 3. 31.
[7] Stat. Theb. ii. 418-9.   [8] Tarr. Pat. Dig. L. 6. 7.

Putator.--Another person who served as an agricultural
worker was the putator. Putatores appear in two capacities, as
pruners of vines and as trimmers of trees. Large estates seem
to have had several pruners of vines, all slaves counted as part
of the instrumentum of the estate - "De putatoribus quoque ita
respondit, si eius fundi causa haberentur, inesse."[1] The pruning
of the vines is mentioned a second time, though the person doing
the work is not mentioned - "Idcirco placuit, si quis....vineam
putet."[2] Pruning hooks also are mentioned as part of the instrumentum of the estate.[3] This function of the putator is mentioned
most frequently in Latin literature.[4]

The function of the putator most common in the Digest,
however, is that of trimming trees. The situation that the jurists are interested in is that of the man who, when he cuts the
limb from a tree either on public or private ground, fails to
shout a warning, and, as a result, kills a person passing by. The
decision of the jurist was that the putator was not guilty under
the Lex Cornelia de sicariis et veneficis - "Quare si....putator,
ex arbore cum ramum deiceret, non praeclamaverit et praetereuntem
occiderit, ad huius legis coercitionem non pertinet."[5] The same
jurist, Paulus, does adjudge him guilty under the Lex Aquilia.
He says:

> Si putator ex arbore ramum cum deiceret vel machinarius
> hominem praetereuntem occidit, ita tenetur, si is in publicum
> decidat nec ille proclamavit, ut casus eius evitari possit.
> Sed Mucius etiam dixit, si in privato idem accidisset, posse
> de culpa agi: culpam autem esse, quod cum a diligente pro-
> videri poterit, non esset provisum aut tum denuntiatum esset,
> cum periculum evitari non possit.[6]

Paulus elsewhere tells us the penalty, relegation to the mines.[7]
This putator who trimmed trees appears in Latin literature also.[8]

Saltuarius.--The saltuarius also served on estates.[9] As

---

[1]Paul. Dig. xxxiii. 7. 18. 7. [2]Ulp. Dig. xxxix. 1. 1. 12.
[3]Idem, Dig. xxxiii. 7. 8.
[4]Ov. Met. xiv. 649; Col. iv. 24. 11; x. 228; Mart. iii. 58. 9.
[5]Paul. Dig. xlviii. 8. 7.   [6]Idem, Dig. ix. 2. 31.
[7]Idem, Sent. v. 23. 12.
[8]Varro L. L. vi. 63; Plin. N. H. xxvii. 69.
[9]The saltuarius has been discussed fully and impeccably
by Rostovzeff (M. Rostovzeff, "Die Domänenpolizei in dem römischen
Kaiserreiche," Phil. 64, 1905, pp. 297-307). The discussion has
been retained here for the point on squatter sovereignty which is
deemed important.

he appears in the _Digest_, the _saltuarius_ was always a slave.[1] One
of his functions was the protection of the estate from robbers.
Both Alfenus and Pomponius offer evidence on this. The former
says: "Saltuarium autem tuendi et custodiendi fundi magis quam
colendi paratum esse."[2] The statement of the latter is: "....
sicuti saltuarius: par enim ratio est: nam desiderant tam vil-
lae quam agri custodiam, illic, ne quid vicini aut agri aut fructuum occupent."[3] It was also his duty to police the boundaries
of the estate against trespass - "Saltuarium autem Labeo quidem
putat eum demum contineri, qui fructuum servandorum gratia para-
tus sit, eum non, qui finium custodiendorum causa: sed Neratius
etiam hunc, et hoc iure utimur, ut omnes saltuarii contineantur."[4]
Lecrivain thinks that in these capacities the _saltuarius_ was subject to the _vilicus_.[5] Orth connects the _saltuarius_ closely with
hunting in the _saltus_ and calls him _Revierförster, the ranger of
the game preserve_.[6] In spite of the use of the _saltus_ for hunting, evidence of any connection of the _saltuarius_ with hunting
is lacking. Later the chief function of the _saltuarius_ became the
maintenance of the correct boundaries of the estate.[7] The necessity for maintaining boundaries suggests actual appropriation of
land and of such squatter sovereignty in the _saltus_ the _Digest_ offers evidence - "....quamvis saltus proposito possidendi fuerit
alius ingressus, tamdiu priorem possidere dictum est, quamdiu
possessionem ab alio occupatam ignoraret."[8] One can see readily
the desirability of a _saltuarius_ to patrol borders and keep an
estate intact. The owner of an estate could maintain such sur-
veillance even against the will of a fructuary because it was very
much to his interest that his borders be protected - "Dominus
proprietatis etiam invito usufructuario vel usuario fundum vel
aedes per saltuarium vel insularium custodire potest: interest

---

[1]_Dig._ xxxii. 60. 3; xxxiii. 7. 8. 1; 12. 4; 15. 2; 17. 2.

[2]Alf. _Dig._ xxxii. 60. 3.   [3]Pompon. _Dig._ xxxiii. 7. 15. 2.

[4]Ulp. _Dig._ xxxiii. 7. 12. 4.

[5]Lecrivain, DS _s. v. Latifundia_, p. 966.

[6]Orth, PW _s. v. Jagd_, p. 558.

[7]W. M. Ramsay, _The Cities and Bishoprics of Phrygia_ (Oxford, 1895), pp. 281 and 615, n. 527, cites inscriptional evidence.

[8]Papin. _Dig._ xli. 2. 46.

enim eius fines praedii tueri."[1] This last function became very
important and especially so on large imperial estates, where the
saltuarius was subject directly to the imperial procurator.[2]

      Bubulcus.--Another slave who worked on the rural estate
was the bubulcus. The Digest explicitly states that a bubulcus
might have either one of two functions. He either guided the oxen
at ploughing or he took the plough oxen to pasture - "De bubulco
quoque ita respondit, sive de eo, qui bubus ibi araret, sive de
eo, qui boves eius fundi aratores pasceret, quaereretur, deberi."[3]

      The latter work is recognized by Cato.[4] Glosses in which
the bubulcus is called pastor bovum also refer to this function.[5]

      Columella especially stresses the former task.[6] He men-
tions especially the work of ploughing between grapevines,[7] services in caring for his oxen, his use of the pick axe as well as
the plough,[8] his assistance in fertilizing fields.[9] In this last
task he is performing the task that Ovid mentions especially, the
driving of wagons.[10] Cato always suggests that there be one bubulcus for each pair of oxen.[11] Columella advised that bubulci
be housed near the animals that they cared for.[12] Apparently bubulci were slaves of uncertain temper,[13] who had to be handled
discreetly that the stock might not suffer.[14] They were under the
direct supervision of the vilicus.[15] Varro differentiates the
armentarius from the bubulcus by the connection that the latter
had with agriculture.[16]

      Opilio.--Another slave that worked on estates was the
opilio. The Digest makes it clear that he had the care of sheep.
We are told that when an estate was given as a legacy those sheep
that were kept to fertilize the place were included in the legacy,
and the opilio, if he cared for sheep of that sort. The words of
Alfenus are: "Praediis legatis et quae eorum praediorum colendo-

---

[1]Pompon. Dig. vii. 8. 16. 1.

[2]Ramsay, op. cit., p. 281. See also O. Hirschfeld, Die
Kaiserlichen Verwaltungsbeamten (Berlin, 1905), p. 133, n. 3.

[3]Paul. Dig. xxxiii. 7.18. 6.   [4]Cato R. R. v. 6.

[5]CGL II. 570. 33.   [6]Col. ii. 2. 25; 28; vi. 2. 8.

[7]Col. v. 5. 13.   [8]Col. ii. 2. 25.

[9]Col. ii. 5. 2.   [10]Ov. Trist. iii. 12 (13). 30.

[11]Cato R. R. x; xi.   [12]Col. 1. 6. 8.

[13]Mart. x. 7. 5; Petr. 39. 6.   [14]Cato R. R. v. 6.

[15]Ibid.   [16]Varro R. R. ii. Pr. 4.

rum causa empta parataque essent....item oves, quae stercorandi
fundi causa pararentur: item opilionem, si eius generis oves
curaret."[1] Cato tells us that one _opilio_ was required for the
one hundred sheep necessary for fertilizer for two hundred forty
jugera of olive orchard.[2] A second citation from the _Digest_ dealing with the same general situation says that if live stock was
excepted from the legacy, the _pastores_, _oviliones_, and _ovilia_ also were omitted - "Item cum instrumentum omne legatum esset ex-
cepto pecore, pastores oviliones ovilia quoque legato contineri
Ofilius non recte putat."[3] This last citation implies a distinction between _opiliones_ and _pastores_ of sheep, but what it is is
not apparent. The references to the _opilio_ that give any hint
as to the sphere of his operations mention him in close connection with the cultivated estate.[4] Possibly he was responsible
for flocks about the villa, but did not take sheep from one pasture to another, nor care for them in distant pastures.

Pastor.--_Pastores_ were another group of slaves serving
on estates. The word _pastor_ seems to have been the general term
used for a slave who had charge of animals. _Pastores_ appear in
citations that offer no information other than that they were
slaves included in or excepted from legacies.[5] One citation defi-
nitely connects them with swine. After wolves had fallen upon
swine in spite of the efforts of the _pastor_, they were rescued
by the tenant farmer of a neighbor and his strong dogs. Ulpian's
account of the incident is as follows:

> Pomponius tractat: cum pastori meo lupi porcos eriperent,
> hos viciniae villae colonus cum robustis canibus et fortibus,
> quos pecoris sui gratia pascebat, consecutus lupis eripuit
> aut canes extorserunt: et cum pastor meus peteret porcos,
> quaerebatur, utrum eius facti sint porci qui eripuit, an nost-
> ri maneant..... Et sane melius est dicere et quod a lupo eri-
> pitur, nostrum manere.[6]

Another citation mentions a _pastor_ that had charge of geese.[7] In
another reference is made to shepherds that watched over sheep
in _saltus_ and pasture lands - "Si fundus saltus pastionesque ha-

---

[1]Alf. _Dig._ xxxii. 60. 3.   [2]Cato _R. R._ x.

[3]Iavol. _Dig._ xxxiii. 7. 25.2.   [4]Varro _R.R._ ii. 1. 18.

[5]Paul. _Dig._ xxxiii. 7. 18. 8. See Note 7, p. 79. Iavol.
Dig. xxxiii. 7. 25. 2. See Note 3.

[6]Ulp. _Dig._ xli. 1. 44.

[7]Paul. _Dig._ xxxii. 66. See Chapter I, Note 10, p. 20.

bet, greges pecorum pastores saltuarii....."[1] The direct connection of the <u>saltus</u> with pasturage is made more than once in the
<u>Digest</u>.[2]

Varro recognizes the <u>pastor</u> in charge of animals other
than sheep when he suggests that Gauls make good herdsmen (<u>pasto-
res</u>) especially in charge of beasts of burden,[3] and when he assigns two such herdsmen to five hundred horses.[4] In the old
prayer for lustration of the fields, <u>pastores</u> are linked with <u>pe-
cua</u>, there probably stock in general.[5] The <u>pastor</u> is usually mentioned, however, in connection with sheep. Varro is our authority
for the ways of the shepherd. He says that shepherds must be
sturdy, swift, adaptable.[6] He suggests that the older shepherds
be used with larger flocks, boys with smaller ones, and again that
full-grown men be sent to the <u>saltus</u>, while boys and even girls
may be used on the estate.[7] Both in the winter pastures and in
summer ones he advises that the shepherd have wife and family with
him.[8] The shepherds drive the flocks from one pasture to another
and to market.[9] They have dogs to assist them.[10] Suetonius suggests that they sheared the sheep, though possibly less skillfully
than a <u>tonsor</u>.[11] The word <u>pastor</u> appears in an inscription that
shows clearly how keenly some Romans felt the error of giving over
the best lands to grazing instead of agriculture.[12]

<u>Tonsor Pecorum</u>.--Shearers of sheep also appear in the <u>Di-
gest</u>. They were slaves and are expressly listed as part of the
<u>familia</u> <u>rustica</u>.[13] In the <u>Edict</u> of Diocletian shearers are al-
lowed two <u>denarii</u> for each animal sheared, with living in addition.[14] This indicates either freemen or freedmen working for
themselves, or skilled slaves let out to others.

Sheep were sheared once a year except in Hither Spain,

---

[1]Ulp. <u>Dig</u>. xxxiii. 7. 8. 1.

[2]Scaev. <u>Dig</u>. viii. 5. 20. 1. .... ut ius compascendi habe-
rent.

[3]Varro <u>R</u>. <u>R</u>. ii. 10. 4.   [4]<u>Ibid</u>. 10.

[5]Cato <u>R</u>. <u>R</u>. 141. 3.   [6]Varro <u>R</u>. <u>R</u>. ii. 10. 3.

[7]<u>Ibid</u>. 1.   [8]<u>Ibid</u>. ii. 1. 26.   [9]<u>Ibid</u>. ii. 9. 6.

[10]<u>Ibid</u>. 3.   [11]Suet. <u>Tib</u>. 32. See also Cal. <u>Ec</u>. v. 66 ff.

[12]CIL I. 551 (1863); 638 (1893).

[13]Ulp. <u>Dig</u>. xxxiii. 7. 12. 5. See Chapter I, Note 5, p.21.

[14]<u>Edict</u>. <u>Diocl</u>. vii. 23.

where the wool was clipped twice a year.[1] What skilled _tonsores_
did at other times than the shearing season we do not know.

      We have no information on method of procedure except that
there was grouping of sheep that wool of like grade might be collected together, and that a covering was spread on which the shearing took place in order that the wool might be easily collected.[2]

---

[1]Varro R. R. 11. 11. 6, 8.   [2]Cal. Ec. v. 67 ff.

CHAPTER VI

OCCUPATIONS CONCERNED WITH SPECIALIZED WORK
OUTSIDE THE HOUSE

In addition to those occupations which have been previously discussed, in which the work was done in or about the house or
estate or emanated from it, at least in some cases, a group of occupations occurs in which the humble worker was engaged, centered
as a rule not about the house, but about some business apart from
the house. Part of these were connected with building trades.
Others were connected with various organized businesses.

Aedificator.--A workman who had some connection with building was the aedificator. He appears once in the Digest and seems
to have been the builder in charge of the erection of a building.
We are told that when he had promised the erection of an apartment
building he ought not to make haste by getting in workmen from absolutely everywhere and summoning an undue amount of help, nor yet
should he be content with one or two workmen, but should use mod-
eration as a careful builder would. The jurist's words are: "Item
qui insulam fieri spopondit, non utique conquisitis undique fabris
et plurimis operis adhibitis festinare debet nec rursus utroque
aut altero contentus esse, sed modus adhibendus est secundum ra-
tionem diligentis aedificatoris."[1] Vitruvius also used the word
aedificator with a like meaning.[2]

The word appears elsewhere with different meanings. In
Justinian's Codex it appears in explanation of structor,[3] though
that is a more usual word in earlier Latin.[4] In the Codex it
seems to mean an ordinary carpenter or builder. In Jerome's comment on Matthew the word is used, explained there by caementarius.[5]
Boethius also uses it in this same sense.[6] In other cases it is

---

[1]Venul. Dig. xlv. 1. 137. 3.

[2]Vit. vi. 6. 7. See Blümner, Technologie, III, p. 88.

[3]Cod. Iust. x. 66 (64). 1.   [4]Cic. Ad. Q. F. ii. 5. 3.

[5]Hier. in Matth. xxi. 42.

[6]Boeth. Diff. Top. M 64, 1184a. (Quoted TLL s. v. aedificator).

used to refer to the man who had the building erected, the owner
of the building, rather than the man who actually worked on it.[1]

    Lapidarius.--Another workman who was connected with build-
ing was the *lapidarius*. In one citation in the *Digest* in which he
appears he is called *faber* as well. In this case he had a slave,
the property of another man, assisting him. A scaffold[2] fell and
killed the slave. The jurist's decision was that the *lapidarius*,
who had tied the scaffold together too carelessly, was liable.
Ulpian's words are: "Nam et Mela scripsit, si servus lapidario
commodatus sub machina perierit, teneri fabrum commodati, qui neg-
legentius machinam colligavit."[3] If the interpretation given for
machina is correct, the *lapidarius* in this case was dressing
stones *in situ*. If, however, the *machina* in question was a der-
rick used for hoisting dressed stones into place, the *lapidarius*
was a man who dressed stones to be used in building, elsewhere
referred to as *lapidarius structor*.[4] The *lapidarius* is mentioned
again in the *Digest* among those whose work is sufficiently important to render them exempt from more severe public duties.[5]

    The *lapidarius* did not extract stone from quarries. The
workman that did that was known as *lapicida*.[6] The latter does
not appear in the *Digest* by name, but we have two references to
the extraction of stone.[7] The man that cut the stone into blocks
after it was quarried was known as a *sector*,[8] or *sector serraris*.[9]
The next step in the dressing of the stone seems to have been the
work of the *lapidarius*. *Opifices lapidarii* appear in an inscription.[10] These are probably the *opifices* to whom Livy refers in a
context that suggests that they dressed the stones to be used in
building.[11] Probably this was the type of *lapidarius* to whom the
second citation refers.

    Another type of *lapidarius* was the maker of tombstones
and monuments that we meet in the person of Habinnas in the *Cena*

---

[1]Cato R.R. 1. 4; Aug. De Civ. xxi. 26; Dig. xxxix. 2. 37;
Iuv. xiv. 86-95.

[2]Isid. Orig. xix. 8. 2.   [3]Ulp. Dig. xiii. 6. 5. 7.

[4]Edict. Diocl. vii. 2.

[5]Tarr. Pat. Dig. L. 6. 7 (6). See Chapter IV, Note 3, p.68.

[6]Varro L. L. viii. 62. Cf. also *lapidicinae*.

[7]Ulp. Dig. viii. 4. 13. 1; viii. 5. 8. 5.

[8]CIL VI. 9887.   [9]CIL VI. 9888.

[10]CIL XII. 1384.   [11]Liv. 1. 59. 9.

<u>Trimalchionis</u>.[1] That sort of <u>lapidarius</u> does not appear in the
<u>Digest</u>. He appears elsewhere in literature under the name <u>lapi-
cida</u> and <u>quadratarius</u>.[2] There is an inscription in which a body
of <u>lapidarii</u> and a body of <u>quadratarii</u> appear.[3] This seems to
indicate that the work of the <u>lapidarius</u> was distinct from that
of the <u>quadratarius</u>. If this is true we should not expect to find
the <u>lapidarius</u> carving inscriptions or engraving stones. The evidence that he did so is very frail,[4] and it has been shown that
that was the work of the <u>lapicida</u> or <u>quadratarius</u>.

 <u>Tector</u>.--The plasterer who works on the walls of a house
appears once in the <u>Digest</u>. A man had obtained the loan of a
slave plasterer who fell from the scaffold. The question is raised
whether the attendant loss is that of the man whom he was serving
or that of the master of the slave. Ulpian's judgment is that if
the owner lent the slave with the understanding that he was to
work on the scaffold the risk was his; but that, if it was expressly agreed that he work on the ground or floor and he was then put
on a scaffold, the risk was that of the man for whom he was working. The latter was true, too, in any case, if the accident happened because the scaffold was tied up carelessly or if the ropes
or supports were old. Ulpian's words are as follows:

> Nam et si servum tibi tectorem commodavero et de machina
> ceciderit, periculum meum esse Namusa ait: sed ego ita hoc
> verum puto, si tibi commodavi, ut et in machina operaretur:
> ceterum si ut de plano opus faceret, tu eum imposuisti in
> machina, aut si machinae culpa factum minus diligenter non ab
> ipso ligatae vel funium perticarumve vetustate, dico pericu-
> lum, quod culpa contigit rogantis commodatum, ipsum praestare
> debere.[5]

 Two illustrations survive clearly depicting this <u>tector</u>.
In one the scaffold is a low one on which ropes are not used.[6]
The other shows the sort of thing that answers the description of
the citation.[7]

 In the second citation in which the <u>tector</u> appears he

---

[1]Petr. 65. 5. Possibly this sort of <u>lapidarius</u> appears
in CIL VI. 8871. There he is a slave.

[2]Sid Apoll. <u>Ep</u>. iii. 12. 5.   [3]CIL VI. 9502.

[4]Petr. 58. 7, <u>lapidarias litteras</u>, interpreted in terms
of Petr. 29. 1, <u>quadrata littera</u>; CGL III. 201. 8 and 271. 14,
<u>lapidarius</u> λιθοξόος.

[5]Ulp. <u>Dig</u>. xiii. 6. 5. 7.   [6]See DS Fig. 6754.

[7]See DS Fig. 4758.

seems to have taken a contract to work on a receptacle full of wine. In working he perforated the receptacle and the wine was lost. He was held responsible. Ulpian says, "Item si tectori locaveris laccum vino plenum curandum et ille eum pertudit, ut vinum sit effusum, Labeo scribit in factum agendum."[1] The receptacle in the case is called laccus. This is probably a variant form of lacus,[2] influenced by the Greek λάκκος.[3] The lacus in this case may have been the vat that received wine from the press,[4] and may have required such service as a plasterer rendered on cisterns.[5]

Frontinus classes the tector as an opifex,[6] and both he and Augustine rate him as essential to the ordinary conduct of life.[7] Varro at an earlier date rated him with the pictor as a workman of the luxury class.[8] Seneca at a later date concurs in this judgment.[9]

The methods of preparing plaster are discussed by Vitruvius.[10] The particular services that a plasterer was prepared to render are listed by Tertullian.[11] He knew how to repair roofs, to put on plaster or stucco, to finish a cistern, and to do various sorts of ornamental work, including incrustations.

Inscriptions of tectores show that many were freedmen.[12]

Balneator.--Other humbler workmen are found connected with various trades and businesses. One of these was the balneator. Two types of balneator appear in the Digest. The first was a slave. In one citation we are told that he was included in a legacy of the instrumenta connected with a bath - "Instrumento balneario legato etiam balneatorem contineri Neratius respondit."[13] The bath was probably one operated for the use of the public. A second passage gives the reason for including the balneator, namely, that baths could not function without balneatores. Marcianus

---

[1]Ulp. Dig. ix. 2. 27. 35.

[2]Cato R. R. xxv; Ov. Fast. iii. 558; iv. 888; Col. xii. 18. 3.

[3]Walde-Hofmann, op. cit. s. v. lacus.

[4]Isid. Orig. xx. 14. 12.   [5]Tert. De Idol. viii.

[6]Frontin. De Aq. 117.   [7]Aug. De Civ. iv. 22.

[8]Varro R. R. iii. 2. 9.   [9]Sen. Ep. 90. 9.

[10]Vit. vii. 3. 10.   [11]Tert. loc. cit.

[12]CIL VI. 5985; IX. 1721; 1722; 3192; X. 6593.

[13]Paul. Dig. xxxiii. 7. 13. 1.

says: "Instrumento balneatorio legato dictum est balneatorem sic
instrumento contineri balneario....cum balneae sine balneatoribus
usum suum praebere non possint."[1] This slave balneator appears
frequently in inscriptions,[2] but rarely in literature.[3] One reference gives the impression that he had the general oversight of the
bath.[4] A scholium on an epistle of Horace's reinforces this impression.[5]

The second type of balneator seems to have been a freeman
or a freedman who conducted a bath of his own or took the contract
for conducting one. In one case he let his bath to an aedile on
contract to serve as a free bath in a municipality for a year. At
the end of three months a fire occurred. During the time that
service was not rendered he was forced to make a contribution of
money. Alfenus says: "Aedilis in municipio balneas conduxerat ut
eo anno municipes gratis lavarentur: post tres menses incendio
facto respondit posse agi cum balneatore ex conducto, ut pro por-
tione temporis, quo lavationem non praestitisset, pecuniae contri-
butio fieret."[6] In another citation in which the balneator is not
mentioned the bath was let for twenty nummi per year, with an allowance of one hundred nummi for the repair of furnace, pipes, and
other parts of the plant. The jurist's judgment was that the balneator must pay the hundred nummi. Labeo said: "Quidam in municipio balineum praestandum annuis viginti nummis conduxerat et ad
refectionem fornacis fistularum similiumque rerum centum nummi ut
praestrarentur ei, convenerat: conductor centum nummos petebat.
Ita ei deberi dico."[7]

The balneator was held responsible for the safeguarding
of the clothing of bathers if it was left with him, whether there
was a fee charged for that service or not. Ulpian says: "Si vestimenta servanda balneatori data perierunt, si quidem nullam mercedem servandorum vestimentorum accepit, depositi eum teneri et
dolum dumtaxat praestare debere puto: quod si accepit, ex conducto."[8] Under the thin disguise of attendants to guard such

---

[1] Marcian. Dig. xxxiii. 7. 17. 2.
[2] CIL VI. 6243; 7601; 8742; 9102. C 13; 9216.
[3] Petr. 53. 10; Lampr. Alex. 42. 2.
[4] Lampr. Com. 1. 9.   [5] Porph. on Hor. Ep. 1. 14. 14.
[6] Alf. Dig. xix. 2. 30. 1.   [7] Labeo, Dig. xix. 2. 58. 2.
[8] Ulp. Dig. xvi. 3. 1. 8.

clothing apparently the balneatores had bands of women slaves of such character that the jurist included the balneator in defining the bounds of lenocinium - "Sive balneator fuerit, velut in quibusdam provinciis fit, in balineis ad custodienda vestimenta conducta habens mancipia hoc genus observantia in officina, lenocinii poena tenebitur."[1] The same charge is made by Martial,[2] and may account for the unsavory reputation that the balneator seems to have had.[3]

Little further information about the balneator appears. He seems to have had to resort to strenuous measures at times to keep order among his patrons.[4] The usual fee paid in the time of Cicero[5] and in the time of Martial[6] was a quadrans. At the Metallum Vipascense the fee for men was a half as, for women one as.[7] By the time of Diocletian the balneator was allowed two denarii.[8]

Fornacator.--The fornacator also was a slave who was connected with a bath. He appears in one passage in the Digest. The context indicates that the bath that the jurist had in mind was one operated for the use of the public, but not a bath in a private house nor yet one of the great public baths. In a legacy which bequeathed the instrumentum of the bath the fornacator was included. The passage together with the context in which it appears is as follows: "Tabernae cauponiae instrumento legato etiam institores contineri Neratius existimat....instrumento balneario legato etiam balneatorem contineri...."[9] "Continetur autem et fornicator (sic)."[10] Probably this fornacator had charge of heating the bath.

Urinator.--Another humble workman not connected with the house or estate was the urinator. The citation in the Digest in which urinatores appear depicts clearly the precarious state of commerce in Roman times. Part of a cargo of a ship caught in a storm was jettisoned in order to save the ship. Subsequently the ship and the rest of the cargo went down. This major portion of the cargo was later rescued by urinatores who received wages for

---

[1] Idem, Dig. iii. 2. 4. 2. [2] Mart. iii. 93. 14, 15.
[3] Cic. Pro Cael. 62; Phil. xiii. 26.
[4] Plin. N. H. xviii. 156. [5] Cic. loc. cit.
[6] Mart. iii. 7. 1-3. [7] CIL II. 5181. 1. 23.
[8] Edict. Diocl. vii. 76. [9] Paul. Dig. xxxiii. 7. 14.
[10] Ibid. 13.

their work. The man whose goods had been jettisoned was entitled to a share of the proceeds from what was thus saved. Afterwards divers rescued his own merchandise and the proceeds from that were his own. The jurist reports the case as follows:

> Sed si navis, quae in tempestate iactu mercium unius mercatoris levata est, in alio loco summersa est, et aliquorum mercatorum merces per urinatores extractae sunt data mercede, rationem haberi debere eius, cuius merces in navigatione levandae navis causa iactae sunt, ab his, qui postea sua per urinatores servaverunt, Sabinus aeque respondit. Eorum vero, qui ita servaverunt, invicem rationem haberi non debere ab eo, qui in navigatione iactum fecit, si quaedam ex his mercibus per urinatores extractae sunt.[1]

No hint is given as to the place at which the wreck occurred. One assumes that it occurred farther from shore and we have references to divers' plying their trade in deeper water.[2] The organized corporation of fishermen and divers, however, is expressly mentioned as an organization for the "entire channel of the Tiber,"[3] and many inscriptions referring to divers come from Ostia.[4] The commercial significance of this, too, is clear in view of the fact that cargoes were transferred from larger to smaller craft there and where other rivers flow into the sea with consequent overturning or sinking of the smaller boat.[5]

No reference to divers for fish or sponges appears in the Digest, though both were known.[6]

Machinarius.--Another worker of humble status was the machinarius. He appears in a citation in the Digest with a putator who was trimming trees. We are told that if he kills a person passing by in a place either public or private, and the accident has occurred because he did not use foresight or shout a warning at the right time, he is to be held accountable for the accident.[7] Clearly the person concerned was manipulating some sort of mechanical contrivance, and not a maker of such a contrivance, the explanation which alone appears in glosses.[8] A machinarius

---

[1]Call. Dig. xiv. 2. 4. 1.

[2]Liv. xliv. 10. 3; Man. Astron. v. 434 ff. See also notes of Housman (A. E. Housman, M. Manilii Astronomicon Lib. v (London, 1930]) on v. 431 ff.

[3]CIL VI. 1872.   [4]CIL XIV. 303; VI. 29700-2.

[5]Call. Dig. xiv. 2. 4; Ulp. Dig. xix. 2. 13. 1, 2.

[6]Plin. N. H. ix. 46. 151.

[7]Paul. Dig. ix. 2. 31. See Chapter V, Note 6, p. 81.

[8]CGL II. 371. 25; III. 308. 54; 500. 16.

may be referred to a second time in a rather unsatisfactory inscription.[1] Blümner recognizes a machinarius (ἀρχιτέκτων) who, he says, did the brain work in the quarries of Egypt.[2] What the contrivance was in the case referred to in the Digest it is impossible to say.

Tonsor Hominum--Another workman who followed a humble trade was the barber. In one citation in the Digest in which there is reference to barbers an incident about one of the class known as circitores is given. The equipment of the itinerant barber consisted of a chair and his instruments. In this case the barber had set up his chair near where a game of ball was going on and he was there shaving a slave. The ball struck the hand of the barber and the throat of the slave was cut. The accident was not fatal. Proculus decided that the fault was the barber's, for working where ball games were usual and pedestrians numerous. Ulpian, however, thought that one that intrusted himself to a barber who had his chair in a dangerous location should blame himself only. Ulpian's report of the incident is as follows:

> Item Mela scribit, si, cum pila quidam luderent, vehementius quis pila percussa in tonsoris manus eam deiecerit et sic servi, quem tonsor habebat, gula sit praecisa adiecto cultello: .... Proculus in tonsore esse culpam: et sane si ibi tondebat, ubi ex consuetudine ludebatur vel ubi transitus frequens erat, est quod ei imputetur: quamvis nec illud male dicatur, si in loco periculoso sellam habenti tonsori se quis commiserit, ipsum de se queri debere.[3]

The only other certain reference that we have to the itinerant barber is in the Lex Metalli Vipascensis, in which, since all tonsorial work had been let as a concession to conductores, circitores were forbidden to ply their trade in the region of the mines to which the Lex applied.[4]

These barbers as well as the proprietors of the barber shops were probably freedmen[5] or plebeian freemen,[6] though no inscription appears that is certainly that of an itinerant barber. This is probably an indication of their poverty and casual way of living. Barbers that had regular shops thronged by the wealthy and centers for the exchange of gossip were in more prosperous circumstances. For this we have evidence both in the time of

---

[1]CIL XI. 634.   [2]Blümner, Technologie, III, p. 82.
[3]Ulp. Dig. ix. 2. 11.   [4]CIL II. 5181. 37 ff.
[5]CIL VI. 4474; 9940; 37822.   [6]CIL XII. 4516.

Domitian[1] and for the fourth century.[2] The fee set for barbers by the Edict of Diocletian, however, was modest (two denarii).[3] There was a trade association of barbers in the neighborhood of the Circus Maximus.[4]

In addition to the proprietors of shops and the itinerant barber with his chair we find slaves serving in the houses of the rich, especially, as we are told in a citation in the Digest, for the retinue of slaves in the country and probably for those in the mansions in the city as well.[5] The proprietors of shops also had slaves, either for the actual work of the trade or for more menial tasks.[6]

The work of the barber was varied. He cut hair, either "over the comb"[7] or short,[8] he shaved his customer,[9] he shaved the head and eyebrows,[10] he curled hair,[11] he gave manicures.[12]

We have two sources of knowledge of the instruments of the barber's trade, the statements of Roman writers and the actual instruments or representations of them.[13] The list includes tweezers (volsellae), a comb (pecten), a mirror (speculum), a curling iron (calamistrum), shears (forfex, axitia),[14] a curved razor (novacula)[15] which had its own curved case,[16] and other razors (culter,[17] cultellus[18]). In addition to these he had a heavy cloth (involucre) to put around the shoulders of the customer,[19] a cloth for dusting him off,[20] and various depilatory salves to take the place of shaving.[21] If the customer was cut, sometimes

---

[1]Iuv. i. 24. 25.   [2]Amm. xxii. 4. 9.

[3]Edict. Diocl. vii. 22.   [4]CIL VI. 31900.

[5]Ulp. Dig. xxxiii. 7. 12. 5. See Chapter I, Note 5, p.21. See also CIL VI. 4359; 6366; Mart. vi. 52. 1-4.

[6]CIL XV. 7172.   [7]Plaut. Capt. 268; Cur. 577.

[8]DS Fig. 3174.

[9]Plin. N. H. xxix. 114; Mart. iii. 74. 1-4; xiv. 36.

[10]Petr. 103. 1-5.   [11]Plaut. Cur. 577-8; Mart. ii. 36.

[12]Plaut. Aul. 312-3; Hor. Ep. i. 7. 51.   [13]DS Fig. 5334.

[14]Plaut. Cur. 577-8; Mart. vii. 95. 7-13.

[15]Petr. 103; DS Fig. 5333.   [16]Mart. xi. 58. 9, 10.

[17]Cic. Of. ii. 7. 25; Val. Max. iii. 2. 15.

[18]Ulp. Dig. ix. 2. 11. See Note 3, p. 94.

[19]Plaut. Capt. 267-9.   [20]See Note 14.

[21]Mart. iii. 74. 1-4.

cobwebs were applied.[1] Instruments were sharpened on whetstones moistened with oil or saliva.[2]

---

[1]See Note 9, p. 95.   [2]Plin. N. H. xxxvi. 164-5.

SELECTED BIBLIOGRAPHY

Barrow, R. H.   Slavery in the Roman Empire.   London, 1928.

Blümner, H.   Der Maximaltarif des Diocletian.   Berlin, 1893.

_____. Die Römischen Privatalterhümer. Vol. II. 2. 2. Handbuch der Klassischen Alterthumswissenschaft, edited by Iwan von Müller. Munich, 1911.

_____. Technologie und Terminologie der Gewerbe und Künste bei Griechen und Römern.   Leipzig, 1875.

Boak, A. E. R.   The Master of the Offices in the Later Roman and Byzantine Empires.   New York, 1919.

Bunsmann, L.   De Piscatorum in Litteris Usu.   Münster, 1910.

Caver, P.   "De Muneribus Militaribus," Ephemeris Epigraphica, IV (1881), 406ff.

Corpus Inscriptionum Latinarum.   Berlin, 1862-

Daremberg, C. et Saglio, E.   Dictionnaire des Antiquites Grecques et Romaines.   Paris, 1873-1912.

Desjardins, E.   Les Tabellarii.   Paris.

Du Cange, C. D.   Glossarium Mediae et Infimae Latinitatis.   Paris, 1840.

Duff, A. M.   Freedmen in the Early Roman Empire.   Oxford, 1928.

Frank, T.   An Economic History of Rome.   2d ed. rev. Baltimore, 1927.

_____. An Economic Survey of Ancient Rome.   Baltimore, 1933-

Friedländer, L.   Darstellungen aus der Sittengeschichte Roms. 9th and 10th ed. rev. by G. Wissowa.   Leipzig, 1919, 1921.

Georges, K. E.   Ausführliches Lateinisch-Deutsches Handwörterbuch.   Hanover and Leipzig, 1918.

Goetz, G.   Corpus Glossariorum Latinorum.   Leipzig, 1888.

Hirschfeld, O.   Die Kaiserlichen Verwaltungsbeamten.   Berlin, 1905.

Jordan, H.   Topographie der Stadt Rom.   Berlin, 1871.

Kaufman, D. B.   "Roman Barbers," C. W. XXV (1932), pp. 145-148.

Kayser, B. von.   Jagd und Jagdrecht in Rom.   Göttingen, 1894.

Liebenam, W.   Zur Geschicte und Organisation des Römische Vereinswesens.   Leipzig, 1890.

Lindsay, W. M.   Glossaria Latina.   Paris, 1926.

Marquardt, J.   Das Privatleben der Römer.   Leipzig, 1886.

_____. Römische Staatsverwaltung.   Leipzig, 1881-5.

Meyer-Lübke, H. Romanisches Etymologisches Wörterbuch. Heidel-
    berg, 1911.

Nicolson, F. W. "Greek and Roman Barbers," Harvard Studies in
    Comparative Philology, II (1891), pp. 41-56.

Pauly, A. F. von, Wissowa, G. and Kroll, W. Realencyclopädie
    der Classischen Alterthumswissenschaft. Stuttgart,
    1894-

Preller, L. Die Regionen der Stadt Rom. Jena, 1846.

Ramsay, W. M. The Cities and Bishoprics of Phrygia. Oxford,
    1895.

Rhode, P. "Thynnorum Captura," Jahrbücher für Classische
    Philologie, Sup. XVIII (1892), pp. 1-78.

Rostovzeff, M. "Die Domänenpolizei in dem Römischen Kaiserreiche,"
    Philologus 64, (1905), pp. 297-307.

_____. The Social and Economic History of the Roman Empire.
    Oxford, 1926.

Ruggiero, E. de. Dizionario Epigrafico. Roma, 1895.

Saalfeld, G. A. Haus und Hof in Rom. Paderborn, 1884.

Vollmer, F. et al. Thesaurus Linguae Latinae. Leipzig, 1904-

Walde, A. und Hofmann, J. B. Lateinisches Etymologisches Wörter-
    buch, 2d ed. Heidelberg, 1910.

Waltzing, J. P. Étude Historique sur les Corporations Profession-
    nelles chez les Romains. Louvain, 1895.

ROMAN HISTORY

An Arno Press Collection

Accame, Silvio. **Il Dominio Romano in Grecia Dalla Guerra Acaica Ad Augusto.** 1946

Berchem, Denis van. **Les Distributions De Blé Et D'Argent À La Plèbe Romaine Sous L'Empire.** 1939

Bouché-Leclercq, A[uguste]. **Histoire De La Divination Dans L'Antiquité.** Four Volumes in Two. 1879/1880/1882

Cagnat, René [Louis Victor]. **L'Armée Romaine D'Afrique Et L'Occupation Militaire De L'Afrique Sous Les Empereurs.** Two Parts in One. 1913

Chilver, G[uy] E[dward] F[arquhar]. **Cisalpine Gaul:** Social and Economic History From 49 B.C. To The Death of Trajan. 1941

Crook, John [A]. **Consilium Principis;** Imperial Councils and Counsellors From Augustus To Diocletian. 1955

Cuntz, Otto. **Die Geographie Des Ptolemaeus:** Galliae, Germania, Raetia, Noricum, Pannoniae, Illyricum, Italia. 1923

Déléage, André. **La Capitation Du Bas-Empire.** 1945

Delehaye, Hippolyte. **Les Légendes Grecques Des Saints Militaires.** 1909

Dessau, Hermann. **Geschichte Der Römischen Kaiserzeit.** Three Parts in Two. 1924/1926/1930

Doer, Bruno. **Die Römische Namengebung:** Ein Historischer Versuch. 1937

Fritz, Kurt von. **The Theory of the Mixed Constitution in Antiquity;** A Critical Analysis of Polybius' Political Ideas. 1954

[Fronto, Marcus Cornelius]. **M. Cornelii Frontonis Epistulae, Adnotatione Critica Instructae.** Edited by Michael Petrus Iosephus van den Hout. 1954

Grosse, Robert. **Römische Militärgeschichte Von Gallienus Bis Zum Beginn Der Byzantinischen Themenverfassung.** 1920

Hardy, E[rnest] G[eorge]. **Roman Laws and Charters** And **Three Spanish Charters and Other Documents.** Translated With Introductions and Notes. 1912/1912

Hasebroek, Johannes. **Untersuchungen Zur Geschichte Des Kaisers Septimius Severus.** 1921

Hatzfeld, Jean. **Les Trafiquants Italiens Dans L'Orient Hellénique.** 1919

Hirschfeld, Otto. **Kleine Schriften.** 1913

Holleaux, Maurice. ΣΤΡΑΤΗΓΟΣ ΤΠΑΤΟΣ: Étude Sur La Traduction En Grec Du Titre Consulaire. 1918

Hüttl, Willy. **Antoninus Pius.** Two Volumes in One. 1936/1933

Laet, Siegfried J. De. **Portorium**: Étude Sur L'Organisation Douanière Chez Les Romains, Surtout À L'Epoque Du Haut-Empire. 1949

Magie, David. **Roman Rule in Asia Minor to the End of the Third Century After Christ.** Two Volumes. 1950

Marquardt, Joachim. **Römische Staatsverwaltung.** Three Volumes. 1881/1884/1885

Meltzer, Otto and Ulrich Kahrstedt. **Geschichte Der Karthager.** Three Volumes. 1879/1896/1913

[Nicephorus (Patriarch of Constantinople). Edited by Carl Gotthard de Boor]. **Nicephori Archiepiscopi Constantinopolitani Opuscula Historica.** Edited by Carolus de Boor. 1880

Nissen, Heinrich. **Kritische Untersuchungen Über Die Quellen Der Vierten Und Fünften Dekade Des Livius.** 1863

Oost, Stewart Irvin. **Roman Policy in Epirus and Acarnania in the Age of the Roman Conquest of Greece.** 1954

Paribeni, Roberto. **Optimus Princeps**: Saggio Sulla Storia E Sui Tempi Dell' Imperatore Traiano. Two Volumes in One. 1926/1927

Ramsay, W[illiam] M[itchell]. **The Cities and Bishoprics of Phrygia**: Being An Essay of the Local History of Phrygia From the Earliest Times to the Turkish Conquest. Two Parts in One. 1895/1897

Rosenberg, Arthur. **Untersuchungen Zur Römischen Zenturienverfassung.** 1911

Sands, P[ercy] C[ooper]. **The Client Princes of the Roman Empire Under the Republic.** 1908

Schulten, Adolf. **Geschichte Von Numantia.** 1933

Schulten, Adolf. **Sertorius.** 1926

Scriptores Originum Constantinopolitanarum. Edited by Theodorus Preger. Two Parts in One. 1901/1907

Smith, R[ichard] E[dwin]. **The Failure of the Roman Republic.** 1955

Studies in Cassius Dio and Herodian: H. A. Andersen and E. Hohl. 1975

Studies in the Social War: A. Kiene, E. Marcks, I. Haug and A. Voirol. 1975

Sundwall, Johannes. **Abhandlungen zur Geschichte Des Ausgehenden Römertums.** 1919

Sydenham, Edward A[llen]. **The Coinage of the Roman Republic.** Revised with Indexes by G. C. Haines, Edited by L. Forrer and C. A. Hersh. 1952

Taylor, Lily Ross. **The Divinity of the Roman Emperor.** 1931

Two Studies on Roman Expansion: A. Afzelius. 1975

Two Studies on the Roman Lower Classes: M. E. Park and M. Maxey. 1975

Willems, P[ierre]. **Le Sénat De La République Romaine,** Sa Composition Et Ses Attributions. Three Volumes in Two. 1885/1883/1885